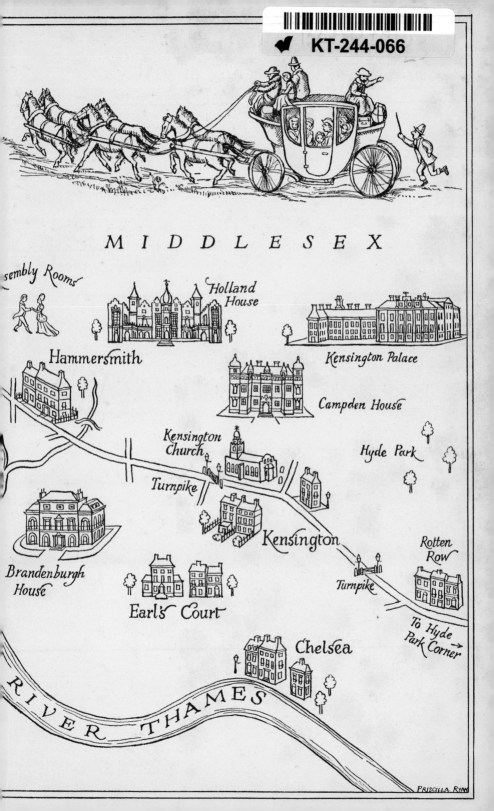

MIDDLESEX

sembly Rooms

Holland House

Kensington Palace

Hammersmith

Campden House

Kensington Church

Hyde Park

Turnpike

Brandenburgh House

Kensington

Rotten Row

Earl's Court

Turnpike

To Hyde Park Corner

Chelsea

RIVER THAMES

PRISCILLA RYAN

SIR JOSHUA REYNOLDS
A Personal Study

Other books by DEREK HUDSON

A POET IN PARLIAMENT
Life of W. M. Praed
(*Murray*)

THOMAS BARNES OF "THE TIMES"
(*Cambridge University Press*)

BRITISH JOURNALISTS AND NEWSPAPERS
(*Collins*)

NORMAN O'NEILL: A LIFE OF MUSIC
(*Quality Press*)

CHARLES KEENE
(*Pleiades Books*)

MARTIN TUPPER: HIS RISE AND FALL
(*Constable*)

JAMES PRYDE
(*Constable*)

LEWIS CARROLL
(*Constable*)

(*Editor*) MODERN ENGLISH SHORT STORIES: SECOND SERIES
(*O.U.P.*)

———

(*with Kenneth W. Luckhurst*)
THE ROYAL SOCIETY OF ARTS 1754–1954
(*Murray*)

(*with Anthony Goldsmith*)
ON THE SLANT (*a play*)
(*Quality Press*)

JOSHUA REYNOLDS. *By Angelica Kauffmann.* 1767
(49″ × 39″)

DEREK HUDSON

SIR JOSHUA REYNOLDS

A PERSONAL STUDY

With Reynolds'
Journey from London to Brentford
now first published

LONDON
GEOFFREY BLES

Printed in Great Britain by
Butler & Tanner Ltd., Frome and London
for the publishers
Geoffrey Bles Ltd
52 Doughty Street, London, W.C.1

Contents

FOREWORD   *page* ix

INTRODUCTION: A Man and His Time   1

I   Plympton   5
II   The Years of Preparation   17
III   Italy   31
IV   Reynolds Conquers London   48
V   Leicester Fields   70
VI   The Royal Academy   88
VII   The Road to Richmond   107
VIII   Page and Monarch   119
IX   Women, Wine and Snuff   133
X   King's Principal Portrait Painter   158
XI   The Friend of Johnson   180
XII   The Silver Spectacles   194
XIII   "Count No Man Happy"   211
XIV   After the Funeral   230

APPENDIX A. Reynolds' "Journey from London to
    Brentford"   239
APPENDIX B. Reynolds' Painting Technique. By Horace A.
    Buttery   248
APPENDIX C. The Recognizance in John Bampfylde's Case   251
SELECT BIBLIOGRAPHY   252
NOTES AND REFERENCES   254
INDEX   265

The endpaper map *A Journey from London to Brentford* was designed by Priscilla Ryan.

Illustrations

With the exception of the Frontispiece, all the works reproduced are by Reynolds.

JOSHUA REYNOLDS. By Angelica Kauffmann. 1767

Frontispiece

('The Earl of Morley)

I JOSHUA REYNOLDS. The earliest self-portrait in oils, *circa* 1746   *Facing page* 22
(*Mrs A. T. Copland-Griffiths*)

II*a* DRAWING OF A LADY. From an Italian sketch-book. 36
1752
(*Trustees of the British Museum*)

II*b* CARICATURE GROUP of Sir Charles Turner, Sir William Lowther, Lord Milltown and M. Huet. Painted in Rome, *circa* 1751   36
(*Lord Richard Cavendish*)

III HON. AUGUSTUS (LATER VISCOUNT) KEPPEL. 1753–4   52
(*Trustees of the National Maritime Museum, Greenwich*)

IV JOSHUA REYNOLDS. Self-portrait. 1753–4   68
(*Trustees of the National Portrait Gallery*)

V*a* DR SAMUEL JOHNSON. 1756–7   72
(*Trustees of the National Portrait Gallery*)

V*b* DR SAMUEL JOHNSON. 1769   72
(*Lord Sackville*)

VI*a* GEORGIANA, COUNTESS SPENCER, AND LADY GEORGIANA SPENCER, LATER DUCHESS OF DEVONSHIRE. 1759–61   84
(*Earl Spencer*)

VI*b* PAGES OF REYNOLDS' NOTEBOOK. 1760   84
(*Royal Academy of Arts*)

VII*a* EDMUND BURKE. 1767–9   100
(*Earl Fitzwilliam*)

vii

ILLUSTRATIONS

VII*b* OLIVER GOLDSMITH. 1770   100
        (*Lord Sackville*)

VIII*a* ANGELICA KAUFFMANN. 1777   108
        (*Earl Spencer*)

VIII*b* GIUSEPPE BARETTI. 1774   108
        (*The Earl of Ilchester*)

IX   THE THAMES FROM RICHMOND HILL   116
        (*Trustees of the Tate Gallery*)

X*a*   JOSHUA REYNOLDS. Self-portrait, *circa* 1773   124
        (*Royal Academy of Arts*)

X*b*   SIR WILLIAM CHAMBERS, R.A. 1780   124
        (*Royal Academy of Arts*)

XI   REV. GEORGE HUDDESFORD AND J. C. W. BAMPFYLDE.
        1779   154
        (*Trustees of the Tate Gallery*)

XII*a* THEOPHILA PALMER (MRS GWATKIN), NIECE OF JOSHUA
        REYNOLDS. 1776, altered 1781   172
        (*Mrs A. T. Copland-Griffiths*)

XII*b* MARY PALMER (LADY THOMOND), NIECE OF JOSHUA
        REYNOLDS. 1785   172
        (*Present whereabouts unknown*)

XIII   THE FAMILY OF GEORGE, 3RD DUKE OF MARLBOROUGH.
        1778   196
        (*The Duke of Marlborough*)

XIV*a* "HEADS OF ANGELS" (FRANCES ISABELLA GORDON). 1787   212
        (*Trustees of the Tate Gallery*)

XIV*b* SARAH SIDDONS AS "THE TRAGIC MUSE". 1784   212
        (*The Huntingdon Foundation, San Marino, California*)

XV*a*   JOSHUA REYNOLDS. Self-portrait. 1788–9   228
        (*Mrs A. T. Copland-Griffiths*)

XV*b*   GEORGIANA, DUCHESS OF DEVONSHIRE, AND HER
        DAUGHTER, GEORGIANA, LATER COUNTESS OF CAR-
        LISLE. 1786   228
        (*Trustees of the Chatsworth Settlement*)

The specimens of Reynolds' handwriting reproduced in the text, pages 98 and 135, are taken from a notebook at the Royal Academy of Arts and from a manuscript in the possession of Mrs A. T. Copland-Griffiths.

The author is indebted to the various private owners, art galleries, etc., who have courteously given permission for the reproduction of these pictures.

Foreword

"I DARESAY it is a good thing that from time to time the great figures of the past are re-presented," wrote Sir Gerald Kelly, P.P.R.A., when I told him that I was engaged on this book. I share that hope, and I feel that this may be an appropriate time to attempt a re-assessment of the first President of the Royal Academy.

Though there have been a number of Lives of Sir Joshua Reynolds, no full-length biography has been published for half a century. During that period our knowledge of him has been greatly advanced, especially by three admirable books from Professor F. W. Hilles of Yale University, the *Letters of Sir Joshua Reynolds* (1929), *The Literary Career of Sir Joshua Reynolds* (1936), and a collection of his character sketches and other writings based on new material in the Boswell Papers and published under the title *Portraits by Sir Joshua Reynolds* (1952). The past fifty years have also seen the appearance of *The Farington Diary*, containing much new information on Sir Joshua, and W. T. Whitley's *Artists and their Friends in England 1700–1799*, a useful and generally reliable miscellany, unfortunately not documented but compiled from papers now in the British Museum. There has also appeared a revised and enlarged edition by L. F. Powell of Birkbeck Hill's *Boswell's Life of Johnson*.

I have paid particular attention to these recent publications in my references at the end of this book, but I have also worked through as much original manuscript material as possible, including the pocket-books and sketch-books at the Royal Academy, the British Museum and elsewhere, in the hope of providing a fresh and unhackneyed picture. I have not tried to displace the two fat volumes of the *Life and Times of Sir Joshua Reynolds* by C. R. Leslie and Tom Taylor (1865). These are filled with essential material, as well as with much unnecessary gossip and many inaccuracies. To supersede Leslie and Taylor would require not only an entirely new reading of the Royal Academy notebooks—

which is badly needed—but also much more time, and space, than I have had at my disposal. I have been indebted throughout to Leslie and Taylor, to Malone's memoir, and to Northcote's *Life*, but I have not attempted regular references to them. I have something to say about Northcote in Chapter VIII; his apology to Mrs R. L. Gwatkin (p. 130) makes it impossible to rely on the literal accuracy of Hazlitt's "Conversations" with him, but Northcote's biography of Reynolds must always remain an important source of information.

I did not expect, when I started work, to be able to incorporate, at this stage, much unpublished material, other than what I could glean for myself from the original notebooks and sketch-books. I have in fact, however, been able to include half a dozen letters of Sir Joshua's which I believe to be unpublished—four to Burke and one each to Sir William Chambers and Warren Hastings—and I have added many other new details. But where I have been singularly fortunate is in obtaining the generous co-operation of Sir Joshua's collateral descendant, Mrs A. T. Copland-Griffiths, who not only gave me the great pleasure of seeing her own remarkable collection of family treasures but has also allowed me to publish some unknown Reynolds' manuscripts, including his "Observations on Hogarth"; his rudimentary drinking-songs; and, most notably, his entertaining parody of Baretti, "A Journey from London to Brentford", which is printed for the first time in Appendix A. Mrs Copland-Griffiths has also lent me two scrap-books which she has herself compiled, as well as the commonplace book of Reynolds' sister Frances (Fanny), and has helped me in many other ways. I could not be more grateful to her.

I have called my book "a personal study", and so it is, in two senses. There is such a vast amount of information available about this great eighteenth-century figure that it was obvious from the start that much would have to be left out. I have economized on the historical elaborations and the gossip about Reynolds' sitters, of which there is perhaps enough in print already, and instead have devoted more attention to Sir Joshua as a man, to his personal life, to his relations with his friends and with his sisters, his two nieces and other members of his family. In particular, my researches have led me to say a great deal more than has been said by previous biographers about Reynolds' relations with that enigmatic figure

Sir William Chambers, who played a very important part in his life. A full-length biography of Chambers is badly needed; meanwhile I have done what I could, with the help of the material available at the British Museum, the R.I.B.A., and the Courtauld Institute, to give him his necessary place in the story.

This book is personal in another sense, in that its judgements and selective approach are necessarily my own. I am not qualified to decide on many difficult questions in Reynolds' art-history. Where I have chanced my arm, I must hope for indulgence; but I have in general leaned heavily on Professor E. K. Waterhouse's expert knowledge, as shown in the catalogue of his *Reynolds* (1941) —a remarkable achievement—and elsewhere. I am most grateful to Mr Horace Buttery for contributing the notes on "Reynolds' Painting Technique" (Appendix B); these, also, I owe to a suggestion from Professor Waterhouse.

The illustrations are largely drawn from Reynolds' own paintings and drawings, but they have been chosen primarily as illustrations to this biography, and not to indicate the range of his artistic achievement, though they do so up to a point. I am deeply indebted to Mrs A. T. Copland-Griffiths for her permission to include the first and last self-portraits of Sir Joshua, which have never before been reproduced in a book about him, and the portrait of Theophila Gwatkin. I am much obliged to Messrs Agnew for a photograph of the portrait of Mary Palmer (Lady Thomond), formerly belonging to Sir Robert Edgcumbe, the present whereabouts of which are unknown to me; and to Lord Richard Cavendish for giving me photographs and for permission to publish the caricature group in his possession. Lord Ilchester has kindly allowed me to reproduce the portrait of Baretti; he wishes me to state that he retains the copyright, and that no further reproductions may be made without his permission. I am grateful to Lord Morley for leave to publish Angelica Kauffmann's portrait of Reynolds, and to various other owners, public galleries, museums, etc., noted in the List of Illustrations, for similar permissions. I thank the Middlesex Standing Joint Committee for permission to publish the Recognizance in John Bampfylde's case of 1779 (Appendix C).

I am most grateful to Professor Hilles and Professor Waterhouse for their encouragement and advice, and to the latter for the loan of photographs; to Sir Gerald Kelly, P.P.R.A., Sir Albert Richardson, P.P.R.A., Mr Sidney C. Hutchison, the librarian of the Royal Academy, and Mr Humphrey Brooke, its secretary, for their unfailing helpfulness and for permission to make use of material in the possession of the Academy; to Earl Fitzwilliam and the trustees of the Fitzwilliam Settled Estates for permission to publish Reynolds' letters to Burke; and to Dr M. J. Mannheim for his great pains in making an analysis of the handwritings of Sir Joshua and of Mary Palmer which has, in part at least, tended to confirm deductions of mine from all the other evidence.

Finally I should wish to remember with gratitude the help of the following, and to apologize to any others whom I may have inadvertently omitted to thank: Colonel A. L. Hadow, Mr Rupert Colomb, Sir Norman Gwatkin, Mr Aubrey Edgcumbe, Commander Geoffrey Snagge, Lord Inchiquin, Professor Thomas W. Copeland, Mr Rupert Scott, Mr John Summerson, Mr Charles Mitchell, Mr Iolo A. Williams, Mr R. B. Beckett, Mr Oliver Warner, the Librarian of the R.I.B.A., the Librarian of the Royal Society of Arts, the City Librarian, Sheffield, the Clerk of the Beaconsfield Urban District Council, Mr W. G. Brown of Richmond Public Library, Mr N. de Bazille Corbin of the National Trust, the Chairman of Brooks's Club, Sir Samuel Scott, Sir Owen Morshead, Mr Robert Mackworth-Young, Mr C. K. Adams of the National Portrait Gallery, Mr Martin Davies and Mr Cecil Gould of the National Gallery, the City Curator of Plymouth, the Rev. H. E. Bennett (Rector of Plympton St. Maurice), the Clerk of Plympton St Mary Rural District Council, the Curator of the Iveagh Bequest, Kenwood, the Clerk of the East Barnet Urban District Council, Mr Edward Croft-Murray of the Department of Prints and Drawings, British Museum, Miss Mary Chamot (Assistant Keeper of the Tate Gallery), the Witt Librarian of the Courtauld Institute of Art, Mr W. Ison of the Architects Department, L.C.C., the Staffs of the Archives Department of the Westminster Public Library and of the Middlesex County Record Office, Mr Harold Beaver, Mr K. S. Thompson, the Rev. C. J. Barker (Vicar of Great Torrington), Dr Oswald Goetz, Mr Willard B. Pope.

April, 1957   D. H.

Introduction: A Man and His Time

Go back beyond the electric light,
The radio and the works of steam,
And look on England dark at night
Or lit but by a taper's gleam.

Go back the last two hundred years
And there another nation find,
Of primal toils practitioners,
And men of self-supporting mind.

C. W. BRODRIBB

IT was with relief that England moved away from the severe Gothic mysteries and from the nightmare of civil war. The closing years of the seventeenth century brought a new understanding of the ordered clarity of Nature and of the laws of reason that was to shape the lives and purposes of Englishmen throughout the century to come. To Joshua Reynolds, painter, philosopher and man of letters, fell not only the honour of establishing the first great age of English art and of recording, as no one else, the likenesses of the outstanding men and women of his time; it fell to him also to attempt to rationalize that spirit of cultured and artistic progress which was characteristic of his age, and which he exemplified by a steady determination in his own life. Reynolds was not the least of those who, "at last, across the vast gulf of the monkish and deluded past", as Basil Willey has put it, "could salute the ancients from an eminence perhaps as lofty as their own".

There is a sense of respect and dedication in the gesture of the young Reynolds, at a crowded auction room on his first visit to London, pressing forward to take the hand of Alexander Pope—the hand that had written:

Nature and Nature's laws lay hid in night:
God said, *Let Newton be!* and all was light!

Reynolds never forgot his glimpse of the great little hunchback,

I

and at the end of his life told Boswell that "he had an extra-ordinary face, not an everyday countenance—a pallid, studious look; not merely a sharp keen countenance, but something grand like Cicero's".[1]

On an August day in 1704, nineteen years before Reynolds was born, Marlborough and Eugene had fought in the stubble fields of Blenheim, and among its white-walled cottages, to secure for Reynolds and his friends those spacious days of civilized progress and taste that we think of vaguely as "the eighteenth century". A world dominated by Louis XIV could never have afforded to Englishmen the same chance of displaying either their creative intellectual power or their native genius as explorers and colon-izers. Part of the nation's thanks to Marlborough was Vanbrugh's vast palace of Blenheim at Woodstock—a masterpiece of the Baroque scantily appreciated at the time of its building. It was left to Reynolds, who was born as Blenheim neared completion, to discover its full merits, to defend Vanbrugh in his masterly Thirteenth Discourse to the Royal Academy of 1786, and to praise his originality of invention, his understanding of light and shadow, his skill in composition. "This is a tribute," said Rey-nolds, "which a painter owes to an architect who composed like a painter; and was defrauded of the due reward of his merit by the wits of his time."

Not all Sir Joshua's judgements were so happy. The effect of his Tenth Discourse, as Mrs Arundell Esdaile has pointed out, was to fill our churches and cathedrals with sculptured worthies in classical togas instead of in the delightful costume of their period. That may be cause for complaint. But, despite his incon-sistencies and aberrations, England still owes to the achievement of the dignified and level-headed first President of its Royal Academy a greater debt than is always realized. For all their quali-ties, neither Hogarth nor Gainsborough brought English art into communication, as Reynolds did, with the artistic traditions of Europe. It was Reynolds who decisively rescued the English artist from a routine mediocrity; Reynolds who, in Ruskin's words, was "among the seven supreme colourists of the true painters that exist", who was "the prince of portrait painters", who "arose from the feet of the greatest masters of Italy to share their throne"; Reynolds who had the grace and patience to formu-

2

late with lasting clarity and authority a set of abstract principles
and practical conclusions which became a classic of our literature.
Because his teaching belittled instinct and genius, his practice
(which was full of both) quarrelled with his theory. Yet the freedom of the English artist to breathe a larger, intellectual air and
the standing of contemporary English art to-day, outside as well
as inside the Royal Academy, are still the measure of Reynolds'
greatness two hundred years ago. No other English artist has occupied the commanding position in his lifetime that he did.

He remains one of the most interesting of great Englishmen—
a challenge to biography that neither Boswell nor Burke would
accept. For although Reynolds as a person was probably more
widely and sincerely esteemed by his contemporaries than any of
our artists before or since, he was nevertheless, in Northcote's
words, "a mixed character", a man of infinite complexity. His
whole life is a testimony to successful ambition, a ceaseless
struggle for self-improvement. Art alone could not satisfy him;
he must succeed in literature, and in society. Thus he contrived,
with infinite pains, to shape a flowing prose, and to mould a
social character of calm dignity and poise. In his idealism and his
heroic perseverance there is much to admire; with it appears a
touch of the coolness that so often accompanies leadership and the
calculating of policy, the blandness that preserves the chairmen
of councils and committees—manifestations which, in a long
view, must be less heartening.

But, looking further, we find a man without conceit who discovers relaxation and loses his sense of inner loneliness among
small groups of friends; an amiable companion who is always
welcome and whose judgement is always respected; a philosopher
and student of beauty; a man of humour with a gift of impish
caricature, officially suppressed, which we can now fully appreciate; one with innumerable kindnesses and courtesies to his credit;
the gentle lover of children and the affectionate flatterer of women.
Far beneath the surface, again, lurks the irritable Reynolds,
emotionally frustrated, releasing occasional bursts of temper—
the combative Reynolds, increasingly evident in his last years,
when failing sight and health kept him from his easel.

It is a strange mixture, though the good predominates. And a
biographer, too, must show Reynolds as a man of his time—one

3

of those little men in bright clothes who hurries across Whitehall to his gaily painted coach in a picture by Canaletto. He walks through a London whose atmosphere is clearer than we have known; a London where the grass is greener, the bricks and roofs redder. There are chickens in a stable-yard off Whitehall; and Paul Sandby, noting a red-coat talking to a housemaid over a white-painted fence, anticipates the artful restorations of Hugh Thomson and the sentiment and lavender of Quality Street.

A man and his time, however, are seldom all that they may seem in a general view. London and its river may look neat and placid in the landscapes of Samuel Scott; yet when Reynolds first came to town the streets were noisy, filthy, ill-paved and at night of stygian blackness; traitors' heads still decorated Temple Bar. Hogarth brought some of Canaletto's innocent little figures into violent action at Tottenham Court turnpike to expose the debauchery and drunkenness against which Reynolds contended for the rational life. From his home in Leicester Fields where he listened for the postman's bell, Reynolds saw Hogarth's funeral and the proclamation of George III in front of Savile House; he saw, too, the burning of that mansion by the Gordon rioters. But in general London was a better place at the end of Reynolds' life than it had been in his youth. The city took on a new air in the fifty years during which he knew it. "Fine streets and squares, most of them regularly laid down and well paved," reported Wedenborn in the 'eighties, "present palaces to the eye . . . where a little while ago nothing was to be seen but uncultivated grounds, brick-kilns and even dung hills."

It was with the inhabitants much the same as with their city. The sum of a man's life, balancing detail and incident, leans either to good or evil. Sir Joshua Reynolds knew his failings, and was on his guard against them. By his civilized example, he did as much as one man could do to improve the manners and taste of the eighteenth century. A gentleman, "not a connoisseur of art", who saw an exhibition of Reynolds' works after his death, told Northcote "that it had raised his idea of mankind, and gave him a better opinion of the world than he had ever before conceived". Let us approach him in this spirit.

I

Plympton

I

BEFORE the rise of Plymouth, the ancient town of Plympton, five miles distant, surrounded by the well-wooded hills of South Devon, was a busy centre with a flourishing market. The Plym river formerly spread more widely; the tidal waters reached nearer the town. From 1241, Plympton was a borough which, until disfranchised by the Reform Act of 1832, sent members of Parliament to Westminster.

The traveller who comes into Plympton to-day by the road beside the Plym, noticing Lord Morley's fine stretch of woods on the farther bank, sees that the river is chalky-white from the china clay. In 1552 Leland observed that the Torry-brook near Plympton was "always redde, by reason of the sand it runneth on, and carryeth from the tynne works with it". The grey streets of the old "Stannary" town likewise reflect traces of an importance that has wandered away—the castle ruins; the remaining rows, or covered arcades, reminiscent of Chester; the guildhall front, bearing the date 1688, which juts out over the pavement. The church of St Maurice still neighbours the seventeenth-century Gothic school-house, raised above its open arcade on graceful pointed arches and columns of Roborough stone.

The south-west corner of the school grounds was once occupied by the schoolmaster's house, older than the school and externally of Tudor character. Delightful to look at, it was in its last days neither sanitary nor convenient, with rambling passages, long rooms and shabby walls. A plaque records its fate: "Here until 1871 stood the house in which Sir Joshua Reynolds was born A. D. 1723." [1]

The Reverend Samuel Reynolds, father of Joshua, came to this house on his appointment as schoolmaster in 1715, when he was thirty-four. The deed of appointment describes him as "of Tor in the said County of Devon, Clerk". A clerical and scholarly

B   5 tradition was already firmly established in his family, for he was the son of Rev. Prebendary John Reynolds (1641–92), Vicar of St Thomas's, Exeter, and the younger brother of a John Reynolds who was Fellow of King's College, Cambridge, and Fellow of Eton, and of a Rev. Joshua Reynolds who was Fellow and Bursar of Corpus Christi College, Oxford.

Samuel Reynolds had followed valiantly in his brother's footsteps by winning a scholarship at Corpus and a Fellowship at Balliol. Thereafter he faltered. His relations may have known him too well. It is alleged that he refused a living worth £700 a year because his brother John thought that "Sam would not like the situation of the Living, it was too much in the World".[2] The appointment to Plympton Grammar School, founded in 1658 under the trust of Elize Hele, must have been something of a second-best. His stipend, derived from the rental of a neighbouring farm, was £120 a year, with additional fees from those boys who were not foundation scholars. The income was by no means a large one for the support of his six children (and there were five more who did not survive their infancy).

Joshua appears to have been the third son and seventh child. He was born on July 16, 1723, and baptized on July 30, his baptism being mistakenly entered in the register of Plympton St Maurice as that of "Joseph son of Samu[ll] Reynolds Clerk". This is later corrected in a crabbed hand: "In the entry of Baptisms for the year 1723 the Person, by mistake named Joseph son of Samuel Reynolds Clerk Baptized July 30th was *Joshua* Reynolds the celebrated Painter, who died February 23, 1792."

The mother of Joshua was Theophila Potter, of Great Torrington, and she was married to Samuel Reynolds at Monkleigh, near Torrington, on December 9, 1711. Until recent years the generally accepted story of her parentage was that she was the daughter of Matthew Potter, Perpetual Curate of Great Torrington, by Theophila Baker, only child of Thomas Baker, Vicar of Bishop's Nympton, a celebrated mathematician. The story went on to relate that Matthew Potter had been Curate to Baker, that he had married his daughter against his wishes, that Baker had disinherited her, and that on her husband's death a few years later, leaving her with three young children, she became blind through grief and anxiety. The researches of O. A. R. Murray, published

6

in *Devon and Cornwall Notes and Queries*,[3] have corrected this melancholy legend, at least in part. "Matthew Potter"—a mythical figure—was never Perpetual Curate of Great Torrington and Theophila Baker was not disinherited; nor was she an only child; she benefited from her father's will after his death in 1689, and she was then unmarried.

It appears much more likely that the maternal grandmother of Joshua Reynolds was Mary Baker, the elder sister of this Theophila Baker, and that his maternal grandfather was Humphrey Potter, Rector of Nymet Rowland and Curate-in-charge of Lostwithiel, who was baptized in 1659 and died in 1690. Humphrey Potter was the son of Philip Potter, a physician (or, alternatively, apothecary) of Great Torrington, and grandson of the Rev. John Potter, Rector of Newton St Petrock. There were three children of this marriage, Elizabeth, Theophila and Thomas, all born between 1686 and 1690. Of these Theophila, who, if this identification is accepted, was to become the mother of Joshua Reynolds, was born in June, 1688, at Lostwithiel. She would thus have been twenty-three at the time of her marriage, seven years younger than her husband Samuel Reynolds.

One advantage of the new theory is that, while retaining the eminent mathematician, the Rev. Thomas Baker, as Reynolds' great-grandfather, and providing two more clergymen from the Potters as his grandfather and great-great-grandfather, it gives him the apothecary Philip Potter as a great-grandfather. We shall see when we come to consider Joshua Reynolds' character and his choice of a career, that this is a consideration of some significance.

Joshua's mother remains a shadowy figure; but Samuel Reynolds, his father, comes to life as a lovable and kind-hearted man. It has been stated that he was inefficient as a schoolmaster; of this there is no evidence. His neat, modest handwriting reveals him as a learned man of little consequence, and, in the worldly sense, a failure of great respectability. But this verdict does less than justice to one of those amiable, scholarly eccentrics who so often inspire the affection of their contemporaries and whose obvious worth and probity sometimes give them a more lasting influence on the young than is acquired by men of greater ability. He reminds one very much of Praed's Vicar:

His talk was like a stream, which runs
  With rapid change from rocks to roses:
It slipped from politics to puns,
  It passed from Mahomet to Moses;
Beginning with the Laws which keep
  The planets in their radiant courses,
And ending with some precept deep
  For dressing eels, or shoeing horses.

Samuel Reynolds was something of an astrologer, who cast horoscopes. He also wrote a treatise on the gout and a Theological Chronology. He read political pamphlets and sermons, and he dabbled in medicine and pharmacology. He was absentminded, and his generosity could be exploited by the unscrupulous. His daughter Elizabeth records that he once gave half a guinea to that notorious rogue, "the King of the Gypsies", Bampfylde Moore Carew, "which was (her mother said) all the money they had in the world". He was an affectionate father, and at times, according to his daughter, "would call in his children into his study & give them lectures on different subjects, once she remembered the lecture was on a human skull which he had procured for the purpose".

Joshua Reynolds was fortunate in his father—whose gentle and benign countenance he recorded in an early portrait—and in the many scholars and literary men who were among his forbears. They influenced profoundly the philosophical cast of his mind and of his developing character. The strongly religious atmosphere in which he was brought up at Plympton may have been partly responsible for the marked distaste which he later showed for formal religion; but his surroundings induced a compensating taste for homely philosophy. "The great principle of being happy in this World is, not to mind or be affected with small things", was a saying of his father's which he treasured; "If you take too much care of yourself, Nature will cease to take care of you", was another. He learned these lessons better than his sister Fanny who became a great fuss-pot.[4]

2

The literature and philosophy which they found at home, imparted in a strong Devonshire accent, must have influenced not only Joshua's and Fanny's leanings towards the literary and artistic life, but also his sister Mary's aptitude for reducing local manners and customs into the terms of dialect conversation. Joshua himself became an authority on the Devon dialect, and was consulted on that subject by Edmond Malone,[5] while Mary's *Devonshire Dialogue* is acknowledged as a minor classic of its kind. In one passage of the latter work, Betty, a farm servant, describes how her mistress brought her quickly out of church lest she be tempted to go to the local inn with her sweetheart Rab:

> Good now, her can't abide zich may-games and high-de-lows sabbath days. Gracious! what a hurly-burly 'twas! How the volks veased out o' church—higgeldy piggeldy, helter skelter: zich jitting, driving, and dringing. I thort no other, but that I shou'd be squat to death. . . .
>
> RAB. It was who shou'd get virst to the Pigeons, to get a good place.[6]

If this was a piece of local observation common to Joshua's youth, it may help to explain why, after spending his boyhood in the pews at Plympton, he later made unerringly for the Turk's Head in Gerrard Street. But his religious upbringing left its mark; Professor Hilles has shown him to us, in later life, writing careful notes on certain passages in the Apocrypha.[7] He told Bishop Lowth in 1778 that Isaiah "was allways my favorite Book of the old Testament" and that he remembered much of it by heart.[8] When he was President of the Royal Academy he drafted a letter to Nathaniel Hone, who had submitted a caricature of two monks carousing before a crucifix, in which he declared that the President and Council "have that fear about them of offending against the rules of decency, and have no desire to ridicule religion or make the Cross a subject for buffoonery".[9]

Joshua was not, however, a goody-goody little boy. When Joseph Farington visited Plympton long after his death, he had a talk with the then schoolmaster and noted a piece of lingering gossip:

> Adjoining the school there is an Orchard into which Sir Joshua confessed He sometimes stole to get an apple, & when he was at Plympton with Dr Johnson, He left the dinner party to pick an apple in the orchard which had afforded Him formerly such gratification.[10]

In later life, Joshua displayed a versatility in spelling that is a little unusual even for the eighteenth century. Perhaps this was part of his determination not to "be affected with small things". It would, however, be a mistake to suppose that his education was neglected. He acquired, at least, some Latin at Plympton Grammar School, and his school Ovid shows signs of careful reading and annotation. But he benefited still more from living as a child in a house full of miscellaneous books. He soon made acquaintance with the classical writers and with Pope, Shakespeare, Milton, Dryden, *The Spectator* and *The Tatler*. Other volumes stimulated his artistic interest. On a window-seat in the parlour, he discovered, at the age of eight, a translation of Padre Pozzo's treatise called *The Jesuit's Perspective*, which he read to his lasting profit. He devoured with a growing excitement Jacob Cats' *Book of Emblems* and an English translation of Félibien's *Tent of Darius Explained*, thus obtaining an early liking for old engravings and woodcuts; the Royal Academy preserves his signed copy of Jost Ammon's *Kunstbüchlin*, printed at Frankfort in 1599. But the book which particularly influenced him as a schoolboy was Jonathan Richardson's *Essay on the Theory of Painting* (1715) and this as much for its moral and philosophical qualities as for its art theory.

William Cotton transcribed a number of passages from Richardson which show very clearly how Reynolds was influenced in his aspirations by the *Theory of Painting*:

> The pleasure that painting, as a dumb art, gives us, is like what we have from music; its beautiful forms, colours, and harmony, are to the eye, what sound and the harmony of that kind are to the ear. . . .
>
> Painting gives us not only the persons, but the characters of great men. . . .
>
> In order to assist and inform the invention, a painter ought to

converse with, and observe all sorts of people, chiefly the best, and
to read the best books, and no other: he should observe the different
and various effects of men's passions, and those of other animals, and
in short all nature, and make sketches of what he observes, to help
the memory. . . .

It is not every picture-maker that ought to be called a Painter, as
every Rhymer, or Grub-Street Tale-writer is not a Poet or Historian.
A Painter ought to be a title of dignity and understood to imply a
person endued with such excellencies of mind and body as have ever
been the foundation of leaders amongst men. . . .

The way to be an excellent Painter is to be an excellent man, and
these united make a character that would shine even in a better world
than this. . . .

Reading Richardson, and appreciating his cherished longing
to see an English revival of "the ancient, great, and beautiful taste
in painting", we begin to understand how it was that Reynolds
adopted his exacting ideals so early in life. His aims were set so
high that it was likely that he would be continually dissatisfied
with his achievement and committed to a ceaseless struggle for
improvement. We see, too, how the pursuit of an ideal career
such as Richardson advocated might lead him deliberately to seek
the acquaintance of the great writers and intellectuals of the time,
and even to try his own hand with the pen. Reynolds' family
background had already given him an inclination to literature;
Richardson's precepts made it a duty for a true painter to be a man
of wide culture.

Joshua Reynolds was not a natural scholar. He was born into
a household where every penny counted. The example of his
book-loving father and the narrow routine of the grammar
school needed to be reinforced by a strong wit and a steady perseverance if they were to lead to greatness. He was, in the best
sense, a self-educated man. From his schooldays until his last illness, he remained in essentials the same person—ever quick to
seize the opportunity for self-improvement, to make a harmonious
synthesis of borrowings and experience, to capture and maintain
each new position.

Such a career demanded strict self-control, vitality, physical
health. Joshua Reynolds had all these from an early age. He caught
measles at nine, and at eleven survived an attack of smallpox

which scarred his face for life. Tom Taylor quotes his own account from an early commonplace book:

1734-5, Mar. 5.—I was seiz'd with the small-pox.

Mar. 10.—Munday, the 6th day of the Distemper, nothing amiss in my Regimen hitherto. I had a blister at 4 this morning.

Mar. 11.—Tuesday, the 7th day, perhaps the 8th, seems to have been the worst day: then most outragious.

Mar. 12.—Wednesday, the 8th day, extremely low.

Mar. 13.—Thursday, the 9th day, being low, and somewhat hungry, I had broth at night, tho' contrary to Mr Ruport's express order.

Mar. 14.—Friday, the 10th day, having slept well, I was brave.

Mar. 15.—Saturday, the 11th, rather the 12th day, taken out of bed.

Mar. 16.—Sunday, the 13th day, I sat up.

Mar. 17.—I ventured down stairs.

3

Nearly sixty years later, and two months before Reynolds died, James Boswell sat beside him, taking notes for a biography that was never to be written. These notes are important, for a dying man remembers essentials.

Boswell enquired what first moved him to become an artist, and Reynolds replied that "His Father was very fond of drawings, & loved to encourage his children in drawing. His two elder sisters did little things & he copied them." He told Boswell that he used to copy all the frontispieces and plates in books, particularly those in Plutarch's Lives, and that his "great fund of imitation" was Jacob Cats' book. He told him how he had read *The Jesuit's Perspective* at eight years old, and that it had taught him so well, "he has never studied any book on it more". Thereupon he had drawn the school at Plympton—a difficult subject, with its pillared arcade—and "he did it so well that his Father said: 'Now this exemplifies what the Author says in his Preface that by observing these rules a man may do wonders; for this is wonderful.'" Reynolds added that "he then began to try likenesses of relations & friends—rubbed them out & did them again. When he read

Richardson's Principles of Painting he was struck with admiration of the Art—thought it beyond all others—thought Raphael beyond Pope & all eminent persons—and indeed (said he smiling 20 Decr. 1791) I have indulged that notion all along." [11]

According to his sister Elizabeth, Joshua's earliest artistic attempts were made with burnt sticks on the whitewashed walls of a long passage of the schoolmaster's house. Some more permanent early drawings in pen and ink are now at the Royal Academy—for example, a drawing of a fish, inscribed "A Perch drawn not from another Picture, but from the Life"; a neat perspective arrangement of cubes signed "I. R. fecit" (among the collection of drawings formerly belonging to Sir John Herschel); and the perspective drawing of a window, done on the back of a Latin exercise and charmingly inscribed by his father: "This is drawn by Joshua in school out of pure idleness."

Joshua was friendly as a boy with Richard Edgcumbe, later the second Baron Edgcumbe, who was seven years older than himself; his earliest surviving portrait is a souvenir of this friendship. It is a likeness of "Dick" Edgcumbe's tutor, the Rev. Thomas Smart, Vicar of Maker near Mount Edgcumbe, and was painted when Joshua was about twelve. This robust impression of a large round face with a lusty red complexion, set between a white woolly wig and clerical bands, now hangs in the office of the *Western Morning News* at Plymouth. According to tradition, it was derived from a drawing "taken in church on the artist's thumb nail", and was painted in a boat-house at Cremyll beach under Mount Edgcumbe, on sail canvas and with shipwright's paint. One would hardly approach this schoolboy lark with large expectations; yet, for a boy of twelve, it is a remarkable effort. The colours are crude; there is an element of caricature; but Joshua tackled his subject fearlessly and the portrait has a primitive strength.

There is a tradition that before he was seventeen Joshua painted a portrait of Dick Edgcumbe's father patting a very large dog. The artist treated him rather more respectfully than he had treated Mr Smart. This picture, re-painted in the 1740's, was unfortunately destroyed by enemy action in the war of 1939-45.

Clearly Joshua was showing unusual artistic talent. Before he was fifteen his father was in correspondence with Mr Bulteel of

Flete, six miles from Plympton, who strongly recommended that he be sent to London and promised to introduce him to "those in artistic circles". In a letter to Bulteel of May 16, 1738, Samuel Reynolds says: "I believe, there will come something from it, if not for the present"; and he reveals that Joshua, who was then away from home, was already an indifferent correspondent ("He told the messenger he would write me a long letter the next day, but he has not hitherto been as good as his word, and now, I perceive he will not").[12]

It was not until two years later, however, that Samuel Reynolds embarked on the important correspondence with his friend Mr Cutcliffe, a Bideford lawyer, from which extracts are printed in Leslie and Taylor's biography. This correspondence lasted for the remainder of Samuel Reynolds' life and tells us most of what we know about the opening phase of Joshua's artistic progress.

In his first letter to Cutcliffe, of March 17, 1740, Samuel Reynolds mentioned that a Plympton neighbour, Mr Craunch, had already taken a friendly interest in Joshua's future. The boy's father indicated that he had seriously contemplated making him an apothecary, hinting that, if this career was chosen, he might be able to instruct him personally; he was also contemplating apprenticing Joshua to that local doctor who had ordered him not to take broth during his attack of smallpox. The consideration thus given to an apothecary's career for Joshua is the more interesting in the light both of our knowledge that his great-grandfather was an apothecary and of the fact that he later showed an absorbed interest, fully worthy of that profession, in devising quack nostrums for his paints (with unfortunate effects, in many cases, on the stability of his colours).

But Samuel Reynolds went on to tell Cutcliffe that he was examining the alternative of making Joshua a painter:

> . . . Joshua has a very great genius for drawing, and lately, on his own head, has begun even painting; so that Mr Warmell, who is both a painter and a player, having lately seen but his first performances, said, if he had his hands full of business, he would rather take Joshua for nothing than another with 50£. Mr Craunch told me, as to this letter, he could put me in a way. Mr Hudson (who is Mr Richardson's son-in-law) used to be down at Bideford, and would be so, he believed, within these two months; he persuaded me to propose the

matter to you, and that you should propose it to Mr Hudson, that
Joshua might show him some of his performances in drawing, and,
if the matter was likely to take effect, should take a journey to Bideford himself. I mentioned this to Joshua, who said he would rather
be an apothecary than an *ordinary* painter; but if he could be bound
to an eminent master, he should choose the latter; that he had seen a
print from Mr Hudson's painting which he had been very much
pleased with. . . .

The vision of Joshua, unknown to fame, passing a blameless
life as a Devonshire apothecary among his jars and bottles, fades
before his determination to be no "ordinary" painter. Naturally
he would be excited at the prospect of having Thomas Hudson
for a master. Hudson's father-in-law, Jonathan Richardson, had
already fired him with the highest ambitions, suggesting the
career of artist-cum-writer as a remote but attainable ideal, and
Hudson himself, in 1740, was rising to the head of his profession
as a fashionable portrait-painter in the succession from John Riley.
The established tradition was mechanical and dull, although,
remarkably enough, it was in 1740 that Hogarth presented his
"Captain Coram" to the Foundling Hospital—a healthy portent
for the future but a masterpiece in isolation. Hudson was not
without original talent; unfortunately he exerted it rarely. His
studio throughout the next fifteen years was to be a remorseless
factory of hard and unimaginative portraiture, now largely rele-
gated to the dark passages and staircases of our country houses;
for a boy like Joshua, who hoped to do better, the experience of
attending that studio proved salutary and useful.

After this letter from Samuel Reynolds to Mr Cutcliffe, events
moved rapidly. Hudson inspected Joshua's specimens, and Joshua
made the journey to Bideford. It was arranged that Joshua Reynolds should be bound apprentice to Thomas Hudson for four
years. His father and his elder sister Mary Palmer provided him
with the necessary premium of £120.

Craunch and Cutcliffe, their parts accomplished, recede into
the background of Joshua's life, to be gratefully remembered.
We can poetically imagine them now joining in symbolical farewell with his excellent parents and with such "formative influences" as the Edgcumbes, red-faced Thomas Smart, Mr Bulteel
and Mr Warmell. The group would be incomplete without one

ROR

additional figure, a friend of Joshua's father who had a name worthy of the *Devonshire Dialogue*—Zachariah Mudge, of Exeter, "a very learned and thinking man", as Edmund Burke said, "& much inclined to Philosophy in the spirit of the Platonists", who early "disposed" young Joshua to his habit of generalizing.

They raise their hands in valediction as the coach leaves the cloistered school-house of Plympton, climbs past the church tower, and makes for the London road.

II

The Years of Preparation

I

JOSHUA travelled up to London on October 13, 1740, with Thomas Cutcliffe, the son of his father's friend, and a gentleman called Mr Lantrow. "He had a most prosperous journey," recorded Samuel Reynolds, "(which is a most prosperous beginning of this affair, and I pray God, it may be as happily accomplished)." Out of the warm valleys and woods of the West, over the bare Wiltshire plains, through the many compact little towns of eighteenth-century England, and always onward to the incomparable metropolis—it was a road that, with many of the great houses along it, Joshua Reynolds was eventually to know well, for he never forgot that his roots were in Devon.

Reynolds nevertheless became as great a townsman as his friend Samuel Johnson, who—at the time of Reynolds' first arrival—had been living in London for three years on very little money. "Slow rises worth, by poverty depress'd!" wrote Johnson pointedly in his poem "London", but he told Boswell that he had dined very well for eightpence at that time, and that a friend had assured him a man could then live in London for thirty pounds a year "without being contemptible". Reynolds no doubt had more than this, but not perhaps much. He was able, however, on coming to London, to lodge for a time with his uncle John Reynolds at his chambers in the Temple. Hudson was temporarily out of town, in Bath; when he returned, Joshua went to live at his house. It has often been stated that Hudson then occupied Nos. 55-6 Great Queen Street, but investigation has conclusively shown that Hudson's residence in the street did not begin until after Reynolds had left him, and moreover that his house was never Nos. 55-6 but a house several doors away, demolished in the latter part of the eighteenth century.[1] The scene of Joshua Reynolds' apprenticeship to studio life cannot therefore be identified.

Though Joshua walked through dirty, noisy streets, under huge creaking signs, the manners of London had improved since the days of Jonathan Wild. A pedestrian naturally preferred to keep as far from the gutter as possible, but already, as Johnson pointed out, there was no longer a quarrel between "those who gave the wall and those who took it . . . if one is taking the wall, another yields it; and it is never a dispute". Joshua, we may assume, would have "given the wall"; but, threading the streets on this first visit to London, he had other things to think about.

A chalk self-portrait in Lord Harcourt's collection at Nuneham gives an idea of him at seventeen—a plump, purposeful face with hair falling to the shoulders, and in his eyes a hint of determination and surmise. It is a capable, straightforward drawing such as Hudson would have encouraged. As a student Joshua was most diligent. Samuel Reynolds told Mr. Cutcliffe that "he has behaved himself mighty well in this affair, and done his duty on his part". On December 30, 1740, he was able to add: "Joshua is very sensible of his happiness in being under such a master, in such a family, in such a city, and in such an employment. . . ." Some personal distresses cloud the picture, for Joshua's elder brother Humphrey and his younger brother Martin both died at this time, the former, a lieutenant in the Navy, being drowned on a return voyage from India. But, with Sir Robert Walpole, the Prime Minister, coming to sit in Hudson's studio, Devonshire seemed a long way away; and it was while running an errand for Thomas Hudson at an auction that he had the thrill of taking the hand of Alexander Pope, the memory of which remained with him throughout his life.

The near-presence of great men stimulated Joshua's ambition no less than the easel and canvas of a fashionable studio. He was early conscious of a double motive in his own advancement. If he was to go down to posterity as a great painter, it was not as a genius in an attic that he wished to be remembered but as an equal among the first intellects of his time. Meanwhile, and more important still, he found a painter's life enjoyable. His father was able to report to Mr Cutcliffe on August 3, 1742, that Joshua had told him: "While I am doing this I am the happiest creature alive." This is something to be remembered alongside Lord

Melbourne's remark to Haydon that "Reynolds was a hard working old dog" who "worked too hard to be happy".[2]

What Hudson could teach him of the tricks of the portrait-painter's trade was probably soon learned. As an artist Joshua already had larger intimations. Hudson's best service to him, perhaps, lay in his recommending him to make copies of some drawings of Guercino's, which were so well done, Northcote tells us, that they passed for originals. Joshua must also have benefited from studying Hudson's famous collection of prints and drawings, and to it he probably owed his first acquaintance with Rembrandt, whose work was profoundly to influence his own.[3]

Joshua later deplored his want of facility in drawing. "The disadvantages I have been under cannot be enough regretted," he wrote:

> I began late. Facility of invention was therefore to be given up. I considered it impossible to arrive at it, but not impossible to be correct, though with more labour. I had the grace not to despise the riches I could not attain, and sometimes administered to myself some comfort in observing how often this facility *ended* in common place. . . .[4]

Much though he regretted that his profession had not been "determined in the cradle", he made up for it by a continuing passion for self-improvement. Defects of proportion and drawing were compensated by an instinctive sense of harmony in composition. He improved so rapidly in Hudson's studio that he may soon have been able to earn small sums of money from casual commissions. Long after Reynolds' death, Joseph Farington recorded a significant conversation he had had with Thomas Coutts, the banker, about his early days. Coutts told Farington that he had known Reynolds while he was a pupil of Hudson, but this must have been a misunderstanding because Coutts was not born until 1735. There is, however, no reason to doubt the general truth of Coutts' statement, applied to this period, that "when Sir Joshua began to get money he did not know what to do with it being totally ignorant of such matters". Coutts goes on to tell the story of a sum of money entrusted by Reynolds to a friend for investment in "the Long Annuities" which was eventually discovered not to have been invested at all but used by the "friend" for his own speculations. "This unprincipled conduct gave cause of alarm, but by proper management the money was gradually recovered." That some such incident occurred is inherently probable and may go far to explain Reynolds' subsequent wariness in money matters.[5]

He did not stay with Hudson for the full four years of his indentures but returned to Devonshire before three years had passed. Farington alleges that Hudson was jealous of Reynolds because he had painted a remarkable portrait of one of his servants and that he dismissed him because of his failure to deliver a picture to the drapery-painter on a rainy evening. If these actual incidents did not occur, probably others very like them did. Obviously Reynolds realized that, having learned all that Hudson could teach him of the workings of a fashionable portrait-painter's studio, it would be a great mistake to stay longer with an insensitive master whose lack of conscience had greatly disappointed his early idealism. But Reynolds was too prudent a youth to depart from an influential senior in open hostility, and his father benignly poured on the troubled waters whatever oil was available, writing to his friend Cutcliffe on August 19, 1743: "I shall only say, there is no controversy I was ever let into, wherein I was so little offended with either party. In the mean time I bless God, and Mr Hudson, and you, for the extreme success that has attended Joshua hitherto. . . ."

What is certain is that by the beginning of 1744, Joshua, aged twenty, had already been back in Devon for several months and was rapidly establishing himself as a portrait-painter in Plymouth Dock (now known as Devonport). Samuel Reynolds told his friend Cutcliffe on January 3, 1744, that Joshua had then painted twenty portraits, including that of the commissioner of the dockyard, and that he had engaged to paint ten more. Several of these portraits, signed and dated 1744 on the back, were of the Kendall family of Pelyn; they are workmanlike efforts, showing the Hudson influence. Tom Taylor says that he painted Mrs Kendall twice and received seven pounds for the two pictures.

Reynolds was soon back in London, however, and on good terms with Hudson, for his father told Cutcliffe on December 7, 1744: "I understand that Joshua by his master's means is introduced into a club composed of the most famous men in their profession"—perhaps the club that met at Old Slaughter's in St Martin's Lane. Where Reynolds lived in London at this time is unknown; but it was probably now that he first settled in this neighbourhood, which was to be associated with the greater part of his professional life. If he did not remain in London throughout the whole of the next two years, he was certainly there again in May, 1745, when we find his father writing to Cutcliffe:

> . . . Joshua's master is very kind to him; he comes to visit him pretty often, and freely tells him where his pictures are faulty, which is a great advantage; and when he has finished anything of his own, he is pleased to ask Joshua's judgment, which is a great honour. . . .

This indicates that the balance between pupil and master was being readjusted; there are even suggestions, in some of Hudson's later pictures, that he had looked at Reynolds' work rather closely, though it is improbable that he would ever have admitted a debt.

2

The next phase of Reynolds' career was determined by the death of his father. C. R. Leslie states that, after this happened, he took a house at Plymouth Dock which he shared with his two unmarried sisters. The schoolmaster's house at Plympton would have had to be given up; Reynolds' mother went to live at Great Torrington with her married daughter Mrs Palmer.

It is usually said that Samuel Reynolds died on Christmas Day, 1746, and a tablet to his memory over the north door of the church of Plympton St Maurice gives 1746 as the year of his death. But the parish burial register has the entry "Mr Samuel Reynolds, Minister, X^ber 26" under the heading "Burials in 1745". His name appears between "Mary Smith Single Woman" and "Samuel Coggin a Stranger", and all are firmly ruled off from "Burials in 1746". This piece of evidence, coupled with the fact that there is no record of Reynolds having worked in London during 1746, suggests that he returned to Devonshire earlier than has been generally believed. Yet a successor at the school was not appointed until early in 1747, and the family may have been allowed to live in the schoolmaster's house until the Rev. John Davis arrived.

Probably the date of Samuel Reynolds' death, which we must now assume to have taken place at Christmas, 1745, can be accounted decisive in fixing the time of Joshua's return. His elder brother Robert was already established as an ironmonger in Exeter; and Joshua, his father's favourite son in whom he took great pride, will have been welcomed at home. It is therefore reasonable to conclude that Joshua returned to Devon at Christmas, 1745, and to affirm that the group of portraits dated "about 1746" were painted at Plympton or Plymouth.

These include a number of family portraits such as the painter would have been likely to undertake for purposes of record before the household broke up. There is no portrait of Mrs Reynolds, but there is the profile portrait of his father, now at Plymouth, which breathes affectionate admiration and may well have been painted as a posthumous memorial; there are portraits of his sisters Frances and Elizabeth (later Mrs William Johnson), both dark, intelligent, temperamental-looking girls with pronounced thyroid tendencies; and, most important for our purpose, there is a self-portrait (Plate I), still in possession of his collateral descendants.

This first self-portrait in oils, painted in his early twenties at the outset of his career, will be studied with the greatest interest by all admirers of Reynolds. It makes a fit companion for the last of his self-portraits (Plate XVa). The two pictures suggest an absorbing contrast between the stirrings of youthful ambition and the pride of recognized achievement.

While painting this early self-portrait, Joshua looked at himself critically. He saw a young man in his early twenties, not downright handsome but not ill-favoured, wearing a dark cloak and a white collar open at the neck, his thick hair, unpowdered, hanging long and carelessly. One might suppose from the expression of the face—painted with a native insight and delicacy that owes little to Thomas Hudson—that its possessor was a man of intelligence, of talent and almost effeminate sensitivity, but that he was not yet sure of himself, was conscious of some weakness or of a coming trial of strength. Such might well be the face of a young man who had lately lost the guidance of his father and who had his own way to make in the world.

This reading of Reynolds' portrait at twenty-two or twenty-three accords with what little we know of his character at this

1. JOSHUA REYNOLDS. The earliest self-portrait in oils, *circa* 1746
$(29\frac{1}{2}'' \times 24\frac{1}{2}'')$

time. Edmond Malone says that "after some little dissipation, he sat down seriously to the study and practice of his art". Reynolds himself told Malone that he "passed about three years in company from whom little improvement could be got; and when he recollected this period of his life, he always spoke of it as so much time thrown away—so far at least as related to a knowledge of the world and of mankind, of which he ever afterwards lamented the loss".

Reynolds' biographers have generally assumed that the whole of the period from the death of his father until his departure for Italy was spent at Plymouth. This is most unlikely. Accepting Christmas, 1745, as the date of Samuel Reynolds' death, it is probable that the following year, 1746, was spent in Devonshire; but there is evidence in three letters to a Miss Weston[6] (written while he was abroad between 1749 and 1752) that in 1747-9 Reynolds was frequently in London and familiar with the artistic life of the capital. His request to her to look after some "goods" of his during his absence indicates that he had a *pied-à-terre* in London. Probably he divided his time between London and Plymouth during these years.

C. R. Leslie implies that Reynolds' alleged "dissipation" occurred after his father's death; Malone specifically dates it to the years following 1743. Whatever the truth about this, there are signs in the letters to Miss Weston, that Reynolds did not live an unduly cloistered life in the years before he went to Italy. He asks her to remember him to his friends "not forgetting the little Girl at Westminster by the Park". And in a later letter, after acknowledging the pleasure with which her English news had been received by him and his friends in Rome, he adds: "But nobody but me knew the westminster Girl a lack a lack she has been brought to bed and tis a fine Chumning boy but who is Lord John? Well who would have thought it oh the nasty creature to have to do with a man."

In another letter to Miss Weston, describing an accident in Minorca in 1749, Reynolds mentions—if this is the correct interpretation of a damaged manuscript—that his "lips are spoiled for kissing". For kissing whom? Miss Weston? The notorious gossip "Anthony Pasquin" declared that she professed an unrequited love for Reynolds. There is no evidence in the letters that Reynolds was in love with Miss Weston, but they leave open the question whether she was in love with him.

With Reynolds, the sowing of wild oats was secondary to his pursuit of his profession. Any suggestion of youthful cynicism and world-weariness that we can trace in the self-portrait of 1746 had vanished by the time that Reynolds came to paint the famous self-portrait in the National Portrait Gallery, in which he shades his face with his left hand as he gazes towards the spectator (Plate IV). According to the best modern opinion, this picture was painted in 1753-4, after Reynolds' return from Italy; and it shows a new confidence and determination, a striking broadening of character which is reflected in the features.

But even between 1746 and 1749 Reynolds applied himself to portrait-painting with assiduity and a considerable measure of success. The local gentry of Devon and the naval officers of Plymouth provided many of his subjects. A group of the Eliot family shows the Van Dyck influence. He also painted the painstaking landscape at Port Eliot of "Plymouth Sound from Cattedown". His portrait (1746) of Captain the Hon. John Hamilton, in the Duke of Abercorn's collection, demonstrates a remarkable strength and virility, foreshadowing the achievement of his prime. Malone tells us that when Reynolds saw this picture again in later life he was agreeably surprised and lamented that he had not made greater progress.

Two further interesting examples of his work at this time are the portraits of the unknown "Captain Roberts", in his white stock and red waistcoat, signed and dated 1747, and of George First Earl of Mount-Edgcumbe, attributed to 1748. Both can be seen at the National Maritime Museum, Greenwich. They show that Reynolds' struggle to emancipate himself from the heavy hand of his master was not an easy one, and that his progress was uneven and subject to set-backs. Commodore Edgcumbe, as he then was, makes a pompous, conventional, Hudsonian figure—a flat piece of painting enlivened only by a long-tailed bird in a tree and a ship at anchor in a theatrical sunset. By contrast, the head-and-shoulders of Captain Roberts is a masterpiece of direct observation and vigorous confident handling.

Like several of Reynolds' portraits of this period, the Captain Roberts is painted in a feigned oval. The firmly modelled head is remarkable for the lightness of the flesh tints and the thinness of the shadows. The portrait is scarcely excelled in freshness and candour by any that Reynolds painted after his visit to Italy.[7] Comparing it with his own early self-portrait (Plate I), we note that he already had a firm grasp of contrasting shades of character.

Portraits like those of Captain Hamilton and Captain Roberts induce some intriguing speculations as to the course that Reynolds' art might have taken if he had never gone to Italy; for he was already showing the unmistakable signs of mastery. His first portrait groups of the Eliot and Neate families, naïve and immature as they are, have graceful and amusing touches; and, seasoning the Hudsonian stolidity of some of the portraits, there are passages of painting—such as the white turban worn by the black boy in the portrait of Captain Ourry in Lord Morley's collection—which, as Professor Waterhouse has pointed out, are as agreeably handled as any in his later work. The frankness of the best of these early portraits suggest that the influence of Hogarth and Allan Ramsay was engaged in moulding a native English genius. Another more surprising influence Reynolds himself acknowledged—that of William Gandy of Exeter, whose example taught him the vital lesson that "a picture ought to have a richness in its texture, as if the colours had been composed of cream or cheese, and the reverse of a hard and husky or dry manner".

It was no amateur, then, but an artist of proved accomplishment who on a May morning in 1749 saw Drake's Island and the Hoe fade into the skyline behind him and began the first stage of his voyage to Italy.

3

Reynolds' visit to Italy, which had such an important effect on his career and such epoch-making results in the history of English art, was entirely the result of chance. Like many another young artist, he may have thought longingly of an Italian journey, but he had little money and there were no scholarship grants to take him oversea. If strong westerly winds had not been blowing in the Channel at the end of April, 1749, it is unlikely that Reynolds would ever have realized his dream or trod the floor of the Vatican.

Augustus Keppel, two years younger than Reynolds and destined to be his life-long friend, was in 1749 one of the most gallant and popular naval officers of the day. Descended from a noble Dutch family and grandson of the first Earl of Albemarle who came over with William of Orange, pride of birth mixed in him with a natural charm and frankness that made him generally beloved. He was short of stature ("little Keppel"). In early manhood a broken nose spoiled his looks and in later life he was paunchy. But his eyes were gay and eager, his step confident; seamen remembered his smile.

Keppel had proved himself by sailing round the world with Anson in the *Centurion*, and now held command of this famous vessel. The *Centurion's* main deck was narrow, forty feet wide at the most; her bows were so lean that she was lively in a head sea. She was a handsome ship, formerly of sixty guns but reduced by 1749 to fifty. The graceful model at Greenwich shows that she had adequate cabin space for a Mediterranean cruise but testifies to the endurance of the men who sailed with Anson.

In January, 1749, Captain Keppel was entrusted with a diplomatic mission to the States of Barbary and appointed to the chief command in the Mediterranean with the rank of Commodore. The *Centurion* left Spithead in company with the *Lyme* on April 22, but unexpectedly had to make for Plymouth. Keppel explained to the Admiralty that, meeting "strong westerly winds, it occasioned my springing both topmasts,—damaging some of my rigging which obliged me to put in here the 26th instant".[8]

Keppel took the opportunity of the enforced stoppage to stay with his friend Lord Edgcumbe at his home nearby. What could be more natural than that he should be introduced to young Joshua Reynolds, the friend and chosen painter of the Edgcumbe family? The pair liked each other at sight, and, while the rigging was being repaired, Reynolds had time to explain himself. With Lord Edgcumbe's encouragement, Keppel soon offered him a free passage to the Mediterranean, which was accepted with enthusiasm. Reynolds' sisters, Mrs Palmer and Mrs Johnson, came forward with loans of money for his expenses in Italy.

"11 May Plymouth. At 10 A.M. Made the Signal & Weigh'd", thus runs the Captain's log of the *Centurion*.[9] Reynolds spent much of the time at sea reading Keppel's excellent collection of books. He had the run of Keppel's cabin, and shared his wine. The next entry in the log is "24 May Tagus. At 6 (A.M.) Anchored in Tagus River". Reynolds went ashore with Keppel at Lisbon and told Lord Edgcumbe that he was lucky enough to see "a bull feast, and the procession of *Corpus Christi*".[10] They stayed five days before going on to Cadiz. There he saw "another bull feast". On June 10 they reached Gibraltar.

From Gibraltar Keppel sailed over to Tetuan, in an attempt to assist the British Consul, who was held in confinement by the Moorish Governor with four Gibraltar fishermen captured by a Tetuan cruiser. He had some success in alleviating the lot of these and other captives of the Moors, but soon had to return to Gibraltar, whence he set out with his newly formed squadron for Algiers at the end of July.

Keppel's purpose at Algiers was to seek audience of "His Highness Mahomet Effendi, Bashaw and Dey of Algiers, etc., etc.", and endeavour to persuade him to refrain from molesting British shipping. The *Centurion*, flying Keppel's red broad pendant at the main-top-mast, was received by a salute of twenty-one guns and returned the compliment. By mistake Keppel's twenty-first gun was loaded. The shot did not reach the shore, but the Dey made the most of it, telling Keppel that, "added to the red flag you wear" he looked upon it "as a mark of your being on no good design".

There followed an awkward interview with the Dey, at which Reynolds was present. "Whenever the Commodore went *a shore* at Cadiz Lisbon Gibraltar he allways took me with him," Reynolds told Miss Weston, "and even when he waited upon the Day or King of Algiers I went with him and have had the honour of shaking him by the hand three several times." The Dey being an elusive old brigand, the negotiations were inconclusive and had to be continued at intervals for the next two years.

4

The *Centurion* proceeded to Port Mahon, Minorca, and on August 18 "Made the signal & Anchored off Quarantine Island". Reynolds landed soon afterwards. He remained in Minorca until January, 1750, which was much longer than he intended. Keppel introduced him to the Governor, General William Blakeney,* "in so strong a manner" that the General insisted on being Reynolds' host throughout his stay. A number of English ladies graced the island; the Governor and his naval visitors gave a series of balls; and Reynolds at first spent a most agreeable time.

A riding accident kept Reynolds in Minorca longer than he wished. He fell from his horse down a precipice, damaging his face so badly that he was confined to his room. But he made the best of this misfortune by devoting himself to his painting and told Miss Weston that he earned a hundred pounds while at Port Mahon. Allowing for the very low prices that he was then charging, he must have painted twenty-five or thirty portraits, mostly of army and naval officers. Few of these pictures have been traced. One of them, at Greenwich, is the first of his portraits of Keppel, slim, nervous, Nelson-like, with his hand in his tunic. Another may be the portrait at Greenwich of a naval lieutenant carrying a telescope; it has a ship in the background that could be the *Centurion*. Reynolds may also have painted a portrait of himself at Minorca—a stout young fellow in a red coat with full cheeks and a tanned complexion wearing a broad-brimmed gold-laced hat casting a deep Rembrandtesque shadow over his face.[11]

Years later, when Reynolds was at his zenith, Fanny Burney had a talk with an Irish ex-commissary who had been one of his sitters in Minorca. "He drew my picture there, and then he knew how to take a moderate price; but now, I vow, ma'am, 'tis scandalous—scandalous, indeed! to pay a fellow here seventy guineas for scratching out a head!" "Sir," demurred another member of the company, "you know not how much he is improved since you knew him in Minorca."

A remark of Dr Johnson's is also apposite. He once declared that "a man cannot know modes of life as well in Minorca as in London. But he can study mathematics as well in Minorca." And no doubt he can study painting equally well. Yet for posterity the main interest of Reynolds' stay in Minorca has lain less in the thirty portraits he painted there than in his fall down the cliff and the damage it did to his face. His upper lip was badly bruised and gashed, and the whole face suffered.[12] The extent to which

* Blakeney had defended Stirling during the '45 and was destined to conduct a gallant but unsuccessful defence of Minorca against the French in 1756.

Reynolds recorded these injuries in subsequent self-portraits has been exaggerated. The rendering of the lips in the National Portrait Gallery self-portrait (Plate IV) affords little of the evidence that assists the dating of this picture to 1753-4; the lips are very much the same as those in the self-portrait of about 1746 (Plate I). And later self-portraits, such as that of the Royal Academy which presents him in his D.C.L. robes, show only a faintly perceptible scar.[13]

The truth appears to be that the somewhat uncouth, thick formation of Reynolds' upper lip was his own from birth, though his accident did not improve it. It has even been argued that he had a slight hare-lip; there have been other instances of this defect among the descendants of his sister Mary Palmer.[14] A defective palate might be a better explanation, again, of Reynolds' indistinctness of speech—of which we hear a lot in his later life— than the accident in Minorca to which it has been attributed.*

Reynolds was not absolutely consistent in his treatment in his self-portrait of the deficiencies of his upper lip, but he usually did indicate, as in the Althorp portrait and in the Tate Gallery portrait of himself holding his hand to his ear, that there was something distinctly unusual about it. Angelica Kauffmann, obviously willing to please, introduced into her portrait of him (*Frontispiece*) a formation of the mouth and lips that was entirely normal and unblemished. However, once the bloom of his youth had departed —as it soon did—Reynolds could not be turned into a handsome man by her or any other means. He was of medium height (five feet six) with a stocky figure inclining to plumpness; smallpox had left its marks on his face; his upper lip was disfigured. In middle life his complexion was ruddy, and painting his own portrait in old age he had the honesty to put a dab of red on his nose. But in matters of appearance the sum total is more important than the parts; the intelligence of his face, his good spirits and friendliness made Reynolds always an attractive figure.

The impression that he gave to those who knew him socially from youth to age was one of geniality and placidity, though the apparent placidity was, as so often, misleading. "That most

* Dr Ernest Irons, in his careful study of Reynolds' medical history, questions this assumption and, in view of Reynolds' subsequent deafness, points out that indistinct and low-toned speech is frequently noted in the deaf.

SIR JOSHUA REYNOLDS

ingenious and amiable man—I had almost used the lady's word
charming," Boswell once wrote.[15] Reynolds was indeed a charmer.
His charm was not only the secret of his success in life and in art
but perhaps the reason for some envy and mistrust. Zoffany's
group of the Royal Academicians in the life-school at Somerset
House shows him as so many knew him, stocky, plump, modestly
dressed, friendly and gesticulating.

This is partially to anticipate; but it may help to explain why
the busy young artist with the bruised face left so many friends
behind him in Minorca when he sailed thence for Leghorn on
January 25, 1750, on his way to Rome.[16]

30

III

Italy

Rome has seldom produced anything peculiarly its own throughout its
entire history, but there has always been inherent in its very soil the power
of lifting above themselves those already formed and mature.

OSKAR FISCHEL

I

TEN years before Reynolds came to Italy, Charles de Brosses,
in his *Lettres Familières*, had written some stinging criticism
of English visitors to Rome. He said that the English were
popular in Italy because of their wealth; he added that the money
they spent on the grand tour did not, apparently, do them much
good. "There are some men of culture who seek for knowledge,
but they are few in number. Most of them have a hired carriage
stationed in the Piazza di Spagna, which waits for them throughout the day, while they get through it by playing billiards or some
similar game with each other. I have known more than one
Englishman who left Rome without meeting anybody except
their fellow-countrymen and without knowing where the Colos-
seum was. . . ."

Eighteenth-century Italy, apart from her music, was intellec-
tually and artistically in the doldrums. She produced no great
artist with the possible exception of Piranesi who, as Dr Trevelyan
has said, "represented her, only too truly, as a land of gigantic
ruins overgrown by verdure and crawled under by monks,
beggars, and dilettanti". Yet Greece, occupied by the Turks,
was remote and uninviting; fashion impelled the moneyed
eighteenth-century Englishman, nurtured on latinity, towards
Roman ruins and classical art. Edward Gibbon, Horace Walpole
and Joshua Reynolds spectacularly repaid their debt; others
acknowledged it conscientiously; but there were empty-headed
English visitors in plenty who provided fit material for caricature
as they drifted towards their masked balls and opera boxes and,
more purposefully, into the coffee-houses.[1]

Reynolds echoed de Brosses' criticisms. He complained particularly that English visitors to the art galleries, content with learning the subject of a picture and the artist's name, scarcely bothered to look at the paintings themselves. But although Reynolds kept largely to the society of his compatriots while in Rome, he was emphatically one of those few "men of culture" who sought for knowledge. The legendary days of "dissipation" were past. Reynolds enjoyed himself in Italy, but most of his time was given to serious study; this may largely explain why so few of his letters written home have survived—he probably did not write many.

On the other hand, he was assiduous in making sketches and jottings in a series of notebooks of varying shapes and sizes. Most of what we know about Reynolds' Italian years is derived from these notebooks, of which half a dozen or more are to be seen in the British Museum, the Soane Museum, in Mrs Copland-Griffiths' collection, in the Metropolitan Museum of Art, New York, and elsewhere. The task of interpreting both these and the later notebooks of Reynolds is one of remarkable complexity. To begin with, the handwriting, especially when it is in pencil, must always have been very difficult to decipher; successive biographers have accepted readings in Leslie and Taylor's biography which are often debatable and sometimes demonstrably wrong. Another difficulty arises from the higgledy-piggledy nature of the contents of the notebooks themselves; sketches of pictures he had studied, notes and critical comments on their composition and on the practice of the artists concerned, mingle with Reynolds' intermittent diary entries and a bachelor's reminders of duties to be done:

> Put out linnen
> Pay Colourman
> Sword
> Write Letters
> Pack my things
> Wait on Mr Long.

For a solitary young man away from home, washing and darning have always been disagreeable problems:

> Sent to Mr Edgar
> 5 Shirts

1 white Wastcoat
5 Stocks
2 p^r of Stocking
Coat and Wastcoat
2 Handkerchiefs

Left to be mended
5 Shirts
7 p^r of white Silk Stockings
3 p^r of black
1 p^r of worsted
1 p^r of white thread
1 Stock
p^r of Sheets.

The last entry has a stroke through it—perhaps, after all, Reynolds with his usual thrift decided that the sheets could be made to last a little longer.[2]

Reynolds' Italian laundry lists do not suggest the wardrobe of a dandy; that he never was; but throughout his life he dressed with unostentatious taste and as soon as he could afford it wore "cut velvet" with quiet distinction. In one of the Italian notebooks he recorded an apparent determination "to look more like a man of some Business and consequence no dangler nor Idler"[3]. This may not have prevented a little snuff getting on his waistcoat.

Outward appearances began to reflect a thoughtful mind. At this time Reynolds was reading such books as Shaftesbury's *Letter Concerning Enthusiasm*, Pliny in Melmoth's translation, *Don Quixote*, and Vasari's *Lives of the Painters*. He makes a note to "Bye a Virgil" and mentions expenses "at the Library". This was not the Englishman's joy-ride in a hired carriage that de Brosses had postulated, but rather a careful experiment in self-education which was to continue for a lifetime. Reynolds early acquired the habit of taking haphazard notes of his reading, many of which have been gathered together by Professor Hilles.[4] "Few have been taught to any purpose, who have not been their own teachers," he assured the students of the Royal Academy in his Second Discourse to them, delivered twenty years after he first set out for Italy.

For some time Reynolds was very pleasantly lodged in rooms in the former Palace of the Queen of Sweden on the Trinita del Monte, near the Villa Medici. It is not known how long he spent there.[5]

Soon after he had settled in Rome he wrote a letter of thanks to his benefactor Lord Edgcumbe. "I am now (thanks to your Lordship)," he declared, "at the height of my wishes, in the midst of the greatest works of art the world has produced." There was only one way, he felt, in which he could express his gratitude, and that was by copying a picture for Lord Edgcumbe. He looked "about the palaces" for something suitable but without success. Eventually he offered to paint "any one you choose, the larger the better, as it will have a more grand effect when hung up, and a kind of painting I like more than little".[6] This was a painter's naïve but endearing way of registering unbounded indebtedness for the great opportunity of his life.

The gesture must have been a painful one for Reynolds to make. If he ever did present a copy of a painting to Lord Edgcumbe, it has not been recorded. During his first six months in Rome, he is known to have made copies from Raphael, Rubens, Titian, Rembrandt and Guido, but on the whole Reynolds did very little copying—"and that little I always considered as so much time lost", he later told James Barry. "I consider general copying as a delusive kind of industry," he declared in his Second Discourse: "How incapable those are of producing any thing of their own, who have spent much of their time in making finished copies, is well known to all who are conversant with our Art." Nor did Reynolds pay much attention to the mediocre contemporary artists then practising in Italy, though he recognized, in the same Discourse, that "to a young man just arrived in Italy, many of the present painters of that country are ready enough to obtrude their precepts. . . ." Lord Edgcumbe had urged him before he left to become a pupil of Pompeo Battoni; he had no intention of becoming anything of the sort.

It is true that Reynolds struck up an acquaintance with Francesco Zuccarelli, who later became a foundation member of the Royal Academy. Malone tells us that he visited him at his home and that Zuccarelli, seeing him at work on a portrait, exclaimed "what a spirit this man has!" There is a note in the larger of the British Museum notebooks which can be interpreted: "Seⁿ. Zuccherelli, pay him palate." Reynolds was grateful for the help and encouragement of the older artist, but not blindly so. After his fantastic description of the beauties of Turnham Green in his *Journey from London to Brentford* (see Appendix A below), we notice that he adds slyly: "I wish'd for the fanciful pencil of Zuccerelli to have taken a Sketch of it."

Reynolds has made it quite clear that his main object in Italy was to study the works of the "great masters", and in particular those of Michelangelo and Raphael. "The works of those who have stood the test of ages," he said, "have a claim to that respect and veneration to which no modern can pretend." For his students, twenty years later, he did not advise any large-scale copying, but urged them rather to select "those choice parts . . . which have recommended the work to notice. If its excellence consists in its general effect, it would be proper to make slight sketches of the machinery and general management of the picture. Those sketches should be kept always by you for the regulation of your style. Instead of copying the touches of those great masters, copy only their conceptions. Instead of treading in their footsteps, endeavour only to keep the same road. Labour to invent on their general principles and way of thinking."

Reynolds not only gave this advice in his Second Discourse of 1769 but spoke to the students of the Academy on very much the same lines in his Twelfth Discourse in 1784. Looking back to the days in which he first arrived in Italy, he said that he "would rather wish a student, as soon as he goes abroad, to employ himself upon whatever he has been incited to by any immediate impulse, than to go sluggishly about a prescribed task". He distrusted elaborate methods for the student that evaded "the real labour of thinking", and felt that "a passion for his art, and an eager desire to excel" could "more than supply the place of method". Reynolds' tendency to argue general rules from his own highly individual experience, is one of the faults of his Discourses; and there is no doubt that he is here describing the manner of his own zealous and impulsive entry into the world of Italian art.

The Italian notebooks are full of small sketches, both of figures and landscapes; the former are mostly notes of pictures he had seen; the latter are sketches from nature made on perambulations of the towns or on coach rides through the countryside. There are, for example, some attractive drawings of the garden of the Pitti Palace in Florence and of a gate at Perugia, while the smaller note-book at the Soane Museum contains numerous studies of animals, especially dogs. These are obviously the notebooks that Reynolds had in mind when he said in his Twelfth Discourse: "I would recommend to every artist to look over his portfolio, or pocket-book, in which he has treasured up all the happy inventions, all the extraordinary and expressive attitudes, that he has met with in the course of his studies; not only for the sake of borrowing from those studies whatever may be applicable to his own work, but likewise on account of the great advantage he will receive by bringing the ideas of great artists more distinctly before his mind, which will teach him to invent other figures in a similar style."

Mr Charles Mitchell, Professor Wind and others[7] have shown how Reynolds, in his search for "the composite style", was wont to borrow attitudes from earlier artists, and sometimes indeed was indebted to more than one artist for different parts of the same picture. These borrowed inventions (many of them first noted in the Italian sketch-books) were so transmuted by Reynolds that they became part of his own personal creation, like the borrowings of Raphael from Masaccio. Reynolds was far from condoning the clumsy borrowings of painters like Carlo Maratti, whom he accuses, in Mrs Copland-Griffiths' notebook, of not being able to think for himself and of stealing whole figures "without adding or diminishing the least turn of pencil!"

Horace Walpole defended Reynolds' practice as "quotation . . . with a novel application of the sense". The word "quotation" was not very happily chosen (except for one or two special instances, such as the amusing adaptation of Holbein's Henry VIII to the boyish dimensions of "Master Crewe", which might equally well be called parody); and Reynolds would hardly have been pleased to see his own carefully concealed "quotations" exposed by the Warburg Institute. But then Reynolds was a genius—much though he distrusted the term—who drew his pictorial material from poetry and history as well as from earlier painters, and used it to enrich a vigorous originality and graceful

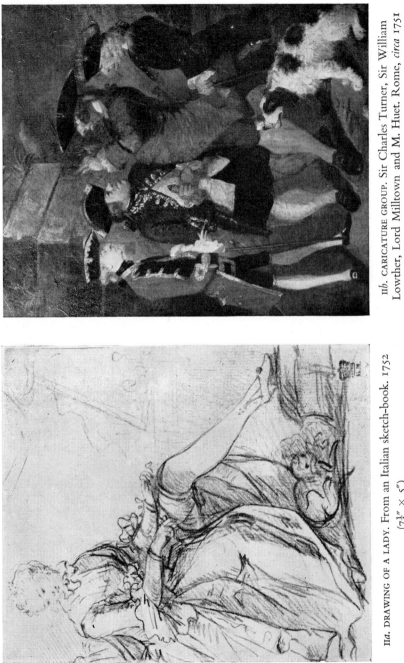

11b. CARICATURE GROUP. Sir Charles Turner, Sir William Lowther, Lord Milltown and M. Huet. Rome, *circa* 1751

(24″ × 19″)

11a. DRAWING OF A LADY. From an Italian sketch-book. 1752

(7¼″ × 5″)

fancy of his own; Reynolds' own amazingly versatile achievement is the best justification of his philosophical method. Horace Walpole's conclusion will therefore stand: "Sir Joshua was not a plagiary, but will beget a thousand. The exuberance of his invention will be the grammar of future painters of portrait."[8] This has been abundantly demonstrated.

Individual borrowings of detail must be carefully distinguished from those broad influences of the style and vision of particular masters, to which all young artists are properly susceptible. Reynolds himself maintained that he owed most to Michelangelo, of the great Italians; in practice he was profoundly influenced by the Venetians, by Rembrandt and Rubens, and by Velasquez; but it seems incontestable that in his search for "the grand style", Reynolds found most in common with the spirit of Raphael, whose superb sense of decorative composition challenged him and whose essential tenderness he saw to be not incompatible with firmness in portraiture.

There is surely much significance in a passage in Mrs Copland-Griffiths' Italian notebook, which shows most vividly how Reynolds felt himself drawn to Raphael by a process of exclusions. It is printed as it was written:

> in Raffiele nothing of the affectation of Guercins Painting not dark nor light no ridicolous affected contrasts no affected masses of lights and shadows he is the medium Annibal Carrach too wild
> D° Michael Angelo
> Domenicino too tame Guido too effeminate.

To which may be added a sentence from his Sixth Discourse, written many years later:

> If your ambition, therefore, be to equal Raffaelle, you must do as Raffaelle did, take many models, and not even *him* for your guide alone, to the exclusion of others.

When Reynolds first visited the Vatican, he was profoundly impressed by the work of Michelangelo in the Sistine Chapel and walked up and down the Chapel for the best part of a day "with great self-importance", but the Raphael rooms disappointed him. As he studied and copied Raphael's great decorations, however—so different from anything he had known before—something of the creative force and vitality of that wonderful youth dawned on him. His versatility, his dramatic power, the sweep of his visual imagination overpowered him. He felt himself in the presence of one whose harmony and humanism, whose patience and gift of assimilation, he could wish to make his own.

Returning to the Vatican again and again, Reynolds fell from the sublime to the ridiculous. He caught a severe cold, "by painting for a long time near a stove" (to quote Malone) "by which the damp vapours of that edifice were attracted, and affected his head". This cold is said to have brought on the deafness from which he suffered for the rest of his life, but deafness was hereditary in his family (two of his nieces became deaf) and it is not unlikely that he would eventually have acquired that disability in any event.[9] Reynolds did not let his deafness worry him; it assisted his natural gift for reading character, though it may incidentally have hindered his clarity of speech, and even, in some cases, his spelling of words; in talking to one person, he heard very well, and he could enjoy a general conversation with the use of an ear-trumpet. He certainly never regretted his hours spent in the Vatican. "If you neglect visiting the Vatican often, and particularly the Capella Sistina," he warned James Barry, "you will neglect receiving that peculiar advantage which Rome can give above all other cities in the world."[10]

In recommending Barry to the study of Michelangelo, he was indirectly responsible for the most interesting essay in the "great style" that eighteenth-century England produced—Barry's paintings at the Society of Arts. Reynolds' veneration for Michelangelo never left him, but Reynolds at thirty must already have known that the god-like attributes of Michelangelo could never be his. "Raffaelle had more Taste and Fancy; Michel Angelo, more Genius and Imagination," he said in his Fifth Discourse. Instinctively, and modestly, he ranged himself among the followers of Raphael.

Apart altogether from the great Italians, another influence, less often mentioned, affected Reynolds in Rome to a considerable degree. It was derived virtually from a single portrait—Velasquez's "Innocent the Tenth" in the Pamphili Palace, which he told Northcote was "the finest portrait in the world". Northcote also recorded that Reynolds said of Velasquez: "What we are all attempting to do with great labour, he does at once." Although

Reynolds never quite touched those heights of portraiture, it was a salutary experience for him to see this great Spanish painting in the midst of Italian influences, and our knowledge that he did so helps to an understanding of his later achievement.

In the eighteenth century the work of Velasquez was still little known outside Spain, so that Reynolds had small opportunity of studying it. That he retained a lifelong interest in the Spanish master we know from Northcote, who tells us that Reynolds twice restored pictures that he believed to be by Velasquez— though it is very doubtful that they were genuine. "See, there is a fine picture by Velasquez," said Reynolds on one occasion. "Indeed it is very fine," replied Northcote guilelessly, "and how exactly it is in your manner, Sir Joshua?"*

Supposing that Reynolds had been able to visit Spain and had felt the full force of Velasquez, would this counterpoise to his Italian influences have given us an even greater painter of portraits? It is an intriguing speculation.

3

Reynolds' letters to Miss Weston show him enjoying Rome to the full in the coffee-house society of artists, antiquarians and noblemen on the grand tour ("You must know when a Letter comes from England we are all impatient to hear news"). John Astley, formerly a fellow-pupil of Hudson's, was one of his friends in Rome; Nathaniel Hone, who attacked him in later life, was another; and towards the end of his stay he saw something of Richard Wilson, who came south from Venice still debating in his mind whether to devote himself to landscape or portrait. Acquaintances such as Lord Charlemont, Lord Bruce, Sir William Lowther, Lord Mayo, Charles Turner, and Joseph Leeson (later Lord Milltown) brought him into the circle of artistic patronage which was to make him prosperous when he returned to London. Reynolds was eager to share his excitement with English visitors and urged Miss Weston to tell two mutual friends "that if it was possible to give them an Idea of what is to be seen here, the

---

* Justi says that Reynolds advised Morritt of Rokeby to buy the Velasquez "Venus" now in the National Gallery. But this is impossible, and must be a mistake for Sir Thomas Lawrence.

Remains of Antiquity the Sculpture, Paintings, Architecture etc., they would think it worth while, nay they would break through all obstacles and set out immediately for Rome". Meanwhile, the letters were read over the coffee-house table; those who listened were "all extremely afflicted for the loss of the Prince of Whales who certainly would have been a great Patron to Painters". (And, in all this personal and cultural advancement, there is still no sign that Reynolds would ever be able to spell.)

The smaller of Reynolds' Italian notebooks at the British Museum contains a caricature of a man, with legs splayed out, sketching in the open air in a book held close to his face. Reynolds has labelled it "Master Hone". This friendly early caricature of Hone may be contrasted with Hone's later satirical comment on Reynolds' methods in his picture "The Conjuror". But Hone was more than a casual subject for a jotting in Reynolds' notebook; it is possible that he introduced Reynolds to the practice of caricature, which Reynolds pursued with considerable success while he was in Rome.

Many have felt it incongruous that an earnest young artist like Reynolds, ambitious to succeed in the grand manner, should have painted frivolous caricatures in the Eternal City. But this will no longer seem so surprising to those who can appreciate his natural gift for parody in the *Journey from London to Brentford*, a gift which he was compelled to suppress in the interests of his career. It is true that in his *London to Brentford*, in 1771, he was only parodying an absurd book of travels by a fantastic though lovable Italian, Giuseppe Baretti; at Rome twenty years earlier he went so far—in the elaborate picture now in the National Gallery of Ireland—as to caricature the "School of Athens" of his beloved Raphael. But a mischievous urge to ridicule was never far beneath the surface of Reynolds' official decorum; it was part of an earthy sense of humour that verged on the Rabelaisian. As he engagingly put it to Miss Burney, he "naturally loved a little of the blackguard".[11] Few great artists have been without this necessary and saving propensity.

The art of caricature, invented by Agostino Carracci, had long flourished in Rome. Bernini had shown a gift for it. Eighteenth-century caricaturists, such as P. L. Ghezzi, were probably inspired by the random humorous excursions of Domenichino, Guercino and Maratti. All these were artists in the grand manner; and to them, as to Reynolds who studied them, it may be that caricature came as a necessary relief. Nathaniel Hone owned a caricature of two men walking and talking by Pier Francesco Mola (1612–1666), which it is tempting to think that he may have shown to Reynolds.[12]

There was ample incentive to caricature in Rome, and Reynolds enjoyed himself—as did Thomas Patch—in poking crude fun at his fellow countrymen, whom he saw mainly in egregious profile and as belonging to one or two stock types. Sir William Lowther and Lord Milltown particularly excited his humour; they are shown with two others in Plate II*b* along with a likeable dog. It is a measure of his confidence and of his social talent that he felt himself in no danger of losing influential friends. Indeed his caricatures increased his popularity; they reflect the gaiety of those Roman years and show that Reynolds was still at heart the twelve-year-old boy who had daubed a likeness of the Reverend Thomas Smart on sail canvas. They also brought him a little pocket-money, which he needed.

Fortunately Reynolds had already accomplished too much in portraiture to be tempted by his success as a caricaturist. Eighty years later a young Frenchman, Jean-Pierre Dantan, who went to Rome with ambitions in serious sculpture, returned to Paris to become a master of caricature statuettes. Reynolds was already on firmer ground; realizing that a reputation in caricature would be a dangerous advertisement for a portrait-painter, he suppressed this mischievous talent. His Italian notebooks reveal him as studying continually to improve his equipment as a serious artist, and, while the sketches that he made in them were not pretentious, the drawing reproduced in Plate II*a* is sufficiently graceful and attractive to suggest that his ability as a draughtsman has been somewhat underestimated.

He was not a great draughtsman, a fact of which he was fully aware and which he often lamented; he himself said that he "began too late". Although he told Academy students that "the port-crayon ought to be for ever in your hands", he went on to urge them whenever possible "to paint your studies instead of drawing them". That was largely his own method during his long and busy career as a studio painter. Few advanced sketches for his paintings survive simply because they are, in fact, usually hidden beneath the finished pictures themselves.

There is, however, an unpublished book of Reynolds' drawings, formerly in Sir John Herschel's collection and now at Burlington House, which shows (though not all the drawings are from Reynolds' hand) that his range of accomplishment as a draughtsman was considerable. They include elaborate student drawings of the figure, portrait heads in chalk and charcoal, and surprisingly delicate ink studies, besides many of those rough designs for compositions which are more familiar and more generally characteristic. It is rather surprising that no collection of Reynolds' drawings has so far appeared; they are, of course, primarily of interest in connection with his practice as a painter—and their editing and arrangement would involve a vast labour of research —but the artistic value of individual drawings is perhaps higher than has been estimated.*

4

"This would serve for a fountain"; "This figure will serve for a Fame"; "Serve for Time discovering Truth"—Reynolds annotated his Italian sketches with a keen eye for his professional future. He made many notes on painting methods. His favourable judgements on inferior painters are more generous than discriminating; but these were the private jottings of a young man taking in much that was new to him and inevitably confused by the panorama of many centuries of Italian art. Amid all its splendours, the petty cash was never forgotten:

Caleshes	16 — 5	
for the Corso	2 — 0	
Coffee house	5 — 2 [13]	

On April 5, 1752, Reynolds set out from Rome on a brief

* Besides the Herschel book at the Royal Academy and the sketchbooks at the British Museum, the Soane Museum and in Mrs Copland-Griffiths' collection, there are books with drawings in the Metropolitan Museum, New York, the Ashmolean Museum, Oxford, and in the collections of Mr Furse and Professor C. B. Tinker. The British Museum Print Room has two boxes of drawings, some of them doubtful attributions, and the Tate Gallery has a charcoal head. There is an interesting box of photographs of drawings in the Witt Library at the Courtauld Institute. The Royal Academy has some juvenile drawings, and the sitters' books there contain some engaging "doodles".

visit to Naples. He habitually enjoyed his travels, poking his head out of the carriage window to miss nothing of the scenery, and keeping a rough diary in the first notebook that came to hand. Castel Gandolfo was passed, and the Lake of Albano, "which is eight miles about". He stayed overnight at Velletri, strolling across the market-place to Bernini's statue of Urban VIII ("Brass, base Marble"). There was another stop at Piperno, after a drive that revealed the desolation of the Pontine marshes ("Pliny says in his time there was here 25 towns now not a house"); he also spent a night at Sessa.

But these journeys were slow, and on a dull drive like this a young traveller could chafe at delay. After a rapid survey of the pictures at Naples, Reynolds was soon back in Rome. "Naples journey cost—6-0-0, Expences on the road 2, At Naples 18."[14] He had next to pack his belongings and the accumulations of two years at Rome. The heavy chest went by sea to Leghorn. "Send my chest of Cloaths Linnen &c. to Civita Vecchia to be sent to Leghorn provided it will arrive soon enough; send my colours there. . . ."[15] With the rich experience of Rome stored in his mind and in his notebooks, he set out finally on May 3 for Florence, passing through the poplars and olives of the peaceful Umbrian valleys, visiting Spoleto, Assisi, Perugia and Arezzo, observing and sketching freely as he went. That journey of 150 miles took him a week.

Reynolds painted few serious portraits in Italy. He painted himself in Rome, his features firm now and resolute in the shadow of his large hat; and at Florence he painted his contemporary Joseph Wilton, the sculptor, who long afterwards became Keeper of the Royal Academy. But he left Rome with such confidence in his future that he brought with him an Italian boy of fifteen, Giuseppe Marchi, as his pupil and assistant. The draft of a letter written in Florence shows him still reluctant to return to England and anxious to make as many friends in Italy as possible, so that he might not "arrive in London without reputation". The masterpieces in the Florentine palaces and churches demanded him; gay excursions among the Tuscan hills and cypresses must have tempted him. The drawing of the girl tying her garter (Plate IIa), done in Florence, has a sensuous liveliness which suggests other influences than the Vatican frescoes.

"Departed from Florence the 4 of July after Dinner"—so runs the record—"Arrived at Bologna the 6th being Thursday." [16] Reynolds contrived a little tour of northern Italy, visiting Parma, Mantua and Ferrara, before he reached Venice on July 24. On the following day he notes "Entered my Lodgings", and on the 26th: "The Boy begun to eat at my Lodgings." Presumably this was Marchi, a sensible, good-tempered lad; he had, after all, to be fed, and there are indications that his master was beginning to run short of money.

Reynolds' notes on the pictures he saw in Bologna and in Venice[17] are of the utmost importance to a study of his development. Bolognese classicism remained a powerful latent influence, inspiring many of those elaborate canvases of Reynolds' middle years that we are now inclined to regret. Titian, Tintoretto and Veronese gave him the exciting example of broad handling, of mastery of tone and rich glowing colour; they taught him how to disguise his own weak draughtsmanship and reinforced the understanding of light and shade that he had already learned from the Rembrandt engravings. Then, too, there was the impact of Venice itself, which, in the words of Adrian Stokes, "excels in blackness and whiteness . . . Colour comes between, comes out of them, intensely yet gradually amassed, like a gondola between water and sky." Reynolds' three weeks in Venice were immediately and practically reflected in the great portraits that he painted on his return to England—and we may be grateful for it (though with his usual caution he warned Academy students of the dangers of Venetian practice in his later Discourses).

"A figure or figures on a light ground; the upper part should be as light if not lighter than the ground, the lower part dark, having lights here and there . . . When the second mass of light is too great, interpose some dark figure, to divide it in two." This was "A General Rule" noted by Reynolds in Venice; and here is another:

A light sky of angels, the light by means of clouds, &c. and goes off by degrees; but on one side a dark figure must come smart against the light, to give the picture a spirit. Titian's "Salutation".

Such observations are especially significant, for Reynolds' great strength as a painter, apart from his colouring and his reading of character, lay in his feeling for masses and their placing in a picture. Indeed, in all that might help him to "give the picture a spirit", these three weeks in Venice were of lasting benefit.

But England now called him insistently. He told Northcote that, one night when he was at the opera in Venice, the orchestra played an English ballad which was very familiar in London at the time he had left, three years before. Reynolds found himself in tears.

In the middle of August he set off for home through Milan and Turin. On the Mont Cenis he met his old master Hudson, intent on a rapid tour of Italy with Roubiliac. By the time he reached Lyons, Reynolds was reduced to his last six louis. According to Malone, he gave two of these to Marchi "with orders to proceed as he could, and reserved four to carry him to Paris, where, in eight days, he was joined by Marchi, who had performed the journey from Lyons on foot". No doubt this was necessary, but for young Marchi it may have carried a first faint message of disillusionment.

5

The long pilgrimage, fraught with such significance for the English school of painting, was coming to an end. Reynolds had embarked on it with humility and was returning with renewed confidence, the colours of Venetian ornament glowing in his mind, determined to raise the status of the British artist by bringing the Grand Style into portraiture and, if circumstances allowed, into "history" painting. Because eighteenth-century England yearned towards the Antique, it is difficult to decide—as it often must be in the careers of successful artists—how much of his motive was economic, how much intellectual. His sincerity was, however, within his limits absolute.

During his stay in Paris he found little to admire in French art but met another ambitious young man of his own age, William Chambers, who had studied architecture in Paris and was now about to leave for Rome. The two were drawn together in an equivocal relationship that was to last until Reynolds' death.

Although they had much in common, their backgrounds were distinct. Chambers was the son of a merchant of Scottish descent who had settled in Gothenburg; he felt himself as much Swedish as British. Having already voyaged far and wide in the service of the Swedish East India Company, he had acquired a love of Chinoiserie but felt like Reynolds that he had largely wasted his time. Essentially academic, sharing Reynolds' passion for the antique, he believed "sublimity" to be the principal aim in architecture, and Roman architecture to be the ideal of perfection. He was now on his way to luxuriate in Rome, as Reynolds had done.

> . . . Travelling to an Artist, is what the University is to a Man of Letters, the last Stage of a regular Education, which opens the Mind to a more liberal and extensive way of thinking, diffuses an Air of Importance over the whole Man, and stamps a Value upon his Opinions, it affords him Opportunities of forming Connections with the Great, the Learned, and the Rich, and the Friendships which he makes when abroad, are very often the first Causes of his Reputation, and Fortune at Home.

That was written by Chambers in one of his lectures;[18] it might equally well have been written by Reynolds, summarizing as it does the experience of both men, who used their travels as a key to fame and fortune. Sizing themselves up, they knew that they could be friends—and enemies. Kindly and humorous in one aspect; quarrelsome, pompous, asthmatic in another; always energetic and ambitious for prestige; Chambers could admire Reynolds wholeheartedly with half of his being, and seek to mould himself on his philosophy, but he could be jealous of him as well. Reynolds' poise and wisdom was something he never attained.

The two men probably saw then, in Paris, that they needed each other and might perhaps do a great work together. They struck up a friendship—or was it an alliance?—one of those friendships made on the Grand Tour which might be the cause of "Reputation, and Fortune at Home".

To cement it, Reynolds painted a portrait of Mrs Chambers which now hangs at Ken Wood. Gossip retailed by Farington makes her out as "a milliner girl" who followed Chambers to Paris, and she was accounted a beauty. The plump round face painted by Reynolds, set off by the blue hat and the dark shawl against a stormy sky, leaves that question open. It is an experiment in light and shade, suggesting to some the influence of Rubens and

the French "Rubénistes", to others Rembrandt, to others again
—and as probably—the Venetian experience. Catherine Chambers
looks out at us a trifle smugly, as she gazed at Reynolds and her
husband two hundred years ago, wondering perhaps where the
ambitions of her architect husband and his painter friend would
lead them.

If Malone is to be believed, Thomas Hudson's tour of Italy
was so rapid and perfunctory that he and Reynolds crossed from
Calais to Dover in the same packet. Reynolds arrived in London
on October 16, 1752, and made straight for Devonshire.

IV

Reynolds Conquers London

I

THE journey from Italy left Reynolds tired, and well content to relax after a strenuous year in the mildness of a Devonshire autumn. Probably he went straight to Torrington, the little town on its plateau above the river Torridge, a few miles from Bideford, which was the second home of his family, and where his mother was now living with his sister Mrs Palmer. It is a place with many beauties for a painter; already Reynolds knew and loved its distant view of the blue hills of Dartmoor.

The link between Torrington and Reynolds' family, on his mother's side, had always been maintained, so that it is not surprising that his elder sister Mary should have married a Torrington man, John Palmer. This had been a successful and gratifying match. Palmer was a lawyer by profession, but, more significantly, he was a wealthy landowner. He owned an estate called Burwood, three miles from Torrington, and in 1752 he built himself a handsome red-brick house facing the lime-trees of Torrington churchyard. The Palmers were hospitable; Reynolds on his return from Italy may have been one of the first guests in their large new home.

Reynolds was always on good terms with Mary Palmer, an intelligent and amusing woman, as her *Devonshire Dialogue* shows. He had painted her and her husband in two of his early portraits,[1] and she had twice lent him sums of money which had proved exceedingly useful. Her two daughters, Mary—who in 1752 was a baby in arms—and Theophila, born in 1757, grew up to be good-looking girls of considerable charm. They won their uncle's heart, and he paid his debt of gratitude to their mother by what he did for them in later life.

A second sister, Elizabeth, also lived at Torrington. She, too, had come to Reynolds' aid when he set out for Italy, but she was not so lucky in her choice of a husband as her sister Mary—and in the long run this had a damaging effect on brotherly affection. Elizabeth's husband was William Johnson, the son of a former Vicar of Torrington, and he started his married life respectably enough by being elected three times Mayor of Torrington. Unfortunately he deteriorated, and lost not only his own and his wife's money but also some of Joshua's, which was unforgivable; he then ran away from his wife to live with another woman. So that, altogether, the Johnsons eventually went under a cloud, and the nephews and nieces of that family, though not rejected entirely, perhaps did not receive their full share of avuncular attention.

Reynolds' third sister Frances (Fanny) was six years younger than her brother, a changeable, restless little woman with a round face and sad eyes. Fanny, who remained a spinster, became Reynolds' particular charge—and, as time went on, a thorn in his flesh. But she was at heart a kindly woman, who meant well and was generally liked on a limited acquaintance. She had a small talent as an artist and painted insipid pretty-pretty miniatures with dexterity. Her commonplace book,[2] branching out from the philosophical maxims so dear to all the Reynoldses, reveals her as a pathetic figure, suffering from a nameless unrequited love and regretting, at last, her failure to achieve a harmonious relationship with her brother.

Against this background of three contrasting sisters and their families, Reynolds embarked on his active bachelor life. Though he had one surviving brother, Robert Reynolds, we hear little of him (perhaps because he was an Exeter ironmonger). Reynolds was a man's man at heart, but with a considerable if somewhat cautious sympathy for women. He knew their ways, admired them, flirted with them, joked with them, yet as the years went on grew increasingly determined not to become sentimentally involved with them. The portrait-painter's life requires a stern discipline, and Reynolds had learned his need to restrict himself emotionally. Sensuous as he was in his response to colour and beauty, he found relief as well as purpose in his work, and he worked obsessionally.

During his stay in Devonshire, Reynolds came across a little book which greatly attracted him. No name appeared on the title-page, and Reynolds knew nothing of the author. He told

49

Boswell later that he "began to read it while he was standing with his arm leaning against a chimney-piece. It seized his attention so strongly, that, not being able to lay down the book till he had finished it, when he attempted to move, he found his arm totally benumbed".[3] The book was Samuel Johnson's Life of that fiery, dissipated, destitute but talented Bohemian Richard Savage, and there was a warning in it for ambitious young artists.

While in Devonshire Reynolds painted a portrait of Dr John Mudge, the son of his excellent and philosophical mentor Zachariah. Early in 1753 he returned to London and took lodgings in St Martin's Lane, and there Fanny joined him as his housekeeper.

2

Reynolds' apartment is said to have been at 104 St Martin's Lane, a site now covered by the Duke of York's Theatre; the ratebooks give no help in confirming this. In a studio behind number 104 G. M. Moser ran a drawing-school, to which Reynolds temporarily belonged. He did not stay long in St Martin's Lane, however, but later in 1753, removed to Great Newport Street, close by. The house he occupied in Great Newport Street was at one time numbered 5, but the ratebooks show that his house was not the present number five, which was erected while he was living in the street.*[4]

The noises of London, rich and various, came in at his windows. "Salt—salt—white Wor—ster—shire salt"; "Hot fine oatcakes, hot"; "Small coales here"; "Will you buy any milke to-day?"—these were some of the street-cries at a time when most of London's trade was carried on outside the shops. Along St Martin's Lane and Great Newport Street, an endless procession of merchants offered in their loudest tones to sell Fanny Reynolds lavender, Shrewsbury cakes, hot codlins, wood, brimstone matches and water-cress. The ballad-singers and the drum that encouraged the

* Reynolds' house in Great Newport Street was apparently pulled down in 1766-7 and two houses, numbers 10 and 11, according to the later re-numbering, were built on its site. A flamboyant unofficial plaque on the present number 5 ("Sir Joshua Reynolds Artist Lived Here") is therefore misleading.

performing bear mingled with the din of carts and carriages rattling over the uneven stones. Against this uproar the shop-keepers' 'prentices—and there were many shops in the streets and alleys around St Martin's Lane—competed with cries of "Buy! buy! buy!"

To be somewhat deaf in such a noisy city was scarcely a dis-advantage, especially for a painter who had to read the faces of his sitters. Reynolds lived and worked in the thick of things; beyond doubt, he enjoyed it. Within walking distance of Covent Garden and St James's Park, he toiled at his easel as long as the daylight lasted. He was continually experimenting—most happily, it may seem to us, while the Venetian inspiration came uppermost, or when he trusted mainly to his own direct and intimate percep-tions; least happily when he sought to combine portrait with the elaborate apparatus of Bolognese classicism.

The beauties and elegants of London stepped cautiously over the muddy cobbles and in at Reynolds' door. His masterpieces were as truly London pictures as any of Hogarth's moralities, although it was of Italy that Reynolds dreamed as he thumbed through his parchment-bound notebooks for a remembered attitude. And everywhere in this area where he lived, between the Strand and Oxford Street, were the coffee-houses he visited when the day's work was over—to enjoy the literary society which was his second ambition, or to exchange memories of his travels with his brother artists. Temptingly near was Old Slaughter's in St Martin's Lane.

He captured the town immediately, soon fixing his prices at the level of his master Thomas Hudson's: twelve guineas for a head, twenty-four for a half-length, forty-eight for a whole length. The sitters' books for 1753-4 are missing, but we know that in these years he painted, among many others, the Duke of Beaufort, Lord Cathcart—brilliantly rendered with Venetian opulence in his red coat—Lord Cremorne, Lady Anne Dawson, the Duke of Devonshire, Earl Harcourt, the Earl of Huntingdon, Lady Charlotte Fitzwilliam as a child (the first of his many child-portraits), Sir William Lowther and the Countess of Kildare. It is scarcely an exaggeration to say, of this young man of thirty, that he became a fashionable painter overnight.

An early portrait after the return to London was that of his protégé Marchi which is now at the Royal Academy. This is not one of his masterpieces, but Hudson's remark when he saw it— "Reynolds, you do not paint as well as you did before you went to Italy"—was wishful thinking. Almost at once Reynolds painted two pictures which established his genius for so long as English painting may last. One is the self-portrait in the National Portrait Gallery (Plate IV) of the determined youth in grey-brown coat and blue waistcoat, holding the fan-like palette* and maulstick, and shading the eyes that were to gaze at his contemporaries so intently and so long. The other is the romantic portrait at Greenwich of his benefactor Keppel (Plate III).

It was appropriate, and indicative of gratitude, that the great portrait which made Reynolds' name should have been of Augustus Keppel. The portrait is at once affectionate, heroic and sincere. Reynolds shows Keppel in his early twenties, stepping ashore after the wreck of the *Maidstone*, determined vigour and athletic grace in his bearing. The colouring is all blues and greys, as if by moonlight (colours that Reynolds loved in these years), and Keppel is alive with the thunder of the storm that wrecked him. Allan Ramsay had painted a portrait of "Macleod of Macleod", a few years earlier, which may have suggested the pose— that of the Apollo Belvedere in reverse. But the transformation is startling; the values of light and shade that Reynolds had learned in Italy, the nervous intensity of Keppel's right hand, even the surf breaking on the shore, make Ramsay's portrait look like cardboard.

Reynolds knew that the "Keppel" might mean much to him. After several sittings he took it all out and began again. This portrait, one would like to believe, must have been entirely by his hand. If so, it may be his last large-scale work of which this can be said with confidence. For Reynolds, following the English tradition of Van Dyck and Kneller, began to depend more and more on the help of studio assistants to meet the demands of his practice.

A score of assistants and pupils worked on Reynolds' pictures throughout his career.[5] They were not lavishly rewarded. Marchi

---

* He habitually used these little square-shaped wooden palettes with handles, never the large semi-circular palette of a later generation which Alfred Drury has given him in the statue, otherwise excellent, in the courtyard of Burlington House.

III. HON. AUGUSTUS (LATER VISCOUNT) KEPPEL. 1753–4
(94″ × 58″)

received £100 a year while he worked for him. Soon he was joined by Peter Toms, a costume painter also employed by Francis Cotes, who was given only fifteen guineas for painting the drapery to a whole-length figure.[6] Peter Vandyke was another professional assistant—and there were many student-pupils besides, of whom James Northcote was the most successful. In his relations with his studio assistants, Reynolds was a severe task-master; Marchi said that he "was never pleased with what was done for Him" and that he "hated to pay money".[7] Northcote tells us that he refused to buy expensive frames: "One frame in particular had gone so often that it might almost have found its way to the Exhibition alone, and it had become so black that you could scarcely have known that it had ever been gilt." [8]

Obviously Reynolds' best pictures are those to which he personally devoted most of his time. Yet it was his habit to go over the accessories that were painted for him, "regulating" them, as the phrase was; so that to attempt to distinguish parts of his pictures, as painted by other hands, is unrewarding. For him to have painted all the draperies, curtains, and furniture properties in a total output of pictures that has been estimated at nearly 4,000 would have been physically impossible—and he was little interested in such painting. He was more ready to concern himself with the animals and birds, at least until Northcote was ready to take them on. For landscape, moreover, he had a definite if minor talent (see Plate IX), and his landscape backgrounds generally bear the marks of his individual style. Richard Wright is known to have painted at least one of his marine backgrounds[9] (though Reynolds was capable of seascape). The pose and composition, and of course the face, were always his own. Beyond this, the secrets of his studio—in which he worked so unremittingly day after day (and often on Sundays)—cannot be probed; though Lord Bath had some illuminating things to say about them in a letter to Mrs Montagu:

... I was yesterday with Mr Reynolds, & have fixed Fryday next at twelve, to finish the Picture. I have discovered a secret by being often at Mr Reynolds, that I fancy, he is sorry I should know. I find that none of these great Painters finish any of their Pictures themselves. The same Person, (but who he is, I know not) works for Ramsey, Reynolds, & another, calld Hudson, my Picture will not

E   53

come from that Person till Thursday night, and on Fryday it will be totally finished, and ready to send home. . . .[10]

That Reynolds received studio help need not disturb our appreciation; he imposed his own vision on all that he fathered, and throughout his life continued to paint many small portraits that are clearly autograph. His haphazard experiments with his painting materials must worry us more. Before he went to Italy he was a direct painter; after his return he tried to procure the effects of the Venetians by the use of transparent glazes over a monochrome under-painting. This was a dangerous method, which he continued to employ for about sixteen years, and during this time he used a carmine that tended to fade. The complexions of many of his sitters have turned ashen pale; over-confident attempts by restorers have ravaged other canvases needlessly. That Reynolds' colours were not always "fast" was well known in his lifetime. His niece Lady Thomond (Mary Palmer) who helped to collect the memorial exhibition of her uncle's pictures in 1813 had to admit that one thing

> vexes me very much which is Alas that many of the Pictures look like Ghosts, white as chalk & consequently have a deplorable appearance. There is a picture of Lady Tavistock adorning a statue of Hymen every bit of colour gone almost even the very flowers, while at the same time Lord Tavistock's picture done at the same time is as fresh as if painted last week. A beautiful picture of the Duchess of Marl-borough (which I never saw before) with the little child on her knee standing at arms length is totally ruined, at least the Duchess herself, for some one has been mending it & painted the whole of her face & figure all over so that it is detestable, the little child has been spared, & looks beautifull . . . I grieve to see how miserable many of the pictures look from fading & being crackd & being mended.[11]

Here as elsewhere, we do not love Reynolds the less for his imperfections—they sprang naturally from an eager nature that never tired of experiment. The Royal Academy's canvas of his trials in oils, with notes in his handwriting like "Orp in stone jug", "Prussian Blue Cer", is nevertheless painful to behold. Some of these have cracked badly, though they are first attempts. Reynolds had something of his father's taste as an alchemist and enjoyed pottering about with the little glass powder-bottles in his mahogany painting chest.[12] But perhaps, after all, if his career had lain in medicine, he would have made a better surgeon than an apothecary.*

3

In the same years, 1753-4, that Reynolds rose to sudden fame as a painter, he stepped as surely into the most stimulating intellectual society in London. There were no rigid boundaries to his social life; he was friendly with many of the nobility, yet in the world of fashion, to which so many of his sitters belonged, his acquaintance remained largely professional; he nodded to many of his brother artists but was intimate with only a few; in politics he was a Whig, who never attempted to curry favour at Court. From the fringes of these different worlds he chose as his friends the men of good company, the wits, the Bohemians, the great originals of his time. There were no hampering restrictions of snobbery or false respectability about his private life. And in the main his friends were literary men and women, writers and journalists. He came among them as a painter but cast a longing eye on their literary fame.

It is from the beginning of 1755 that the series of his small leather-bound pocket-books, which continues with some exceptions until 1790, begins to reveal Reynolds' daily life in full detail.[13] *The New Memorandum Book Improv'd: or, The Gentleman and Tradesman's Daily Pocket Journal* was sponsored by Johnson's publisher, Robert Dodsley. It was admirably prepared. As a gentleman and as a tradesman, Reynolds found it indispensable. He entered the names of his sitters on the left-hand pages, using the right-hand pages, intended to be devoted to the "week's Account", for all kinds of illuminating memoranda. His notebook gave him the English value of Portugal Pieces, Louis d'Ors and Pistoles, and the dates when dividends were paid at the Bank. Reynolds scanned the lists of Peers and Members of Parliament for influential acquaintances. In the 1755 notebook he marked the names of the two members for Plympton and also that of William

---

* Mr Horace Buttery, whose experience as a cleaner and restorer has given him an intimate knowledge of Reynolds' pictures, contributes a note on his painting methods in Appendix B below.

Beckford, M.P. for Petersfield (his portrait of Susannah Beckford in the Tate Gallery is signed and dated 1756).

These books did not stay in his studio but went abroad with him in his pocket. He made notes of his excursions in them; they are stained and worn. If ever they were lost—as probably some of them were—this must have been a major disaster.

In 1755 Reynolds had 120 sitters; in 1758 he had 150, the greatest number in any single year of his life. The sittings followed the social round; heaviest in the early part of each year, they slackened in August and September. He usually began work at nine in the morning, and sometimes took a walk in St James's Park before breakfast. There are many entries, in these early years, of "Dog"—the dogs sometimes being brought round by Milord's groom at unfashionable hours and painted in a poor light. He often worked on Sundays, much to the distress of his pious sister Fanny.

Reynolds' energy was equal to a full social life in addition to the daily round in the studio. Wherever he went, he brought humour and a flow of good spirits. He enjoyed playing cards, now and throughout his life, and had a flair for it, though he never played according to the book. That John Wilkes, with his brothers, was a regular companion at Reynolds' card-table in 1755 emphasizes his weakness for an engaging rascal. Despite his close watch over domestic expenditure, he could be a generous lender where his affection was engaged, and when his debtors were friends like Johnson and Burke he did not look for repayment. But "Creditor to Bob", before a note of several small sums in 1755, may suggest loans to his brother Robert Reynolds which were not continued.

As the money came in, he enjoyed forming a collection of pictures. He favoured landscapes by artists of France and the Low Countries. In 1755, besides a flower picture, he acquired one "Landskip" unspecified, "2 Landskips of Momper", "2 Little Dutch Lands", "A Little Brugell", "A Little Rysdale". His pictures, hung in his painting-room, assisted conversation during sittings. Sir George Beaumont told Constable that Reynolds pointed out to him a landscape by Jacques Fouquières of Antwerp "as an excellent model on which to form his style".[14] Beaumont later acquired the Fouquières, while another favourite landscape

56

picture, "The Return of the Ark" by Sebastian Bourdon, was left to Beaumont in Reynolds' will. Reynolds studied Bourdon's picture, now in the National Gallery, with affectionate care; the two interrelated trees at the right of his own Richmond landscape (Plate IX) may owe something to a similar effect in "The Return of the Ark".

The magnificent portrait of Lord Ludlow and the portraits of two Keppel ladies, all at Woburn, together with his Horace Walpole in Lord Lansdowne's collection—the shrewd, bright-eyed little man, with the lace cuffs—are among Reynolds' masterpieces of 1755-6. His first portrait (1756-7) of Samuel Johnson, in the National Portrait Gallery (Plate Va), shows Johnson sitting back quizzically in his chair, enjoying the fame of his Dictionary. Johnson was habitually pallid, but one supposes that if Reynolds' carmine had proved more permanent he would have looked a little less anaemic than he does here.

The year 1756 probably saw Reynolds' first meeting with the man who, excepting his father and Zachariah Mudge, was the chief intellectual influence in his life.[15] "For my own part I acknowledge the highest obligations to him," he wrote in his fine character-sketch of Johnson: "He may be said to have formed my mind and to have brushed off from it a deal of rubbish." [16]

Boswell was probably mistaken in dating their meeting earlier than 1756, but there is no reason to doubt his story that the pair first met at the home of the Misses Cotterell, who were neighbours of Reynolds in Great Newport Street. Reynolds was struck by the conversation of the "huge uncouth figure, with a little dark wig which scarcely covered his head, and his clothes hanging loose about him".[17] The author of that engrossing account of Savage did not disappoint him; for the rest of his life he remained his devoted admirer and friend. Johnson cared nothing for painting, but he immediately found in Reynolds a quality of mind that impressed him. The Misses Cotterell had lately lost a friend to whom they owed much, and Reynolds reminded them: "You have, however, the comfort of being relieved from a burthen of gratitude." In its combination of sense and cynicism, the remark was typical of Reynolds. It shocked the ladies but pleased Johnson. He went home with Reynolds and shared his supper.

No reader of Boswell can be unaware of the importance of Reynolds' relationship to Johnson in the thirty years that followed. It was to Reynolds, "the intimate and beloved friend of that great man", that Boswell dedicated his immortal biography, saying: "You, my dear Sir, studied him, and knew him well: you venerated and admired him." And in the same dedication Boswell commemorated the cardinal virtues of Reynolds as he saw him, his "equal and placid temper", his "variety of conversation", his "true politeness", his "enlarged hospitality". Apart from the Thrales, there are probably more references to Reynolds in Boswell than to any other single individual. Reynolds' long and intimate friendship with Johnson gave him an unequalled authority on his life; and Boswell built largely on his contributions, which included a sketch from Reynolds' own pen —one of the most perceptive studies of genius and its disabilities ever written.[18]

Highly though Reynolds valued Johnson's acquaintance, it took him some time to get accustomed to the frequency and to the length of his visits; they were not an unmixed blessing to such a busy man. Fanny Reynolds never failed to make the Doctor welcome, however, and was always ready with a fresh cup of tea. These two felt an immediate sympathy for each other's eccentricities. Fanny's affection for Johnson was matched by his fondness for his "Renny dear", and beside her tea-table Reynolds and Johnson founded an immortal friendship.

Reynolds was not the man to be impressed by titles (nor, for that matter, unduly influenced by appearances). He talked to the nobility as equals and had no use for "Your lordship". When Reynolds spoke to Johnson as "Sir", the gesture acknowledged a unique master. In his turn, Reynolds became for Johnson "the most invulnerable man I know; the man with whom if you should quarrel, you would find the most difficulty how to abuse". For Johnson he was "the same all the year round" and "a man not to be spoiled by prosperity".[19]

Because he saw his virtues and recognized his steadfastness so clearly, it should not be assumed that Johnson was unaware of Reynolds' weaknesses. Boswell disguised one or two critical references which have since been identified.[20] Thus, on one occasion, Johnson would not allow Reynolds to be termed "good humoured"; and once, when Boswell apparently referred to Reynolds as "a very universal man, quite a man of the world", Johnson pointed to the danger of a man being "zealous for nothing". It was a hint, perhaps, at the inevitable drawbacks of moderation, of easy-going tolerance, even of agnosticism. The friendship of Reynolds and Johnson was so firmly founded that each could afford to see the other's blemishes.

4

To be on intimate terms with Dr Johnson was to know most of the great intellectuals of the time. Reynolds' own circle of acquaintances was already large and growing; his friendship with Johnson immeasurably increased it. Within a few years of their first meeting, he had become the close friend of Edmund Burke (Plate VII*a*), David Garrick and Oliver Goldsmith (Plate VII*b*). He had been introduced to Bennet Langton and Joseph Warton. He knew the tempestuous Giuseppe Baretti (Plate VIII*b*), who was to cause him so much worry and amusement, and had plumbed the tedious depths of conversation with Samuel Richardson.

The world of intelligence and taste was then a small one. To maintain a footing in it required either an aristocratic income or a great deal of hard work, preferably both. A walk through the streets of London was a daily reminder of the most sordid poverty and debauchery, of prostitution and drunkenness. The aim of an ambitious man was to raise himself above that sullen, threatening sea, and to stay above it. Reynolds had long realized that what painting in England now needed was a demonstration of worldly success, an alliance of art and intellect and aristocracy. The literary clubs and public-spirited societies which grew and flourished in the eighteenth century were islands rising out of the deep waters; islands on which like-minded men could gather for comfort and encouragement, with the hope, too, of drawing further deserving strugglers out of the depths; islands which enlarged themselves as the waters slowly receded.

England in the seventeen-fifties was a land of experiment and discovery; the creative minority to which Reynolds belonged worked through small groups of purposeful men to achieve a great social and cultural advance. Reynolds had the project of an Academy of Arts much in mind from the time of his return from Italy. An English Academy had been founded in Rome in May, 1752—the very month that he left the city—and doubtless owed much to his inspiration. He was probably one of those who joined in 1753 with Francis Hayman and F. M. Newton—later the first secretary of the Royal Academy—in an unsuccessful attempt to develop the drawing-school off St Martin's Lane into a public Academy. He was certainly concerned—again with Hayman, a fellow-Devonian—in a much more elaborate scheme of 1755 to establish an Academy under the auspices of the flourishing Society of Dilettanti.* Reynolds already had several friends among the Dilettanti, including Richard and George Edgcumbe and James ("Athenian") Stuart, the painter and architect. His notebook of 1755 contains the word "Academy" opposite March 19, and he has been credited, not very plausibly, with the composition of an introduction to the printed scheme circulated for the occasion by the committee of artists, which included Hudson, Roubiliac, Astley and other friends of his. When this scheme also failed, Reynolds gave his support to a new society, "the Society for the Encouragement of Arts, Manufactures and Commerce"—now known as the Royal Society of Arts—which had been founded by a group of scientists, noblemen and clergy at Rawthmell's Coffee-house, Henrietta Street, in 1754.

Joshua Reynolds, of "Newport Street, near Long Acre", was elected to the Society of Arts on the proposal of James Stuart on September 1, 1756. Soon afterwards Stuart also proposed Samuel Johnson, of "Temple Lane", who was elected on December 1, 1756. The conjunction of their names under the same proposer is a further hint that Reynolds and Johnson first met in this year. It is significant, too, that Reynolds' ambitious friend William Chambers, the architect, was elected to the Society early in 1757.

The aims of the Society of Arts, in so far as they related to the encouragement of "Manufactures and Commerce"—and they always have done so to a large extent—did not interest Reynolds at all. In his *Journey from London to Brentford* (Appendix A), he writes of travel books "stuffed with accounts of the state of Arts, Manufactures and Commerce, the Police of Nations and I

---

* From *delectare*, to delight: a word misleading in its later implication of superficiality.

know not what, which nobody cares one pin about". But in its early years the Society did pay particular attention to the encouragement of drawing in the young, and to the promotion not only of industrial design but of the Fine Arts generally. As the Society had attracted powerful support, Reynolds clearly perceived that it might do a useful work in raising the status and proficiency of artists, and that it could also assist him in his own career.

He attended the committee that judged the competition drawings with some regularity. So did Chambers, who designed the Society's early premises in the Strand. Reynolds was also present in 1759 at meetings of the Committee of Polite and Liberal Arts and of the Committee on History Painting. In 1760 we find him enlisted (more by accident perhaps than by design) to attend a meeting of a committee to encourage the growing of the Zante currant. But in the same year he was much more happily placed on the Society's committee for the promotion of the first exhibition of pictures ever to be held in England.

Though Reynolds had probably worked for this exhibition ever since he joined the Society, it was Francis Hayman who again took the lead as chairman of the Committee of Artists. The whole affair was obviously stage-managed, however, by Reynolds' circle of intimates. Hayman's letter to the Society was written for him by Dr Johnson. The Society's committee that considered it included Hayman himself, Reynolds, Garrick and Chambers.

The historic exhibition of 1760 in the Society's Great Room in the Strand gave Reynolds his first opportunity of showing his work to the public. The four portraits he offered at once established his pre-eminence as a portrait-painter. It was a glorious muddle, that exhibition; undesirable visitors attended, and the Society had to pay a bill for "windows broke"; works by Reynolds, Richard Wilson, Cosway, Morland and Paul Sandby were mixed with the prize-winning entries for the Society's competitions on the over-crowded walls; but there was no doubting the success of the innovation as a whole, nor its importance in Reynolds' public career.

The most distinguished of the artists seceded from the Society's exhibitions after 1760 to form the Incorporated Society of Artists. In future Reynolds exhibited with them at Spring Gardens. He took no further interest in the Society of Arts, which had served its turn; but he did not resign formally until 1764, when Johnson also left the Society.[21]

5

Reynolds' father never had the pleasure of seeing his hopes for Joshua fulfilled, but his mother lived long enough to know that he had become a fashionable portrait-painter and perhaps to learn that he had been admitted to Dr Johnson's friendship. She died at Christmas, 1756, and was buried at Torrington on December 27 of that year.[22]

It is distinctly curious that Reynolds, who spoke affectionately of his father, should never apparently have left anything on record about his mother. Outwardly Mrs Reynolds seems to have made little impression on her son, but her reaction to the easy-going improvident generosity of Samuel Reynolds may have shown itself in Joshua's cautious, acquisitive approach to money matters. His alternating moods of generosity and niggardliness may have reflected an endless remembered debate between his parents in the schoolmaster's house at Plympton. Perhaps his mother gave him the determination, the vital spring of nervous energy, that was lacking in his father.

Studio business thrived on Reynolds' industry; and his Italian friendships provided some unexpected fruit. He could not have anticipated, for example, that wealthy Sir William Lowther, whose ugly humorous face had invited a caricature as well as a portrait, was to die in 1756 at the age of twenty-six, leaving legacies of £5,000 each to thirteen of his friends. Reynolds was not one of the lucky thirteen, but he benefited almost equally because most of the legatees gratefully commissioned copies of his portrait of Lowther. For several years these versions provided employment for Marchi and his collaborators and gave Reynolds a steady income. They helped to establish Reynolds' fortune; and in time they also proved a source of embarrassment to art-historians, for the solid young man with the big nose and chin, his hand thrust into his doublet, recurs in country houses up and down the land.

Not least of the cares of a fashionable portrait-painter was the packing and dispatch of his canvases by road to clients all over the British Isles. Details of the proposed route and method of transport of pictures, noted at the time of the final sitting, continually recur in Reynolds' indispensable pocket-book. In May, 1758, Charles Pigot directs that a picture destined for Shropshire be sent to Blossoms Inn, Lawrence Lane ("goes out Mondays & Thursdays"). In April, 1759, there is a note: "Mrs Ingram Wakefield to be sent to the Swan with Two Necks in Lad Lane". Another picture must be sent "to the Castle in Wood Street by the Stamford Carrier directed to Grantham to be left till calld for". A painter's household was much preoccupied with carriers, stage-coaches, inns and departure times; Reynolds' portraits had to be packed to sustain long and rough journeys.

During the late 'fifties some of his most lovely pictures—natural, intimate and unpretentious—thus set out from Newport Street. The Duke of Richmond went to Goodwood, graceful in his glowing scarlet coat, though inordinately long in the torso; young Jacob Bouverie went to Longford, one of many noble children whom Reynolds was painting with ever-increasing felicity. Although 150 portraits were now coming from the studio each year, it is a marvel how many impress us by the force of their candour and sincerity—none more so than the Countess of Albemarle in the National Gallery, and Lady Spencer and her child, the future Duchess of Devonshire, at Althorp (Plate VI*a*). They give us the experience of age, the pride of motherhood, the innocence of childhood, and prove that Reynolds, having won his laurels with portraits of men, had already mastered the moods and manners of women.

This was a phase of tender simplicity that he only fully re-captured in the last years of his life. The 1760 exhibition at the Society of Arts set Reynolds upon a public platform and, by seducing him into an elaborately artificial and pseudo-classical style of public utterance, broke the spell of his early London years. His public manner had its triumphs, and intermittently his deepening sense of character or his genuine love of children broke through the pomp and circumstance. Sometimes, and usually when he was personally interested in a sitter, he found the confidence to dispense with his prepared canvas and paint directly; the portraits that resulted are among those that we most value. But to take and hold the public eye in overcrowded exhibitions exacted an inevitable price from Reynolds' art and from his spontaneity. Above all, the advent of exhibitions demanded elaboration and grandiosity.

His well-known picture of "Garrick between Tragedy and Comedy" (1762) illustrates the struggle that went on between Reynolds' public and intimate styles. It was the symptom of a similar struggle that was being waged within himself. We cannot fail to recognize the conflict between his simple signatures to private notes and his elaborately embellished signatures on formal occasions; between his brilliant capacity to analyse complexity— as shown in the Discourses, or in a penetrating portrait like that of Laurence Sterne (1760)—and his innate gift for generalization.

With a lesser artist, one style or the other would have conquered—probably the public style. Reynolds' prolific nervous energy ordered a different result. The student of Reynolds who has searched for his work, both in public and private collection on both sides of the Atlantic, will have learned that, within the artist's obvious limitations, he cannot anticipate what he will find. He feels as if he is looking at the work not of one painter but of two or three.

All this was not achieved by placidity, though Reynolds successfully deceived his friends into thinking that it was. It derived from the interplay of a mind that vacillated between daring and caution, between a longing for intimate companionship and a deep desire for independence.

> Dear Knight of Plympton, teach me how
> To suffer, with unclouded brow
> And smile serene, like thine . . .

wrote his friend, Dean Barnard. "To suffer with unclouded brow" —that indeed was the great lesson that Reynolds had learned.

6

How much he suffered for his ideals can only be fully realized by those who have studied the drafts of his literary compositions. He was determined to be a writer, and by dint of immense effort he succeeded. He achieved a literary style with the same recipe of hard work that he had used to acquire a style for living and a style for painting. Whenever he sat down to pen and paper he was under immense strain, continually correcting, even simple words and phrases, and re-writing. He would not be an "ordinary writer", any more than he would be an "ordinary painter"; he intended to be a writer worthy of such friends as Johnson and Burke. His indecision makes his drafts agonizing to read; but he persevered—and his *Discourses* are cited as models of lucid English prose.

Reynolds began his literary career with three essays published in Johnson's *Idler* in the autumn of 1759. In writing these anonymous papers he was obliged to take stock of his views on the theory of painting, for two of them contained indirect critical allusion to Hogarth's *Analysis of Beauty* which had first appeared six years earlier.

Although Reynolds had a constitutional aversion to Hogarth's self-assertion and pugnacity, and although he was on the opposing side in his war with the connoisseurs, he fully appreciated the "extraordinary talents", as he put it in his Fourteenth Discourse, of "our late excellent Hogarth", his "successful attention to the ridicule of life" and his invention of "a new species of dramatic painting, in which probably he will never be equalled". On the other hand, he deprecated Hogarth's attempt at "the great historical style, for which his previous habits had by no means prepared him"; he was unable to give the highest praise to a genius employed on "low and confined subjects" (Third Discourse); and he had no high opinion of Hogarth's theorizing in the *Analysis of Beauty*.

In the *Idler* No. 76 of September 29, 1759, Reynolds ingeniously ridiculed Hogarth's central theories of the serpentine line—the Line of Beauty—and the pyramidal principle by putting them into the mouth of an alleged connoisseur (and we must remember that Hogarth detested connoisseurs) who was supposed to be viewing the Raphael Cartoons at Hampton Court. But this master-stroke was apparently an after-thought. The following unpublished "Observations on Hogarth" [23] in Reynolds' hand are prefaced by the opening "Sir" which was commonly employed for letters "To the Idler", and suggest that he originally intended to reply to Hogarth more directly.

Sir as you desire my opinion of Mr Hogarth's Anylisis of Beauty I will freely give it you, [it] is full of ingenious observations tho I dont think him so profound a Philosopher as it appears he thinks himself, he treats his Brother Artists in his introduction pretty Cavilierly, by telling them that tho they knew the beauty of the line yet they did not know it Philosophically but as a Labourer who make[s] use of the Leaver knows not its powers as a Mecanical Philosopher; one might reasonably expect after this a philosophical investigation of this cause of the beauty of this line. Notwithstanding this air of superiority & self-sufficiency, he has given no philosophical account why this line of Beauty is so pleasing, it is so only because it is so.

Mr H. as he is not so indeed he dont pretend to be the first inventor or the first who found out the beauty of the waving Serpentine line but proves the beauty of it from the practice of all artists, so that yet nothing is done except giving it the name of the line of beauty & the precice line—notwithstanding the high prancing at first setting out & galloping over his poor fellow-artists.

That there is beauty in the form of this Line superior to that of any other kind is beyond all dispute, but the reason of its beauty proceeds as is shown by Mr Hogarth in 1,000's of Instants from our being more used to that line than any other, this may with the appearance of reason be denied, as the line is but seldom met with compleat, but if it [be] considerd that all the lines that can be may be reduced to two, a strait & a circular line, these may be said to be medium or central forms of all lines, but it being necessary to make one line that shall be medium of central form of all line[s] these two must be joind together, perhaps to do this mathematically may be as difficult as squaring the circle, it must have exactly as much of a strait line as it has a circle.

Reynolds' scepticism about Hogarth's serpentine line is perfectly understandable, but all attempts to define beauty are hazardous and he himself was in error when he went on to propose a theory of common use as the reason for the beauty of the line. He developed this unsatisfactory argument of central form and custom in the *Idler* No. 82, of November 10, 1759, and in his Third Discourse of 1770. In the *Idler* No. 82 he even ventured a mild rebuke to Edmund Burke, whose essay on "The Sublime and Beautiful" (1757) had been much influenced by Hogarth's *Analysis*; he might not have allowed himself this comment at a later stage of their intimacy. He was still repeating his argument about the Line of Beauty in a letter to James Beattie of March 31, 1782, when he added: "An artist would act preposterously that should take every opportunity to introduce this line in his works as Hogarth himself did, who appears to have taken an aversion to a straight line." [24]

Hogarth's instance of the labourer and his "leaver" is to be found in the Preface to his *Analysis*.[25] A few pages further on Reynolds discovered another passage [26] which equally aroused his indignation. Hogarth there quotes Pliny's famous account of the Greek painter Apelles' visit to Protogenes: not finding his friend at home, Apelles is said to have drawn a line on a board which would indicate to him who had called; Protogenes took the hint and drew "a finer *or rather more expressive line* within it", much to the satisfaction of Apelles when he returned later. Hogarth maintained that this line must have been the serpentine line, but Reynolds had a simpler explanation:

... the absurdity of supposing it an excellence in a Painter to draw a line with in another line is so frought with ignorance that nothing can be more contemptable. Mr Hogarth in his Analysis of B. has given a much more ingenious tho perhaps not a more true solution of what kind of line was left but it serves his purpose very well; it appears to me that there is no need for the explanation to be far fetchd when a more rational one lies before them that there was a mark left by which Proto[genes] might discover that an able painter had been at his house, he drew what was calld linea which in French is un trait, that linea signifies a drawing or sketch as well as a line, we have Apelles own proverb "nulla dies sine linea"—[and] that the other finist [finished] the outline of the former.

Reynolds concluded these fragmentary notes[27] with some reflections on "the infancy of Painting" which seem to lie behind both his second and third *Idler* essays, and which reappear in different form in the Discourses:

The first Painters in their Historical Characters gave the moles warts and every minute part that the model that was before them exhibited, their cloths were distinguishd whether silk satin or cloth. The succeeding Painters as the Arts advanced extended their practice

67

only to the General Ideas of Nature; the stuffs with which their dresses are made have no minute discrimination of the property of the stuff, it is drapery.

I might have mentiond another circumstance as characteristick of [the] first Artist[s], their ambition turning of endeavouring to excell each other in neatness & high finishing.

Whilst the Art remaind in this state it had no pretensions to a higher rank than a mecanical work or to be rank[ed] as a sister Art to Poetry.

The chief interest of these "Observations on Hogarth" lies in the fact that they may represent, though in an abortive form, Reynolds' first attempt at writing for publication. They were not, however, his only aids to composing the *Idler* essays, for Northcote quotes several pages from a commonplace book which obviously provided much of his material, and Reynolds drew not only on the theories of Hogarth and Richardson, but also on Adam Smith and Johnson.[28]

The "Observations" are also of value as illuminating, however slightly, Reynolds' attitude towards Hogarth. They were too violently opposed, both as men and as artists, for either to be able to estimate the other justly so long as they were competing as contemporaries. Reynolds was well aware of Hogarth's genius and in his Fourteenth Discourse, written towards the end of his life, he assessed him, as we have seen, dispassionately and with a large measure of appreciation. But in 1759, when the *Idler* papers were composed, Hogarth was an embittered man of over sixty; Reynolds, at thirty-five, was already the leading portrait-painter in London. Reynolds must, indeed, have contributed to Hogarth's disillusionment, for to capture the world of fashion he had developed the new style of portraiture initiated by Hogarth himself in his great portrait of "Captain Coram". There could be no rapprochement between Hogarth, the opponent of the Royal Academy, and Reynolds, who became its first President; between the overbearing satirist with his sense of class distinction, and the social charmer with his talent for co-operation and compromise. Only time, in a long view of English art, could reconcile such opposites. That Mrs Hogarth should have received an annuity from the Royal Academy during the last two years of her life is curiously moving.

IV. JOSHUA REYNOLDS. Self-portrait. 1753–4
$(25'' \times 29\frac{1}{4}'')$

In 1760 Hogarth enjoyed one thing, at least, that Reynolds coveted—a house in Leicester Fields. But buying a house on the opposite side of the square brought Reynolds no nearer to Hogarth. They may, perhaps, have touched their hats to each other in the gardens.

V

Leicester Fields

I

Reynolds' move to Leicester Fields was made at a time when
he was very heavily engaged. In 1759 he raised his prices
to twenty guineas for a head, fifty guineas for a half length,
and a hundred guineas for a whole length. He did so with a
double motive; he not only required money for a new house but
felt the need to limit the number of his sitters.

The names of Garrick, Sterne and Lord Ligonier—to mention
only a few of the sittings that gave rise to well-known portraits—
occur in Reynolds' pocket-books of 1759–60. There, too, we
first find the name of the notorious courtesan Kitty Fisher whose
portrait he painted several times, and who also sat to him as an
artist's model. The notebook for December, 1759, has the memorandum "N.B. Miss Fisher's Picture is for Sir Charles Bingham":
a necessary reminder, because Kitty's clients and admirers were
innumerable. They included Augustus Keppel and Lord Ligonier,
either of whom may have brought her to the studio. Reynolds
painted many portraits of soldiers and sailors during these years
of glory in the war with France; he also had to provide the aristocratic equivalent of what was later to be vulgarly known as a
"pin-up".

Kitty's *élan* was continental; she had a German father and could
chatter in French. Reynolds tended to see her in elusive profile,
the portraits at Ken Wood and in Lord Lansdowne's collection
suggesting a petulant vivacity rather than coarseness. She seems
almost fragile beside her leading rival Nelly O'Brien, who also
appears in Reynolds' notebooks at this time. Nelly's eyes look
out of Reynolds' magnificent portrait in the Wallace Collection
with unflinching boldness; a few years later she is overblown and
passée. The charms of these ladies of the town were as evanescent
as Reynolds' carmine. Both were dead before the 'sixties were
out.

For Reynolds, Kitty and Nelly were indispensable items of the social scene, taking their places beside the grave lawyers and statesmen, the soldiers on rearing horses, the refined society hostesses in classical poses, the family groups of patrician respectability, the innocent children skirmishing with domestic tabbies. Kitty Fisher and Nelly O'Brien were painted with the professional impartiality that made Reynolds the supreme recorder of eighteenth-century society.

Other sitters promised a loftier, a royal patronage which was never properly fulfilled. In 1758-60 Reynolds was painting not only the Duke of Cumberland and the Duke of York but also the Prince of Wales, who was soon to become George III. Much might have been expected to flow from that meeting, but in fact the new King never took to Reynolds either as a man or as an artist, and such recognition as he accorded him was grudgingly given. Why George III, after Charles I the greatest contributor to the royal collections both in paintings and drawings, should have patronized Hoppner, Gainsborough, Beechey, Zoffany, and the Americans West and Copley—and have slighted Reynolds— is something not to be fully explained, perhaps, by Reynolds' associations with the left wing in politics.

Both Cumberland and the Prince lived in Leicester Fields, where the adjacent Leicester House and Savile House were royal residences. As he painted them, Reynolds may have finally determined to move his own household to those spacious surroundings. This ambition reached its climax in the summer of 1760. "House bought", he noted on July 3. Opposite August 28 he wrote "House to be Paid for", but he crossed this out. In the week of September 3 he recorded "House Payd", and on September 11 he spread himself in a bold satisfied handwriting across two pages of his notebook: "Paid the remaining £1000 for the House in Leicester Fields" (Plate VIb).

In October George III was proclaimed King before Savile House with splendid ceremony. England had begun a new reign, and Reynolds had secured a home from which he was to be rarely absent for the rest of his life.

2

"Good-bye Piccadilly, Farewell Leicester Square." To recapture the atmosphere in which Reynolds lived and worked requires a vigorous effort of imaginative reconstruction. It is a melancholy place, Leicester Square, two hundred years after, its little garden of asphalt and flower-beds dominated on three sides by the commercial cinema. The site of Reynolds' house, before which his coach once waited, is covered by the headquarters of the Automobile Association; opposite towers a black monstrosity reminiscent of Lenin's tomb, dedicated to "serial pictures" of a kind not contemplated by Hogarth. None of the famous squares of London has suffered more drearily.

In 1760 Leicester Square was agreeably civilized. To the north lay Savile House and Leicester House, with its forecourt; facing them, against the square railings, was a stand for sedan-chairs. Along the east side, and across the entrance to what is now New Coventry Street, ran a line of houses dating from the close of the seventeenth century. A similar row of houses on the west side, where Hogarth lived, ended at Cranbourn Street; some of these were built as early as 1673. There were no kerbstones around the square, but, between the pavements and the cobbles, posts marked off the roadway. Assuming his share of civic responsibility, Reynolds became a trustee under the Act passed "for the better paving and lighting of the parish of St Anne".[1]

Memories of duels in Leicester Fields had already grown dim by the time that Reynolds came there. The Square garden with its grass plots had been enclosed since 1720; on a high pedestal in its centre stood a gilt equestrian statue of George I, in classical armour. This statue fell to bits in the middle of the nineteenth century, and "Baron" Albert Grant, the company promoter, then advanced to the rescue of the dilapidated square. Grant laid out the present garden with the help of Sir James Knowles and gave it to the public in 1874. Shakespeare took the place of George I; busts of former residents—Hogarth, Newton, Hunter, Reynolds —were allotted to the four corners. The unrecognizable Reynolds by H. Weekes is on the north side, heroic under his large marble hat. Cockney sparrows that perch on that hat have changed less in two hundred years than anything else in the Square.

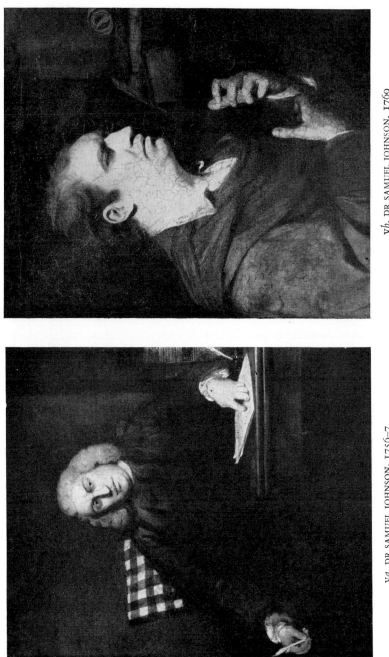

Vb. DR SAMUEL JOHNSON. 1769
(32″ × 26″)

Va. DR SAMUEL JOHNSON. 1756–7
(49″ × 39″)

The house for which Reynolds paid £1,650 for a forty-seven years' lease was, appropriately, number 47, in the middle of the west side. It was built about 1690 and already had an artistic history, having belonged for a time to H. R. Morland, the portrait-painter and picture-dealer, father of George Morland. There were three floors above the ground floor and (fashionable asset of the period) a basement for the kitchen below. With its narrow frontage, it was still not a particularly large house, but Reynolds spent a further £1,500 in building over the back garden a gallery and painting-rooms for himself and his assistants. The approach to this new wing—a self-contained portrait factory— was by way of the first half-landing. Reynolds also rebuilt the staircase up to the first floor, providing stone stairs and wrought-iron balustrades with a graceful outward curve designed to assist the stately progress of ladies in crinolines; above the first floor he retained the original stairs with turned balusters and carved brackets. His alterations raised the rateable value from £80 to £100.

The painting-rooms did not long survive Reynolds' days. They were probably demolished about 1827 when a lecture theatre, with an entrance from Whitcomb Street, was built at the back of the house for the Western Literary and Scientific Institution. Further changes occurred in 1859 when Puttick and Simpson's, the auctioneers, replaced the lecture theatre by a large sale-room. But the front part of the house, though altered by a succession of tenants, remained much the same as Reynolds knew it until it was pulled down in 1937.

A plaque recording that Reynolds "lived and died in a house on this site" is poor consolation to those who remember the old house—neighbour for many years to Thurston's Billiard Hall— with the red plaque of the Society of Arts above its front-door. For the house in which Reynolds entertained Johnson, Burke, Goldsmith, Garrick and Fanny Burney, the hall and staircase which had known so much of the beauty, taste and genius of the time, were not to be lightly discarded. No house in London held more historic associations with the latter half of the eighteenth century than 47 Leicester Square. Lady Oxford and several distinguished artists contended for it in the correspondence columns of The Times.

73

Unfortunately the interior, damaged by long service to a firm of auctioneers, hardly called for preservation on architectural grounds. There were intangible presences for the sentimental, but one or two poor marble mantelpieces and old grates, a little panelling, the staircase and its balusters were all that caught the wary eye of the expert who went round with his notebook. The mantelpieces surviving in 1937 did not include a very handsome one known to have been designed for Reynolds by his friend James Paine[2]—which suggests that this mantelpiece may have been intended to impress visitors to Reynolds' new painting-room. During the last months in the life of 47 Leicester Square photographers and artists tramped over the bare boards to make a record for posterity. A more determined enthusiast, Father J. S. M. Ward, succeeded in carrying off the stone steps of the staircase and the crinoline balusters to his museum at the Abbey Folk Park, New Barnet.

3

Ours being a happier purpose than that of the demolition men, we can still go in at the front-door and up the stairs, pass through the gallery filled with Reynolds' own works, and enter his studio.

The busy professional greeted his sitters cordially but without fuss. If they put themselves at once into a natural attitude, he was likely to tell them not to move and to begin a rapid sketch.

The room was octagonal, about twenty feet long by sixteen feet wide, and lit only by one small window high up in the wall (probably a consequence of the window tax). Reynolds worked beside the window, placing his sitters in an armchair, eighteen inches from the ground, that turned on castors. He used either a large standing easel—William Mason the poet gave him one such—or a solid wooden painting-table that opened ingeniously to make an easel. His wooden palettes were square with a handle and he kept his paints in a small chest containing five drawers. Beside the sitter's chair stood a Chippendale mirror of dark mahogany carved with sprigs of flowers; this served a double purpose—Reynolds could see the sitter's reflection, and the sitter, by way of diversion, would be asked to look in the mirror and watch the painter at work. Northcote maintained that Reynolds' portraits had indeed something of the romantic, visionary character of a looking-glass reflection.[3]

With his long brushes and his maulstick, on which he occasionally rested his hand, the painter conveyed an impression of eager activity. He worked quickly and never sat down. "He took quite a quantity of exercise when he painted," old Lady Burlington told Sir Francis Grant, "for he continually walked backwards and forwards. His plan was to walk away several feet, then take a long look at me and the picture as we stood side by side, then rush up to the portrait and dash at it in a kind of fury. I sometimes thought he would make a mistake and paint on me instead of the picture." [4]

All that we learn from Northcote of Reynolds' studio practice goes to show his absorbed happiness in his work. He approached each fresh canvas with a determination to do better than ever before, with an undimmed zest for experiment both in the composition and colouring of a picture. Hence he never lost interest in portrait, and would never have written as Gainsborough did: "I'm sick of Portraits and wish very much to take my Viol da Gam and walk off to some sweet Village where I can paint Landskips and enjoy the fag end of life..." [5] Gainsborough had learned a sound painting technique from Hayman; perhaps it bored him. Reynolds' experimental interest in his work was paid for in many faulty canvases, but it is arguable that the art was advanced even by his failures.

Northcote quotes Gainsborough as saying: "Sir Joshua's pictures in their most decayed state were better than those of any other artist when in their best." To which may be added Gainsborough's more famous tribute: "D——n him, how various he is!" Gainsborough worked in fits and starts, wondering at Reynolds' "*equal* application".[6]

Reynolds' long-sustained and disastrous preference for carmine instead of vermilion is discussed by Mr Horace Buttery in Appendix B. He was forced to stop using it, though he was obstinate in argument with Northcote, looking at his hand and saying: "I can see no vermilion in flesh." "But did not Sir Godfrey Kneller always use vermilion in his flesh colours?" retorted Northcote. "What signifies what a man used who could not colour?" replied Reynolds "rather sharply".

His secret colour preparations were locked away in his painting-chest; his obduracies were deeply engraved in his character. He much enjoyed painting his "fancy pictures", and admitted that he should have confined his colour experiments to such things; but he found he simply could not do it—to have played safe with portrait would have blunted the zest.

The purchase of the house in Leicester Fields exhausted his savings, but he was soon earning £6,000 a year. A large part of his income went in the purchase of works by the masters, for he considered himself "as playing a great game" and loved to surround himself with treasures. Nevertheless, he destroyed several "capital ancient paintings of the Venetian School", reports Northcote, in his attempts to learn their technical secrets. And so absorbed could he become that, cleaning out a gallipot with turpentine, he once threw some of it into his studio fire. Flames appeared at the top of the low chimney, and when the fire-engine arrived, Reynolds had to pay a fine of five pounds.

This must have seemed a wicked imposition, for Reynolds grudged the smaller household expenses. Looking about the house for old canvases, he once discovered "a mop-stick put up in the corner of the back-kitchen". He told Ralph Kirkley—the servant who came into his employ at about the time of the move to Leicester Fields—that this must be preserved, "in order that its value might be deducted when the next new mop was purchased".[7]

Reynolds' miserly streak may have been accentuated by the knowledge that, though he was now earning a large income, his outgoings were also considerable. He spared no expense in furnishing his home, being influenced by the prevailing taste for Chinoiserie, as might have been expected from the friend of William Chambers, architect of the Kew Pagoda and author of *Designs of Chinese Buildings, Furniture, Dresses, etc.*, published in 1757. One of Reynolds' Chinese gilt and lacquer cabinets was a squat chest decorated with flowering shrubs and flying birds; another, taller, was inset with mirrors and panels carved with Imperial dragons. Both were handsome pieces raised from the floor on stands. Reynolds derived no artistic inspiration from Chinoiserie, but he had a sympathetic interest for it, and when given an oriental subject, such as the page-boy Wang-y-Tong, he painted with particular spirit.

In course of time, Reynolds acquired a blue Chinese Lowestoft dinner service of 150 pieces; his silver spoons and forks bore his crest—a Talbot issuing out of a Coronet; the dinner table was lit by four silver branch candlesticks. He showed an author's interest in his silver inkstand, which he contrived to introduce casually into several of his portraits; with a quill-pen stuck into it, and a handful of papers nearby, Reynolds' inkstand often appears on the tables which eminent lawyers rest their elbows. Then he had his own card-counters, specially designed in mother-of-pearl and packed in a lacquer box. And he attracted gifts from admirers. Margaret Beattie, wife of James Beattie, the author, presented him with a luxurious silver tea-caddy lined with red velvet, containing tongs and silver spoons inscribed "M.B. to J.R." Garrick gave him the chest made out of Shakespeare's mulberry-tree which he received with the freedom of Stratford-on-Avon.

Thus the treasures multiplied over the last thirty years of Reynolds' life, until his house became an epitome of cultivated taste, a little palace for the self-made aristocrat of painting. In his dark blue velvet coat with the plain blue buttons, the lace ruffles, the silver shoe-buckles, he walked out of a room lined with Italian and Flemish masterpieces, down the staircase with the crinoline balusters—and out to that wonder of wonders, the coach.[8]

This crowning extravagance was, frankly, a shrewd piece of advertisement, comparable in the mid-twentieth century to a rich industrialist's opulent motor-car. The panels of Reynolds' rococo coach were painted by Charles Catton with allegories of the seasons; the wheels were adorned with carved foliage and gilding. Perhaps William Chambers, who designed George III's state coach, inspired this piece of ostentation. Was it, after all, as Northcote rumoured, "an old chariot of a Sheriff of London, newly done up"? That might, indeed, have been a private joke which Reynolds would have enjoyed.

His notebook first shows a concern for the coach in 1764. There is a prudent memorandum at the end of the book: "$\frac{1}{2}$ Bushel ever[y] day for two Horses or a sack a week", and in May he makes a note to interview "Timothy Clemiston Coachman". On June 26 of the following year, at nine in the morning, he "Gave warning to the Coachman". The men servants (and Reynolds employed a number), were always difficult, even though he provided liveries laced with silver. He was fortunate in Ralph Kirkley, and he appreciated his devotion. Kirkley's wages will have been small, but he took tips at the door, which in a fashionable painter's household made a great difference.

Reynolds had little opportunity to use his coach in the daytime; but he liked to see his sister Fanny ride out in it. Fanny, being exceedingly shy, was soon embarrassed by this ostentation. When she remonstrated with her brother, he replied "What! would you have one like an apothecary's carriage?" Had he not, after all, once declared that he would rather be an apothecary than "an *ordinary* painter"?

4

Throughout the seventeen-sixties until the establishment of the Royal Academy in 1768, Reynolds regularly exhibited at Spring Gardens with the Society of Artists which had seceded from the exhibitions of the Society of Arts after 1760. He knew its directors well. They included the powerful and influential William Chambers (Plate X*b*), a close friend at this time but a man too fond of intrigue, too self-centred to make a settled ally; they included a loyal old friend like G. M. Moser, a rival portrait-painter in Francis Cotes, and lesser men like Nathaniel Hone and William Tyler who envied his success. Though he was several times invited to become a director himself, Reynolds always respectfully declined.[9] He probably realized that he would only be involved in distracting squabbles. Moreover, the larger design of a Royal Academy was constantly in his thoughts. Reynolds watched and waited. He had acquired style; he had trained himself in social poise; he knew by now that he had the gifts of a conciliator, the chairman's touch. But he realized also that his strength lay in detachment, that with his sensitive, restless nature he must avoid open conflicts. Wisely, he withheld himself from too close an association with a body of temporary significance.

It was not enough for him to be recognized as the most successful painter in England. He must be the artistic leader in an intellectual sense—and the fulfilment of that ambition was his unique achievement. He was not averse to playing cards or to visiting Ranelagh and Vauxhall or the theatre on occasions, but, generally speaking, whatever time remained to him after the day's work in his studio, was given to reading, to writing, and to the pleasures of intellectual society. His three Letters to the *Idler* had been well received; they had been reprinted in the *London Chronicle*, and Johnson had contrived to present them to their author as a small pamphlet. Reynolds then attempted a humorous sketch, in which he wrote as the wife of a man who was a great wit in company but exceedingly dull at home—the sketch was never finished, but the manuscript at the British Museum suggests that in different circumstances Reynolds might have developed as a humorous writer.[10] A life-long interest in Shakespeare, again, enabled him to contribute some notes to the edition on which Johnson was now engaged. Though the notes are of slight importance, they reflect a careful study of the plays, particularly of *Othello*, which is also evidenced by the pages of extracts in his commonplace book.[11] It was Reynolds' view that Shakespeare used to make continual alterations as he wrote—though his principal reason for adopting the theory may have been that Reynolds did so himself.

Johnson's finances had long been a matter of concern to his friend—Reynolds' notebook for 1759 contains the entry "£96 to Johnson", though this may have been money lent to his brother-in-law rather than to Samuel—so that he must have been well pleased to learn in 1762 of the new King's intention to provide Johnson with a pension of £300 a year. The Doctor dearly longed to accept the offer, but his conscience was embarrassed because his Dictionary had unequivocally stated that in England a pension "was generally understood to mean pay given to a state hireling for treason to his country". He called on Reynolds to ask for his advice, allowing him a day to think over the problem. But Reynolds replied immediately that there could be no objection to his receiving a reward for literary merit, and that the definitions in his Dictionary were certainly not applicable to him. This satisfied Johnson, who went off determined to accept the pension. And later he reported to Reynolds that Lord Bute had said much the same: "It is not given you for any thing you are to do, but for what you have done." [12]

In celebration of his good fortune, Reynolds carried the Doctor away with him for a Devonshire holiday in August, 1762.[13] "Sat out from London at two o'clock," says the notebook for August 16 (Reynolds habitually "sat out" rather than "set out"); "at eleven arrived at Winchester." They visited Wilton and Longford before making for Torrington, where Reynolds' relatives entertained them for two days. The rest of the time they spent at Plymouth as the guests of Dr John Mudge, where Johnson met his father Prebendary Zachariah Mudge—Reynolds' revered friend and mentor—who impressed Johnson so much that he later wrote his obituary for the *London Chronicle*.

To have brought these two older men together must have afforded Reynolds unusual pleasure; probably, apart from his own father and Oliver Goldsmith, he loved them more than he loved anyone in his life. Looking from one to the other, he may have reflected how much his lonely, restless nature owed to their wisdom and courage. They did not succeed in making a churchman of him, but they helped to make him a philosopher.

Johnson enjoyed this Devonshire outing, which linked him more closely than ever to Reynolds. We hear of him devouring quantities of clotted cream and honey and drinking a lot of cider. He raced with a young lady on a lawn, kicking off his slippers and leading the girl back in triumphant delight when he had won. To another Devonshire lady (or was it the same?) who asked him how he had come to define *Pastern* in his Dictionary as the knee of a horse, he made his famous reply: "Ignorance, Madam, pure ignorance." He identified himself loyally with the old town of Plymouth, in which he stayed, and some local dispute with the new town of Devonport drew from him the cry: "No, no! I am against the *dockers*; I am a Plymouth-man."

The Devonshire air also inspired Johnson to make an Irish "bull"—the only one, according to Boswell, that he ever perpetrated in his life. While they were out riding, Reynolds "complained that he had a very bad horse, for that even when going down hill he moved slowly step by step. 'Ay (said Johnson,) and when he *goes* up hill, he *stands still*.'"[14]

It was refreshing for these Londoners to be able to relax and make bad jokes in the country—Reynolds introduced Johnson to his friends at Mount Edgcumbe and Saltram; they also spent a day at Plympton. Not all the local admiration went to the Doctor, for it was now that James Northcote—a lad, of about sixteen, who had studied Reynolds' pictures "with wonder and delight"— first caught sight of Reynolds at a public meeting in Plymouth and "got as near to him as I could from the pressure of the people, to touch the skirt of his coat, which I did with great satisfaction to my mind". One is reminded of Reynolds' own hero-worshipping-gesture towards Alexander Pope.

5

On the way home from Devonshire, the travellers passed through Dorset and slept at the Crown at Blandford. It was probably on this homeward journey that they visited John Bankes, M.P., of Kingston Hall. Reynolds recorded[15] an instance of Johnson's eccentric behaviour while he was there. The conversation turning to pictures, Johnson "retired to a corner of the room, stretching out his right leg as far as he could reach before him, then bringing up his left leg and stretching his right still further on". Mr Bankes "went up to him, and in a very courteous manner assured him that though it was not a new house, the flooring was perfectly safe. The Doctor started from his reverie, like a person waked out of his sleep, but spoke not a word."

No one knew more about Johnson than Reynolds. There are signs that he himself had a fear of loneliness; at all events, he well understood Johnson's dread of solitude. Observing that Johnson's odd tricks and movements occurred only when he was not engaged in conversation, he conjectured that this "proceeded from a habit he had indulged himself in of accompanying his thoughts with certain untoward actions, and that those actions always appeared to him as if they were meant to reprobate some part of his past conduct". Boswell considered this theory "very ingenious".[16]

In February, 1764, Reynolds founded the famous "Literary Club", commonly known as "The Club", with the avowed object of giving Johnson every opportunity for conversation. At its beginning the numbers were strictly limited—besides Reynolds and Johnson, the members were Goldsmith, Burke and his father-in-law Dr Nugent, Topham Beauclerk, Bennet Langton, Anthony

Chamier and Sir John Hawkins. The last-named soon displeased the company by attacking Burke, was pronounced "unclubable" by Johnson, and was compelled to retire. The numbers were then brought up to twelve, and later to thirty-five. For about ten years they met once a week at the Turk's Head in Gerrard Street, which was just round the corner from Leicester Fields, "and generally continued their conversation till a pretty late hour". Afterwards they met at Prince's in Sackville Street and at various other places.[17]

Throughout the eighteenth century there was a progressive tendency for dinner to be eaten at a later and later hour. Reynolds in his hey-day made a good breakfast at eight or nine and worked steadily on until his dinner was announced, usually at five. Later in the evening, supper was served, of which he partook sparingly, if at all.

The secret of Reynolds' success as a host lay in the artless informality of his gatherings. So long as Fanny Reynolds was in charge of the housekeeping, there must presumably have been some degree of order, but her brother's instinct was towards a free-for-all. Guests were encouraged to "drop in", invitations were issued on the spur of the moment; often insufficient places were laid. The servants kept an eye on their master, but were not over-attentive to the visitors, who largely had to fend for themselves, calling for knives and forks as well as for bread, wine or beer. Though the food was nothing remarkable, the atmosphere was convivial and unrestrained. Reynolds, deaf to the clatter, presided with great good humour. He was a good listener—through his ear-trumpet—and his active, inquisitive mind ensured that when he spoke he gave a fresh and lively turn to the conversation. Statesmen and noblemen, authors, actors and artists filled his dining-room; they were well satisfied with their own entertainment. The wit and genius of the eighteenth century flourished and expanded at 47 Leicester Square.

Of the chief adornments of Reynolds' circle—Johnson, Burke, Goldsmith and Garrick—their host left a critical account only of the last-named.[18] "Great as Garrick was on the stage, he was at least equal if not still superior at the table," wrote Reynolds, "and here he had too much the same habit of preparing himself, as if he was to act a principal part." Despite their long friendship, despite his deep admiration of Garrick as an actor, Reynolds in the long run judged Garrick's vanity to be insufferable. "It was difficult to get him and when you had him, as difficult to keep him," recorded his host. "He never came into company but with a plot how to get out of it. He was for ever receiving messages of his being wanted in another place . . . Garrick died without a real friend; though no man had a greater number of what the world calls friends. . . ."

This was the considered summing-up, for Boswell's eye alone; Reynolds' portraits of Garrick suggest nothing worse than a jaunty self-confidence. How different was his verdict on Oliver Goldsmith![19] Here was a man of sociable disposition who liked to be sought after, a man who longed to shine in conversation but who habitually chattered the most egregious nonsense. With his "fighting, absurdity, and ridiculous kind of envy, he made always a sort of bustle," wrote Reynolds, "and wherever he was there was no yawning. The conversation never stagnated or languished. The same company that, the moment he had turned his back, were in open cry on his absurdity and folly, were still desirous of meeting him again the next day." Reynolds was as fond of Goldsmith as of any man in his life; he befriended him in his good and bad times, and they were constant companions from 1762, when they first met, until Goldsmith's death in 1774. His portrait of him at Knole (Plate VII*b*) breathes an unusual affection, an intimate understanding of the real man, whom he chose to paint as he worked in his home, with his shirt open at the neck, without his wig and his finery. Goldsmith, in his turn, was devoted to Reynolds, dedicating *The Deserted Village* to him in touching words: "The only dedication I ever made was to my brother, because I loved him better than most other men. He is since dead. Permit me to inscribe this Poem to you."

Reynolds' friends were complex characters, as he was himself. Johnson and Goldsmith displayed their eccentricity lavishly; Reynolds and Edmund Burke, his closest friend in his later years, did not. "Dr Taylor is the same one day as another," declared Johnson enviously; "Burke and Reynolds are the same." [20] So they generally appeared, but we know in Burke's case that he was troubled by a recurrent melancholy which he generally concealed remarkably well.[21] Reynolds enjoyed his prosperity, as Burke pointed out, and so long as he was active he avoided depression, but it may be that Reynolds was no less deceptive, in outward appearances, than Burke.

Political discussion was not encouraged at Reynolds' table, so that Burke was usually at his best there. Fanny Burney first met him at Reynolds' and was greatly taken by that "striking superiority in his demeanour, his eye, his motions, that announced him no common man". Politics made him irritable, she noted later; one should meet "this wonderful man when he is easy, happy, and with people he cordially likes!" [22]

These conditions were fulfilled for Burke whenever he was in Reynolds' house (with the reservation that his contentious political career made him wary of Boswell's note-taking). Throughout life Burke suffered from an inferiority complex; harassed by financial worries, he was reticent and cautious about his personal affairs as a man becomes who is continually set upon by journalists and caricaturists. In Reynolds he found not only an artist whom he admired, a friend who lent him money, but a fellow-philosopher who joined with him in giving shape and direction, in his own way, to the thought of the time. Reynolds was here Burke's disciple, and was criticized by Johnson as being too much his "echo". [23] But although Reynolds inclined to Burke's liberalism rather than to Johnson's Toryism, both men knew that they could put absolute trust in their mutual benefactor. And Reynolds would take as much trouble over Johnson's blind friend Miss Williams as he would over Burke's harum-scarum Irish relatives.

It was the evening hours with such friends as these that gave Reynolds' portraits their lasting authority. He did not gather his friends round him in his dining-room or at The Club to look at their faces—he knew their faces by heart—but he held out his ear-trumpet, humbly enough, to try to understand their minds. If he was an "echo", he echoed only the best. He gave the English painter a place in intellectual society. His successors have not bettered that place, but they have never lost their right to it; they have always been aware of the claim that Reynolds made for them.

VI*a*. GEORGIANA, COUNTESS SPENCER, AND LADY GEORGIANA SPENCER. 1759–61

(48″ × 45″)

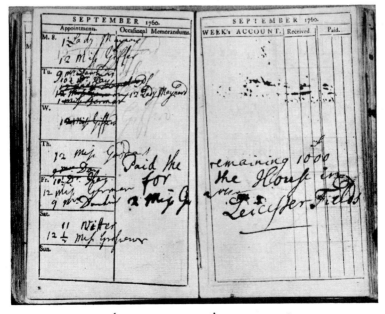

VI*b*. PAGES OF REYNOLDS' NOTEBOOK. 1760

6

The move to Leicester Fields had been a successful gamble. Throughout the seventeen-sixties, until at least 1768, the new studio was busy with a constant succession of sitters. Mothers and their children, lawyers and divines, gallant fighting men, society ladies, frail beauties of the town—for each Reynolds now had a tested approach, a considered setting, an implied unobtrusive comment. Henceforward his portraits were known to thousands from the admirable mezzotints of James MacArdell and of successors like Valentine Green and Charles Turner. But his formula was a matter of style and feeling, and never lent itself to monotonous repetition. The Countess of Mount Edgcumbe in her armchair (1762) inspired a masterpiece of intimate sympathy. Lady Sarah Bunbury, painted about the same time, looks down from a window of Holland House, with a gesture of unaffected simplicity, to the youthful head of Charles James Fox. And yet, within a few years, Reynolds presented the same Lady Sarah "sacrificing to the Graces" in the full amplitude of antique drapery and with all the trappings of neo-classicism.

The struggle between Reynolds' intimate and public styles, that began with his classical portrait of the Duchess of Hamilton at the Society of Arts exhibition of 1760, continued throughout the decade. Lady Sarah, it appears to us, has sacrificed too much to the Graces; she has become an absurdity. We feel the force of Mrs Thrale's criticism:

> A rage for sublimity ill understood,
> To seek still for the great, by forsaking the good.

But Reynolds was now so much a master of his public that he had no difficulty in persuading the ladies that "fancy dress" was the thing. Their husbands, who had to pay for the pictures, did not always agree, as an amusing correspondence between Gainsborough and Lord Dartmouth indicates. Gainsborough had accepted the convention against his better judgement: "I never could have patience to read poetical impossibilities," he wrote, "the very food of a painter, especially if he intends to be knighted in this land of roast beef." [24]

Modern opinion agrees with Gainsborough, but there was no

checking Reynolds' urge to experiment in the classical vein, which had not worked itself out before 1780. He ordered the fashion and dictated the prices to be paid for it, which by 1764 had been raised to thirty guineas for a head, fifty for a kit-kat, seventy for a half-length, and a hundred and fifty for a whole length. No one was excluded from the studio or the dining-room whose presence was likely to be interesting or profitable. Kitty Fisher sailed down the stairs as Kirkley opened the door to the Archbishop of Canterbury. But every commission was tackled thoroughly; nothing was left to chance. Take the sittings for the Speaker, Sir John Cust, in July, 1767. A note "The Speaker's Wig at Thede Perukemaker Middle Temple" is followed by: "Mr Stevens house keeper of the House of Commons to send a day or two before for the Mace." And on October 19 there is a special appointment: "Peruke of the Speaker".

The genius that Reynolds believed in had an infinite capacity for taking pains. There are many jottings like that in the notebook of 1765 (February 19): "Model. Mrs Gibs at a stay-makers opposite the Cambrian coffee house." The notebook for 1769 has a folded paper containing a lock of dark brown hair, inscribed "Lady Carlisle"—a reminder that Reynolds presumably found useful in painting the portrait of the Countess of Carlisle at Castle Howard.[25] Even so, he did not always succeed in getting a good likeness, and after his death his niece had several portraits left on her hands. The Duchess of Gordon refused hers, saying "Her eyes were not green, as those in the picture were." [26]

Reynolds had a great capacity, too, for helping his fellow artists, if he had a mind to do so. He bought a picture of Zoffany's when he first came to London, and when he re-sold it at a profit, he sent the twenty guineas to Zoffany. To Ozias Humphry, who came from Devonshire, he was remarkably generous. Humphry's mother was so grateful that in 1765 she sent Reynolds a piece of lace of her "own manufacturing", and Reynolds assured her that her son's "merit in his profession is so great that a man does honour to himself in recommending him".[27]

His unusual vitality carried Reynolds through a life of almost incessant activity, but there were occasional signs of overstrain. In the summer of 1764 he was taken seriously ill; from a remark of Fanny Burney's it appears that he suffered a slight stroke. Dr

Johnson did not hear of his illness until the danger was past. "If the amusement of my company can exhilarate the languor of a slow recovery," he wrote on August 19, "I will not delay a day to come to you; for I know not how I can so effectually promote my own pleasure as by pleasing you; in whom, if I should lose you, I should lose almost the only man whom I call a friend."

VI

The Royal Academy

I

BEING tolerant and friendly by nature, Reynolds was quickly bored by quarrels and disputations, whether with his sister Fanny or within a closed circle of professional artists. His influence in the Incorporated Society of Artists—it received a Royal Charter in 1765—had been exerted to encourage young painters, such as J. S. Copley,[1] but by 1768 the Society was in such a state of dissension that Reynolds, apart from occasionally exhibiting a few pictures, had virtually nothing to do with it. Nor, as we have seen, did his membership of the Society of Arts continue after 1764, for he was not interested in improved spinning-wheels or machines for slicing turnips. *Candide* had not long been published, and probably Voltaire's satirical reference to the red sheep that were given to the Bordeaux Academy of Sciences would not have been lost upon Reynolds.* If higher responsibilities had not called him, he might well have been content with his card parties, his Monday nights at The Club, his Thursday nights with the men about town at the Star-in-Garter, Pall Mall, his occasional dinners with the Dilettanti, the Royal Society, and—for piety's sake—the Society of Sons of the Clergy. There was enough here to employ his social talents and to exercise his stamina.

But Reynolds' future was now to be shaped, perhaps not intentionally but certainly decisively, by the forceful hand of his ambitious friend William Chambers. Whether Reynolds ever firmly trusted Chambers is rather doubtful, and he was not one of the regular visitors to Leicester Fields, but they were to be closely

* "The Academy proposed as the theme for its yearly prize competition an investigation into the reason for the redness of the sheep's wool. The prize was won by a scholar from the north, who demonstrated by $\frac{A + B - C}{Z}$ that the sheep must of necessity be red, and furthermore that it would die of the rot."—*Candide*, Chapter XII.

88

associated for the rest of Reynolds' life, and it appears that for at least five or six years after 1768 they were intimate friends.

Since they had first met in Paris in 1752, they had developed in different directions. Soon after his return to England, Chambers had been fortunate in obtaining an introduction to the Princess Dowager of Wales, by whom he had been employed to devise ornaments for her gardens at Kew, including the famous Pagoda. He had taught architectural drawing to her son, the Prince of Wales, now George III. On his accession Chambers became one of the Crown architects and, later still, Comptroller of the Works and the first Surveyor-General. He acquired an official residence at Hampton Court, and owned a house in town, as well as Whitton Place between Hounslow and Twickenham, formerly the property of the Duke of Argyll, which Chambers turned into an Italianate villa surrounded by statues, temples and mock ruins.

By 1768 Chambers stood high in the royal favour—as the independent Reynolds, the friend of the Whigs from Burke to Wilkes, could never hope, nor indeed intended to do. With it all, Chambers' Swedish origin gave him a certain mysterious detachment; and he had among his Scottish ancestors some rank Jacobites, a fact which he did not mention. Both Chambers and Reynolds were playing "a great game", but Chambers was a classical architect with political talents; Reynolds an intellectual artist with a passion for art-theory and for broad generalizations. They were drawn together, inescapably, in the foundation of the Royal Academy as complementary but uneasy partners.

Chambers leaned heavily on his own virtue, which had in it an element of priggishness and pomposity not unmixed with kindliness and humour. He liked to have his way. Two excerpts from letters to his son-in-law John Milbanke will best show the sort of man he was. Milbanke and his daughter Cornelia having somehow contrived to offend him at the time of their wedding, Chambers could only give them a qualified blessing: "I wish you both every sort of happiness, and whenever I can reduce myself to that fashionable State of Indifference which Great minds possess, you will certainly find me in the Circle of your Attendants. Till then Adieu." There may well be a hit at Reynolds here. Chambers relished a quarrel; Reynolds did not.

The second letter was written years later. Chambers had then become the heavy grandfather:

> . . . I am Sorry but not Surprised to hear that little Henry has been ill. Cornelia's overmuch Care though arising from the best motives is I fear calculated to produce the worst consequences. Everything, my dear Sir, is to be apprehended for a Child Sucking at the Age of near two years when the nurses milk becoming Acrid from its age has more of poison than Cordial in it, heavily Cloathed all day, Nursed in a Room with a constant large fire, put to bed Swaddled round with blankets and loaded with two or three more on the bed. . . .[2]

Chambers may have been right about little Henry. He was often right; but he could be most provocative in asserting himself. It is not to be wondered that Reynolds held aloof from the business of the Incorporated Society of Artists in 1768, because the struggle for its leadership was waged between two friends of his, both architects—Chambers and James Paine (whom he had painted with his son in an admirable portrait of 1764 now in the Ashmolean). Paine won that battle; Chambers' autocratic rule of the Society was brought to an end, and he and most of his fellow Directors were replaced by members of the rank and file, democratically elected. But Chambers did not take this reverse lying down. He had the abler members of the Society on his side, and when in November, 1768, he and Benjamin West, Francis Cotes, and G. M. Moser had drafted the constitution of a Royal Academy, it was with firm determination that he carried it to his former pupil, the King.

During this autumn, while the battle of the artists was at its height, Reynolds, accompanied by Richard Burke, travelled to Paris, where his sister Fanny was then staying. Passing through Arras on the way home, he thought the Cathedral "not worth seeing". On the road from Dover to London, he noted "lay at Sidereberg", which Tom Taylor printed in his biography as "lay at Sittingbourne". Taylor may have guessed correctly, but one is left wondering again at Reynolds' sublime indifference to the claims of spelling. Could "Sidereberg" possibly suggest "Sitting-bourne", as spoken by a local inhabitant with a cold in the head, heard faintly through an ear trumpet on a stormy night?

Reynolds was back in London on October 23, and dined the

next day with Goldsmith, no doubt telling him how the "axel-tree" of his carriage had broken twice on the roads of Flanders; of the pleasures of "Versails"; and of the pictures by Guido and Mola he had bought. In November he resisted an invitation from Joshua Kirby, the newly elected President of the Incorporated Society, to associate himself with its new management.[3]

The first intimation that the King intended to lend his support to the proposed Academy was given to the unfortunate Kirby—a worthy man, of slight artistic pretensions, who had tried to teach the King the laws of perspective—while he was discussing with him and Benjamin West the merits of the latter's "Departure of Regulus" which George III had commissioned. "Assuredly I shall be very happy to let the work be shown to the public," said the King. "Then, Mr West," put in Kirby hopefully, "you will send it to my exhibition." "No, it must go to my exhibition —to the Royal Academy," declared the King.

According to West's biographer, John Galt, "poor Kirby was thunderstruck . . . His colour forsook him, and his countenance became yellow with mortification. He bowed with profound humility, and instantly retired, nor did he long survive the shock."[4] This was an exaggeration; in fact he lived until 1774, and seems to have fought his losing battle for the Incorporated Society of Artists with considerable courage.

The decisive meetings at which the seceding artists resolved to establish the Royal Academy were held at the house of Joseph Wilton, the sculptor. Reynolds had been the friend of Wilton ever since he had painted his portrait in Florence; but at first he kept away from these meetings. The most interesting account of the events that followed is given in his diary by Joseph Farington on the authority of Benjamin West:

> West told Smirke & me that at a meeting at Wilton's where the subject of planning & forming the Royal Academy was discussed, Sir Willm. Chambers seemed inclined to [be] the *President*, but Penny [Edward Penny, R.A.] was decided, that a *painter* ought to be the *President*. It was then offered to Mr Reynolds, afterwards Sir Joshua, though He had not attended at any of those meetings which were held at Mr Wilton's.—Mr West was the person appointed to call on Sir Joshua to bring him to a meeting at Mr Wilton's, where an offer of the Presidency was made to him, to which Mr Reynolds

replied that He desired to consult his friends Dr Johnson and Mr Burke upon it. This hesitation, was mentioned by Sir Willm. Chambers to the King, who from that time entertained a prejudice against Reynolds, for both Johnson & Burke were then disliked by the King, the latter particularly on political accounts. . . .[5]

This narrative is more or less consistent with that given by Northcote in his *Life*, and Northcote confirms that Reynolds consulted Johnson and Burke, which it is quite likely that he would have wished to do. There is also a high degree of plausibility in Farington's description of Chambers' behaviour, of his disappointment at not being President himself, and of his care to inform the King of Reynolds' desire to be advised by Johnson and Burke. The King's attitude towards Reynolds could, indeed, have been adversely influenced by this circumstance.

John Galt's account of the proceedings,[6] which was followed by Leslie and Taylor, is somewhat different, and leaves out the details about Chambers, Johnson and Burke. According to him, Reynolds was unanimously elected President as soon as West brought him into the meeting at Wilton's. But Galt was not a particularly accurate writer, and it seems best to accept Farington's narrative as substantially representing the course of events.

There is an entry in Reynolds' notebook for December 9: "Mr Wilton's at 6". On December 10, 1768, the King signed the Instrument of Foundation of the Royal Academy. And on December 14 (after an interval which would have allowed Reynolds time to be reassured by his friends) the first meeting of the Royal Academy was held in Pall Mall, at which he was formally elected to the chair and subscribed the minutes with one of his most elaborate signatures: "J. Reynolds, President". Apart from Reynolds himself, the original forty members of the Academy included the following: Benjamin West, Thomas and Paul Sandby, Francis Cotes, Thomas Gainsborough, F. M. Newton (the first Secretary), Francisco Bartolozzi, Charles Catton, Nathaniel Hone, William Tyler, Nathaniel Dance, Richard Wilson, G. Michael Moser (the first Keeper), Peter Toms, Angelica Kauffmann, Mary Moser, William Chambers (the first Treasurer), Joseph Wilton, Edward Penny, Francis Hayman, Francesco Zuccarelli, George Dance, Johann Zoffany.

It is much to the credit of George III that, whatever his personal feelings, he recognized that the professional and social standing of Reynolds made him the only satisfactory choice as the first President. Reynolds had behaved with tact and discretion through an embittered controversy, and in the event his tenure of the office fulfilled, and indeed exceeded, the hopes of the moderate and reasonable men who had supported him. He alone possessed the zeal, the detachment, the idealism, the quality of mind that could import the necessary prestige to the presidency of the newly founded Academy. Without his inspiration, and without his Discourses, its future might have been different. That Reynolds knew himself to be indispensable, and that the presidency represented the end of a long cherished ambition, is probably true; but it is equally true that the Academy was most fortunate in being able to call upon such a leader.

In a letter to the Hon. William Hamilton, written in March, 1769, describing the constitution of the Academy, Reynolds made it clear that, of all its officers and professors, he was the only one whose services were truly honorary. "To the surprise of every body I have the honour of being President, and it is only honour for there is no salary annex'd to this dignity. Mr Chambers the Architect is Treasurer £60 per Ann.", etc.[7] There were shortly, however, to be some further honorary appointments, for which Reynolds was clearly responsible: his eccentric friend Giuseppe Baretti became Secretary for Foreign Correspondence, and Dr Johnson and Oliver Goldsmith assumed the eloquent titles of Professor of Ancient Literature and Professor of Ancient History. He presumably did not know when he wrote to Hamilton that a more tangible reward was soon to be his. But on April 21, 1769, he wrote in his notebook, in his bold happy handwriting: "$12\frac{1}{2}$ The King's Levee", and on the opposite page: "Knighted at St James'". According to Hawkins, Dr Johnson broke his rule of abstinence and "drank one glass of wine to the health of Sir Joshua Reynolds, on the evening of the day on which he was knighted".[8]

There was considerable gossip in pamphlets and newspaper articles of the time[9] to the effect that Reynolds had been seduced from the Incorporated Society of Artists by the promise of a knighthood as President of the Royal Academy. As Reynolds had been interested in the idea of an Academy for fifteen years,

93

and had never taken any large part in the affairs of the Incorporated Society, these charges are not convincing. Moreover, there was an interval of several months between his election as President and his appearance as Sir Joshua. During these months, it appears that he was much disappointed that the King showed no inclination to sit to him for a portrait;[10] the knighthood may have been to some extent a consolation prize. West told Farington that "the King had said to him that He did not knight Sir Joshua Reynolds as President of the Royal Academy but in consequence of an application from the Duke of Grafton", who was then Prime Minister. Reynolds was certainly pleased by his knighthood. "I acknowledge that I do not feel myself possessed of that grandeur of soul sufficient to give me any pretensions of looking down with such philosophical contempt upon titles," he confessed during the last year of his life, in a memorandum found among his papers. "Distinction is what we all seek after, and the world does set a value on them, and I go with the great stream of life." [11]

2

"Sir Willm. Chambers seemed inclined to [be] the *President*," said Farington; and indeed it is not surprising that he should have been so inclined, considering that he had undoubtedly taken the lead in founding and organizing the Academy. Although compelled to cede first place to Reynolds, he was determined to secure effective control of the new body. Thus in Article VIII of the Instrument of Foundation, which Chambers drafted, we find it laid down that, in return for his financial support, the King should have the right to appoint the Treasurer, "that he may have a person in whom he places full confidence, in an office where his interest is concerned; and His Majesty doth hereby nominate and appoint William Chambers, Esquire, Architect of his Works, to be Treasurer of The Royal Academy of Arts". Chambers was, in fact, the only individual mentioned by name in the Instrument, and he was given commanding powers. His duty was "to receive the rents and profits of the Academy, to pay its expenses, to superintend repairs of the buildings and alterations, to examine all bills, and to conclude all bargains". As he was made responsible not only to the Council but to the Keeper of His Majesty's Privy Purse, it will be obvious that his potential influence was equalled only by his opportunity for backstairs intrigue. Joseph Farington informed the Academy, long afterwards, that "Sir William Chambers in many respects had too much considered himself and had assumed improperly great power. . . . That Sir Joshua Reynolds had felt it, & had told him in the Council, that though he (Sir Joshua) was President, Sir Wm. was Viceroy over him." [12]

Chambers did not long allow Reynolds to enjoy any advantage over himself that may have been implicit in the honour of knighthood. But how to make up the lost ground must have caused Chambers some thought, because the King could hardly be expected to confer a second knighthood on an officer of his Academy. An ingenious solution for the difficulty was found, however, in 1771 when Chambers, having received the Order of the Polar Star—the Swedish equivalent of Knighthood—obtained special permission from George III to assume the rank and title of a Knight in England. With this honour in view, Chambers communicated some biographical particulars to the Swedish authorities which show that he was not unaware of his own merits: "His Majesty was graciously pleased to appoint me to treasurership of the Royal Academy, which whole institution was planned by me and was completed through my efforts, a circumstance that affords me great pleasure, as in all probability this institution will cause the arts to rise as high as possible in this country." [13]

There is no doubt that Reynolds' relationship with Chambers was precariously poised, and that to preside over the Council of the Academy required all his coolness and tact. Chambers was the King's appointed officer; he had at all times the easy access to His Majesty which Reynolds lacked. It was inevitable that there should be friction between the two men; but in the early years, while they still rejoiced at the success of their mutual efforts and bent all their energies to the organization of the Academy, serious collisions were avoided. To begin with, all was improvisation; the Academy was something of a picnic. Jealousies were forgotten when members of the hanging committee sat down heartily to dinner in the little passage-room at Lambe's auction rooms, Pall Mall, before the joint which had been roasted for them on a string by Mrs Malin, the housekeeper, or when by special invitation Reynolds and Chambers dined off a veal and ham pie served in a large dish by Mrs Newton, the Secretary's wife.[14]

One of the Academy's first duties at a meeting on December 17, 1769, was to appoint a Porter and a "Sweeper", as laid down in the Instrument of Foundation. The chosen Porter was John Malin, with a salary fixed at twenty-five pounds a year, and the "Sweeper" (whose cooking was not despised) was conveniently found in his wife Elizabeth who received ten pounds a year. The annual exhibitions were held at Lambe's until 1780, when handsome rooms designed to serve all the Academy's requirements were provided in the new Somerset House built by Chambers. But from 1771 onwards the Academy had the use of seven large rooms in Inigo Jones' old Somerset Palace which accommodated the School of Drawing, lodgings for the Keeper, and the Library and Council Room.

Reynolds took his duties as President very seriously. He was assiduous in attending the meetings—there were as many as nine General Assemblies in 1770, besides the meetings of the Council —and the elaborate flourishes of his signature in the minute book soon gave place to an informal scrawl. The annual dinner was originated by Reynolds, and he gave much thought to the exhibitions. He was re-elected president *nem-con.* for several years; later there was occasionally a ballot, at which other candidates— Gainsborough, Chambers, and Penny among them—would receive single votes, which were often, no doubt, cast for them by Reynolds himself. It was as well that he had been earning his £6,000 a year since he moved to Leicester Fields, because between 1769 and 1773 he had much less time for painting and his practice markedly declined. He also lost sitters to Francis Cotes, who was in favour at Court, and who died, not inconveniently, in 1770. Nevertheless Reynolds maintained his quota of at least a dozen pictures at the annual Academy exhibitions in these years. They are not, on the whole, pictures that we now turn to with wholehearted admiration; for Reynolds was feeling the need to set an academic example. He was at his most classical, seeking to show that "history painting", then by common consent the highest form of art, could be allied to portrait and could raise it to fresh dignity. Yet these years of didactic preoccupation gave us moving portraits of Johnson and Goldsmith, as well as one of his noblest experiments, the double-portrait of Lord Sydney and Colonel Acland known as "The Archers", in which he turned for inspiration to Rubens and the Venetians. And it was now, also, that he gave intimate life to Mrs Abington, leaning over the back of her chair, and caught the puzzled charm of his pretty twelve-year-old niece Theophila as she tried to read *Clarissa Harlowe*, or as he saw her, more fancifully, in the character of "The Strawberry Girl", which was always one of his own favourite pictures.

3

The President remained, first and foremost, a painter; but the business of the Academy in its early stages absorbed a great part of his time. Although the robust countenance of Chambers confronted him warningly across the council table, there was one opportunity of his office that lay open to him alone—it was Reynolds' duty to deliver the address at the formal opening of the Academy. Here was his chance not only to establish with authority the principles that would guide the Academy but to show himself in his true and carefully nurtured character as a literary man. He had only a fortnight in which to prepare a discourse on which a whole new reputation might depend, only a fortnight before the momentous day which marked the new year in his notebook for 1769.

With his habitual hesitations and alterations, even in simple words and phrases, writing was always a painful process. For this fortnight Reynolds can have thought of little else than his discourse. He was no speaker; his whole nature rebelled against an affected eloquence. Therefore his address must be meticulously prepared and polished, and he would get through the reading of it as well as he could, relying on the quality of the matter.

"Gentlemen." he began, in his low voice and his Devonshire accent, "an Academy, in which the Polite Arts may be regularly cultivated, is at last opened among us by Royal Munificence. This must appear an event in the highest degree interesting, not only to the Artist, but to the whole nation. It is indeed difficult to give any other reason, why an empire like that of Britain should so long have wanted an ornament so suitable to its greatness, than that slow progression of things, which naturally

Appointments in January, 1769.	MEMORANDUMS, or OBSERVATIONS.
2 Monday	*Opening of the R. Academy*
Tuesday	
Wednesday	
Thursday	*Lady Almeria Carpenter*
Friday	*12 Masters* *4 Engaged at home*
Saturday	*12 Masters*

makes elegance and refinement the last effect of opulence and power."

He could not resist a dig at the Society of Arts, though recollections of the days when he was co-opted to encourage the Zante currant induced him to oversimplify its problems. "An Institution like this," he went on, "has often been recommended upon considerations merely mercantile; but an Academy, founded upon such principles, can never effect even its own narrow purposes. If it has an origin no higher, no taste can ever be formed in manufacture; but if the higher Arts of Design flourish, these inferior ends will be answered of course." Time has shown that Reynolds was mistaken here.

There followed some graceful compliments to George III, which cannot have been produced without effort: "We are happy in having a Prince, who has conceived the idea of such an Institution, according to its true dignity; and who promotes the Arts, as the head of a great, a learned, a polite, and a commercial nation. . . ."

Reynolds proceeded to stress that, "besides furnishing able men to direct the Student", the Academy must be "a repository for the great examples of the Art". It must be remembered that he was speaking fifty years before the foundation of the National Gallery; in fact, the Royal Academy did not develop, in this respect, on the lines which Reynolds laid down, though the early acquisition of Leonardo da Vinci's famous cartoon of the Virgin and St Anne gives a measure of its aspirations. "By studying these authentic models, that idea of excellence which is the result of the accumulated experience of past ages, may be at once acquired; and the tardy and obstructed progress of our predecessors may teach us a shorter and easier way."

Reynolds did not read his discourse from his own much corrected draft. He had before him a fair copy, written in a large round hand by his pupil Charles Gill, who was the son of a pastry cook in Bath.[15] But he made improvements even on this fair copy. For instance, the last half of the sentence just quoted read in the original: "and those slow Approaches which our predecessors have made in Advancing the Art may be by these means accelerated".[16] He was a true writer, and altered for the better. No one who studies his manuscripts can fail to be indignant at the suggestion, which was more than once made in his lifetime, that the discourses were not all his own work. If he took advantage of the experience of Johnson, Burke or Malone in his revisions, their help was purely incidental. The discourses, no less than his portraits, were the fruit of Reynolds' own carefully acquired taste.

In his first discourse, Reynolds addressed himself to beginners, recommending "that an implicit obedience to the *Rules of Art*, as established by the practice of the great Masters, should be exacted from the *young* Students". Every opportunity, he urged, "should be taken to discountenance that false and vulgar opinion, that rules are the fetters of genius . . . How much liberty may be taken to break through those rules, and, as the Poet expresses it, 'To snatch a grace beyond the reach of art', may be a subsequent consideration, when the pupils become masters themselves." He warned them of being early ambitious for, "a facility in composing", which he said was not so hard to attain. "After much time spent in these frivolous pursuits, the difficulty will be to retreat; but it will be then too late; and there is scarce an instance of return to scrupulous labour, after the mind has been relaxed and debauched by these delightful trifles." The text of the last part of this sentence is taken from Gill's fair copy, which the President had propped up before him as he spoke. Once again, later consideration improved and strengthened the sentence, which was altered to: "after the mind has been debauched and deceived by this fallacious mastery".[17]

Reynolds urged that "labour is the only price of solid fame" and insisted that drawing from the model must be exact—"I very much doubt," he said, "whether a habit of drawing correctly what we see, will not give a proportionable power of drawing correctly what we imagine"—a remark which even William Blake approved, for he noted: "This is Admirably Said. Why does not he not always allow as much?"[18] In conclusion Reynolds expressed the hope "that the present age may vie in Arts with that of Leo the Tenth; and that *the dignity of the dying Art* (to make use of an expression of Pliny) may be revived under the Reign of George the Third".

Northcote relates that the whole body of Academicians thereupon "adjourned to an elegant entertainment at the St Alban's Tavern", where Reynolds presided "with his accustomed

VIIb. OLIVER GOLDSMITH. 1770
(32″ × 26″)

VIIa. EDMUND BURKE. 1767–9
(30″ × 24″)

urbanity". They heard a song composed for them "by the good old Mr Hull, the comedian"—presumably Thomas Hull of Covent Garden—and sung by Joseph Vernon, a favourite at Drury Lane.

> '*Tis yours*, O well selected band!
>   To watch where infant genius blows,
> To rear the flow'r, with fost'ring hand,
>   And ev'ry latent sweet disclose:
> So Arts, unrivall'd, long will reign
> Where George protects the polish'd train.
>
> No more to distant realms repair
>   For foreign aid, or borrow'd rule;
> Beneath her Monarch's gen'rous care,
>   Britannia founds a nobler school—
> Where Arts, unrivall'd, shall remain
> For George protects the polish'd train.

The song did not convince Reynolds that there might not still be advantages in a timely journey to Italy.

4

The Royal Academy had opened auspiciously, and its first exhibition in April also proved successful and profitable. For the next twenty years the annual exhibitions called forth all Reynolds' powers—this regular "shop window" was as necessary to him as it was helpful to the Academy. On June 5, 1769, the Academicians gratefully celebrated the King's birthday with an entertainment at their house, the whole front of which was covered by a transparent illumination. Cipriani devised the central panel: the figure of Painting was surrounded by Genii, students were grouped at her feet, while "over her head hovered a celestial form, representing Royal Munificence, attended by several other figures supporting a cornucopia filled with honours and rewards". The crowds in Pall Mall gaped with admiration, and Reynolds must have been reminded that he had to deliver another discourse at the distribution of the prizes in December.

This second discourse was intended for the more advanced

students, and was remarkable for its common sense and psychological insight. It was now becoming clear to those few who heard Reynolds' speeches—and to the many more who read them, for each in turn was printed as a pamphlet as soon as it had been delivered—that they were listening to something rare at any time but almost unique in the eighteenth century: the voice of a practising artist of high achievement who also possessed a power of detachment and generalization that enabled him to speak with lasting authority. Reynolds had already immeasurably raised the status of the artist in England; but it was the delivery of his discourses, and the acclaim with which they were received on the continent when they appeared in translation, that made him the outstanding figure in European art of his period. He must now be read with the caution that comes from a deeper knowledge than was available in his time; the discovery and appreciation of Greek art and of the art of the Middle Ages has upset the balance of some of his theory; we know now that, as Roger Fry pointed out, there is a valid poetic beauty in Van Eyck's altarpiece at Ghent that can exist apart from any strong visible unity of expression such as Reynolds demanded. But it is still true that no young artist to day can fail to read the Discourses without profiting from their enlightened moderation and humility. Above all, Reynolds was right when he urged the student, in his second discourse, not to depend on his own hypothetical genius but to work out his personal salvation. "Nothing is denied to well-directed labour: nothing is to be obtained without it." We may remember, also, Roger Fry's opinion that "Reynolds himself, whose genius is not his most conspicuous trait, was, on the whole, a more important figure in the history of British art than Gainsborough, who had genius of the most striking kind".

A discourse from Reynolds was eagerly expected henceforth at the annual distribution of the prizes. This he provided yearly until 1772, and thereafter in alternate years, until he had delivered fifteen in all. The publication of the first seven discourses in book form in 1778, with a dignified introduction by Dr Johnson, consolidated their reputation. Reynolds actually received £62 9s. 0d. from the sales—the only money, apparently, that his writings ever brought him.[19] The seven discourses appeared in Italian, German and French. And thus at last their author attained the literary fame which had been his second ambition since Plympton days, and which was proper to the founder of the Literary Club.

5

Reynolds was a great critic because he had the gift, rare for an artist, of being able to survey the whole field of art—and this included his own productions—with an unselfish detachment. He has been accused of inconsistency, of failing to practise what he preached, and it is true that he discovered by painful experience that he lacked the poetical imagination to paint history in the grand style of his revered Michelangelo, or even to do it as well as Burke's protégé James Barry. During the early 'seventies he was engaged on what is perhaps his best historical picture, the "Ugolino and his children in Prison", at Knole (in Reynolds' notebook it is always "Hugolino"). The "Ugolino" fostered appreciation of Dante in England, but Horace Walpole's "most admirable" finds no echo today. Reynolds himself probably recognized that there was not enough feeling in the central figure—indeed, when he drew it, he did not intend it to represent Ugolino at all. Knowing his weakness, he made Johnson say, in an imagined dialogue with Gibbon:

> Ask Reynolds whether he felt the distress of Count Ugolino when he drew it.
>
> GIBBON: But surely he feels the passion at the moment he is representing it.
>
> JOHNSON: About as much as Punch feels.[20]

Because Reynolds had the sense to realize that he himself could not imitate Michelangelo with any profit, and in his final discourse admitted "I have taken another course, one more suited to my abilities and to the taste of the times in which I live", that is no reason to doubt the fundamental sincerity of his idealism or to accuse him, as Blake did, of hypocrisy. Blake was, of course, the absolute artistic antithesis to Reynolds. There is no more revealing expression of the point of view of an artist to whom inspiration was everything than the notes written by Blake—long after Reynolds' death—in the margins of Malone's edition of Reynolds' "Works".[18] Blake had been an embittered student at the Academy in 1778 and held Sir Joshua in contempt. It must be remembered that he was an engraver, and that many engravers, headed by Sir Robert Strange, were indignant at the discrimination shown against them in the early days of the Academy. They felt that Sir Joshua, who owed so much to their services, might have done more for them.[21]

"This Man was Hired to Depress Art," Blake wrote in a large angry hand on the title-page, "this is the opinion of Will Blake." And on the back of the title-page he continued:

> Having spent the Vigour of my Youth and Genius under the Opression of Sir Joshua & his Gang of Cunning Hired Knaves Without Employment & as much as could possibly be Without Bread, The Reader must expect to Read in all my Remarks on these Books Nothing but Indignation & Resentment. While Sir Joshua was rolling in Riches Barry was Poor & Unemployed except by his own Energy Mortimer was called a Madman & only Portrait Painting applauded & rewarded by the Rich & Great. Reynolds & Gainsborough Blotted & Blurred one against the other & Divided all the English World between them. . . .

Throughout the book Blake, true to his promise, keeps up a running fire of vitriolic comment. When Reynolds advises against much copying, Blake writes: "To learn the Language of Art Copy for Ever is My Rule." Where Reynolds acknowledges his disappointing first impression of Raphael in the Vatican, Blake adds: "I am happy I cannot say that Rafael ever was from my Earliest Childhood hidden from Me." There are frequent protests such as "Villainy: a lie". And Blake even intrudes his malevolence into Reynolds' personal friendships. Malone quotes Goldsmith's famous mock-epitaph on Reynolds:

> Here Reynolds is laid, and, to tell you my mind,
> He has not left a better or wiser behind:
> His pencil was striking, resistless, and grand;
> His manners were gentle, complying and bland;
> Still born to improve us in every part,
> His pencil our faces, his manners our heart:
> To coxcombs averse, yet most civilly steering,
> When they judg'd without skill he was still hard of hearing:
> When they talk'd of their Raphaels, Corregios, and stuff,
> He shifted his trumpet, and only took snuff.

Against this, Blake can only grumble: "Such Men as Goldsmith ought not to have been Acquainted with such Men as Reynolds."

The whole performance is a startling display of unbalanced egotism by a genius who could never submit to academic discipline (as Blake might well have done to the profit of his art). "The Enquiry in England," growls Blake, "is not whether a Man has Talents & Genius. But whether he is Passive & Polite & a Virtuous Ass & obedient to Noblemens Opinions in Art & Science. If he is; he is a Good Man: If Not he must be Starved."

"A Lie", "A Lie", "A Lie", cries Blake all down one page; "A Folly" on the next. Before the Third Discourse, which Reynolds devoted to a discussion—admittedly not entirely satisfactory— of the nature of beauty, Blake writes: "The following Discourse is particularly Interesting to Blockheads as it endeavours to prove That There is No such thing as Inspiration & that any Man of a plain Understanding may by Thieving from Others become a Mich Angelo". Reynolds fully realized that men's natural gifts are unequal, but when he argued that conscious intelligence had its uses, that art was not the mere sport of a capricious fate, that genius must have its rules—it was then that he most angered Blake. "The Man who on Examining his own Mind finds nothing of Inspiration ought not to dare to be an Artist," Blake comments at one point; "he is a Fool & a Cunning Knave suited to the Purposes of evil demons." And Blake thus answers Reynolds' exposition of the theory of genius in his Sixth Discourse: "When a Man talks of Acquiring Invention & of learning how to produce Original Conception he must expect to be called a Fool by Men of Understanding but such a Hired Knave cares not for the Few. His Eye is on the Many, or rather on the Money."

It might be thought unnecessary to pay much attention to Blake's cheap jibes and maledictions, entertaining as they are; but they have a considerable importance to the student of Reynolds because they serve to focus, if in exaggerated form, an impatient reaction to academic classicism which is still very much alive. The truth is that art needs both a Reynolds and a Blake, and that they never will be reconciled.

As a matter of fact, Blake, reading through the Discourses, often found himself agreeing with Reynolds. "True", "True", "Good Advice", "A Noble Sentence", "Excellent Remarks",

"Fine & Just Notions", "Well Said enough"—these are some of
the friendly comments, which mingle strangely with "Damned
Fool", and with such misguided attacks as: "Why should Titian
& the Venetians be named in a discourse on Art? Such Idiots are
not Artists."

It looks at times as if Blake held a sneaking affection for Reynolds, even while he cocked a snook at him. And, as the brother-
hood of the Arts transcends party, so will other rebels feel to-day
towards the figure on the pedestal in the courtyard of Burlington
House. We like Blake best when he speaks as a poet:

> Reynolds Thinks that Man Learns all that he knows. I say on the
> Contrary that Man Brings All that he has or Can have Into the
> World with him. Man is Born Like a Garden ready Planted & Sown.
> This World is too poor to produce one Seed.

But those were not the sentiments with which "sundry persons,
resident in this Metropolis" established in 1768 a "Society for
promoting the Arts of Design" which was to be honoured by the
membership of Wilson, Turner, Constable and Millais.

VII

The Road to Richmond

What I left open fields, producing hay and corn, I now find covered
with streets, and squares, and palaces, and churches ... Pimlico and
Knightsbridge are now almost joined to Chelsea and Kensington.

TOBIAS SMOLLETT, *Humphrey Clinker* (1771)

I

WHEN they looked for relief from the clatter of expanding
London, the authors, artists and actors of the eighteenth
century drove out through the threatened villages of
Earl's Court or Kensington to relax on the banks of the Thames
in the neighbourhood of Richmond or Twickenham. Garrick
was to be found at Hampton; Horace Walpole had succeeded
Pope as the genius of Twickenham (where Reynolds could still
be found paying a loyal visit to his old master Hudson); William
Chambers had established himself at Whitton; and in 1766 George
Colman, the dramatist and theatre manager, built a house on the
Petersham Road below Richmond Hill. Reynolds well knew
these gentle river meadows and had long admired the view from
the hill. An entry in his notebook for November 15, 1767—
"Richmond to see a h."—may mark the time when he first
thought of acquiring a villa of his own for week-ends and
holidays.

He did not buy that house, but he continued to visit Richmond,
and the notebook for 1769 shows him inclined to escape periodi-
cally from the cares of the Royal Academy. He paid three visits
in that year to Vauxhall, and in September went to the Richmond
Assembly, for which ordeal the notebook suggests that he took
dancing lessons from Noverre. George Colman's friendship—
for Reynolds often acted as his intermediary in theatre matters
with Garrick and Goldsmith—probably kept his thoughts on
Richmond, and he began to covet a house on the hill with a view
over the river. By 1771 he had gone so far as to ask the Earl of

107

Dysart, who was Lord of the Manor of Petersham and a patron of his, for permission to build on the outlying land, or waste, of his Manor, at the top of the hill between the Star and Garter Inn and the Bull's Head (a tavern soon afterwards demolished). Permission being granted, he had to find an architect, and as he was then continually seeing William Chambers, and wished to placate him, it is not surprising that Chambers should have been chosen. Joseph Hickey, father of William Hickey the diarist, drew the conveyance; and Reynolds painted his portrait for the Academy exhibition of 1772.

The house that Chambers built—it was called "Wick House" because it stood on the "waste" of Petersham Manor—was unostentatious and exceedingly plain. This was hardly Chambers' fault, because Reynolds did not want to spend much money on it, and at first thought of having only one large room with attic bedrooms above, though later he decided to make it bigger. The house was not a great success; Reynolds' niece Mary Palmer said that she hated it—"a house stuck upon the top of a hill, without a bit of garden or ground of any sort near it but what is as public as St James's Park".[1] It was isolated, exposed and cold, with Petersham Common reaching to the walls and some poor houses at the back cramping the garden in Reynolds' day. But, of course, to Sir Joshua the view was the thing—and the view, a very soothing and peaceful one, inspired him to the best of his landscapes (Plate IX).* James Northcote, then lately installed as a pupil of Sir Joshua's, commissioned his brother to make a telescope which he intended to present to his master so that he could better enjoy the view.[2]

Reynolds and Chambers were continually together. On January 30, 1771, Chambers wrote to Lord Charlemont: "Sir Joshua is now with me; the chevalier begs to be respectfully remembered to your lordship. He proposes sending you a copy of his dissertations or discourses as he calls them, delivered in the royal academy of which he is president." But he added, typically: "I have also an intention of making discourses on architecture. One I

---

* He was not averse to taking his easel out of doors occasionally. The Victoria and Albert Museum has a slight but not unattractive sketch, attributed to him, of the entrance to the Thrales' park at Streatham, a gate and tree-lined drive, in greys and greens.

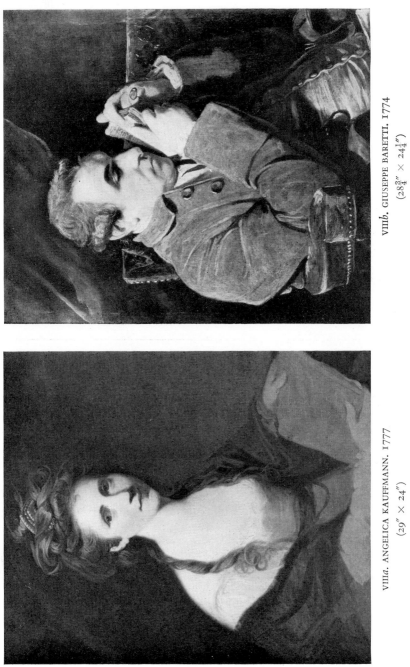

VIII*a*. ANGELICA KAUFFMANN. 1777

$(29'' \times 24'')$

VIII*b*. GIUSEPPE BARETTI. 1774

$(28\frac{3}{4}'' \times 24\frac{1}{4}'')$

have finished which I have shown to a friend or two who tell me it is very well and encourage me to go on. . . .[3]

By the summer of 1771 the walls of Wick House were rising. Reynolds went out to see Chambers on September 15, and on the 29th he visited Richmond to inspect progress. There were some technical difficulties. In October Chambers wrote to Mr Bell, the Richmond carpenter:

S[r]

As I observed a little Settlement in the two Windows under the Bow of S[r] Joshua Reynolds's house, I would have you put the sash frames immediately then shore up the wall and bow, take out the brick arches of the Windows, and put in hard stone ones each composed of three stones, with very close Joints and the Arch about 18 In: deep, and as thick as the other part of the reveal of the Windows, which done I think the whole will be effectually secured. All this must be done directly.

I cannot think of Letting the plaisterers make up their Stuff in any part of the house as eaven the Kitchen must be fitted up Immediately. They must therefore do it in the Vaults which may be paved with flat brick paving of very hard Brentford Stocks immediately.

In the two large rooms bring out the Bracketting at the ends in a line with the projections of the Chimneys as I would have no breaks in the Cieling and do the same in the room towards the Garden next the Kitchen as I mean to have Cupboards on each side the Chimny. In other particulars follow the Directions already given. You may use the bracketting taken down in the little room on the parlour floor in this room and instead of the Cornice first intended for it use the Cornice intended for the little room.

I am, &c &c.
Oct. 14. 1771.[4]

2

The vaults, paved with the "very hard Brentford stocks", must have been extensive. They brought Reynolds into court, because they encroached eastward on to the Manor of Richmond "to the damage of the Lady thereof". The Lady, however, was pleased to forgive Sir Joshua provided he paid rent of a shilling a year.[5] Reynolds was wisely intending to lay in a good stock of coal; his notebook for 1772 has a note on the fly-leaf:

"Andrews Cole-merchant Richmond Hill recommended by Mr Patson."

Meanwhile, however, work on the house proceeded only slowly. Writing to Solomon Browne on November 20, 1771, Chambers said: "I send you the plan and directions for fitting up the Offices of Sr Jos: house which you will communicate to Mr Bell &c, & I beg it may be done as expeditiously as possible. Pray give my Service to Mr Englehart & desire he will loose no time with his Work. I thought it had gone on very slowly when I was there last." [6] In the spring of 1772 he was still complaining, this time to Mr Bell: "I am sorry to see things go on so slowly at Sr Joshua's, pray get done there immediately. . . . I shall send down to have the Chimneys put up next week & I hope you will get so forward with all the floors that you will not prevent their going on. Pray desire Mr Englehart to finish his work all to the whitning immediately." [7]

By the autumn of 1772 the house was virtually completed, but Reynolds was annoyed, not only by the long delay but because he had to pay more for his house than George Colman had paid for his. He can hardly have been pleased to receive the following letter from Chambers:

Dr Sir,

I herewth send you your Bills for the House at Richmond which you will find exceed what you proposed to lay out there cheifly owing to the Changes that have from time to time been made in the 1st Design.

You may remember that your 1st Intention was only to have one large room which was to be on the Parlour Floor & only to have atticks over It. You then desired to have the large room up stairs & an eating Room upon the parlour floor &c: this was done & attended wth some additional Expense when finished. However your friends thought there was not Elbow Room enough so a good part of what was done was demolished & a large eating room wth a Bow Broke out was made at a considerable expence. Your little Garden wth the Pales that enclose it has likewise cost Something & as the Ground was all a very stiff Clay the digging part, of which there is a good deal, exceeded what I expected & I was under a necessity of making a new Sewer of a considerable Length to take off the water as the one w^h runs by your Building was not deep enough to drain it.

All the Bills including my own amount to the sum off 1655-1-4½
You have already paid at

diff^t times 940.-.-
Ballance due . . . 715.1.4½

You will find by the Bills sent you that amongst them there are Bills
paid to the amount of 911-6-9½, the rest is due & as some of the
Tradesmen are necessitous I beleive whenever it is Convenient to you
it will be very agreeable to them to receive their mony.

As I have never examined Colemans House I cannot tell weither it
be Cheap or dear at 1000£s. But since You spoke to me I made some
enquiry about it & was told that the man who undertook to build it
lost 500£s by the Bargain & that it is besides as ill built a house as
can be. Whether all this be true or not I cannot tell but you may be
assured that your own house is worth all the mony it has cost you &
I do not doubt but you might meet wth a Chapman for it any day
you Pleased. I am D^r S^r &c.

Oct: 15, 1772.

N.B. The painting is charged as finished which it is to be whenever
you find it Convenient. In the meantime do not pay the painter
above ½ his Charge.[8]

Reynolds now had his house at Richmond. Fox maintained that
he never enjoyed it—"that he used to say the human face was
his landscape".[9] It is true that he only used it occasionally and
spasmodically, but he liked to invite parties of his friends to Wick
House in the summer, and he never tired of the view. As a gentleman of consequence he was appointed a trustee under the Petersham Highways Act with the duty of superintending the lighting
and repair of the roads; he attended a vestry meeting in 1775.[10]
His easel was set up sometimes at Wick House, but local clients
were discouraged. William Gardiner of Richmond invited him
to paint his portrait in 1774 and said, "I hope it will prove agreable to you to take the Face here, upon your next Retreat to our
little *Alps*";[11] but the portrait was not painted.

Wick House was never beautiful; it was enlarged and altered
in the nineteenth century, and a new wing added, so that the case
for preserving it on historical grounds has not been impressive.
Nevertheless, there were successful protests when the Ministry
of Health proposed to knock it down in 1937—the year in which

Reynolds' house in Leicester Square was destroyed—and in 1950, after further re-building, it was opened as a home for the nurses of the Star and Garter Home. The large sitting-room on the ground-floor, with the "Bow Broke out", still holds the memory of great company and retains some of the atmosphere of Reynolds' day.

3

Reynolds may have had qualms about Wick House when he settled Chambers' bill, but throughout the planning and building he had been on the best of terms with its architect. The busy, dusty coach road to the west, which brought him not only to Richmond, over Kew Bridge, but also through the narrow High Street of Brentford to Chambers' house at Whitton, became thoroughly familiar to him. And he used his knowledge in writing his skit "A Journey from London to Brentford", now first published in Appendix A, which was probably intended particularly as a diversion for Chambers.

Those who knew Reynolds best have testified to his "strong turn for humour" and his "uncommon flow of spirits";[12] there is evidence of it in his Roman caricatures, in the dialogues that he wrote in imitation of the conversational manner of Johnson, and in *The Ironical Discourse* that he composed towards the end of his life in which he turned his own most cherished theories upside-down.[13] But it has not been generally known hitherto that he also amused himself in writing a parody of the travel literature of Giuseppe Baretti, the unpublished manuscript of which has remained ever since Reynolds' death in the possession of his collateral descendants.

Baretti was an engaging but embarrassing character well known to Johnson's circle. He first came to England in 1751, after a violent literary quarrel with Professor Bartoli of Turin, and lived here for most of the rest of his life. Through the recommendation of his friend Giardini, the violinist and composer, he was employed for a time at the Italian Opera House in London. Thereafter he earned a precarious livelihood by teaching Italian, by translating and writing books, and by compiling dictionaries. Though warm-hearted and generous, he was also vain and overbearing. A great admirer of women, with absurdly romantic notions of his own attractions, he was an impetuous and inaccurate writer—and he was always poor. Despite his shortcomings, Baretti was a frequent visitor to the Thrales at Streatham for many years; he could be stimulating company; as Johnson said, he carried his head high in conversation; and he was treated by Johnson's friends, Reynolds included, with that sort of tolerant affection that ends in a sigh.[14]

In 1769 the loyalty of Baretti's friends was tested. Reynolds had not long appointed him Secretary for Foreign Correspondence to the Royal Academy when, in October, 1769, he was involved in a fraças in the Haymarket which brought him into serious trouble. He was approached by a prostitute who asked him to give her a glass of wine. On his refusal, she struck him. Baretti retaliated—and found himself engaged in a running fight with three bullies. Short-sighted and flustered, he lost his head, drew a silver fruit-knife which he always carried with him, and struck out blindly at his assailants, one of whom eventually died. Baretti spent the night in prison at Tothill Fields. The next day he was bailed out on the sureties of Burke, Reynolds, Garrick and William Fitzherbert.

His sureties all spoke up for him at his trial at the Old Bailey, and so did Johnson, and Goldsmith, who called him "a most humane, benevolent, peaceable man". Reynolds testified that he had known him for fifteen or sixteen years, that he was "a man of great humanity, and very active in endeavouring to help his friends", "a gentleman of good temper", and "of a sober disposition". Baretti was honourably acquitted.

In the following year, 1770, Baretti's "A Journey from London to Genoa, through England, Portugal, Spain and France" was published by T. Davies of Russell Street, Covent Garden, in four volumes. It was wildly successful—"I know not whether the world has ever seen such travels before," commented Johnson truly enough. The journey had been made in 1760, and part of Baretti's account, written as a series of Letters, had already been published in Italy. He dedicated the English version "To the President and Members of the Royal Academy of Painting, Sculpture, and Architecture", declaring that he had "neither seen nor heard of a set of artists comparable to that which your

monarch assembled when he formed you into a academy. . . .
You have a right to this small token of an affection, which inclination as well as duty has kindled in the breast of Your most
humble and most devoted servant JOSEPH BARETTI."

This was the book which caused the President of the Academy
so much entertainment. It can still be read with amusement for
its exquisite exaggerations and absurdities, and has besides the
merit of being vividly written and of containing, if allowance
is made for Baretti's extravagances, some genuinely interesting
observation. The adventure in the Haymarket comes as a natural
sequel to a book in which Baretti continually pictures himself in
gallant and improbable situations.

Baretti's description of that part of his journey which lay
between London and Falmouth is comparatively short; and
Reynolds, or "Rinaldo", as he called himself, in writing his skit—
"A Journey from London to Brentford, through Knightsbridge,
Kensington, Hammersmith and Turnham Green"—was concerned to parody Baretti's book as a whole and to give a taste of
his continental adventures in a ludicrous English setting. He has
written a very close parody and has captured Baretti's style and
manner.

Rinaldo pursued his hero along a road which he knew very
well; he did not take him over Kew Bridge to Richmond,
because Baretti would have had to pass through Brentford on the
way to Falmouth. He may also have remembered, if he wrote his
skit largely for Chambers' benefit, that the road to Chambers'
house at Whitton lay through Brentford.

"Many people are of opinion that I might as well have wrote
my travels in my Study as going to Spain for that purpose," says
Rinaldo, in a preface in which he mercilessly pulls Baretti's leg.
The synopsis of the contents of "Letter I" is closely based on
Baretti's book—"A Nota Bene, and a Digression" actually
occurs in the index to the fourth volume. Rinaldo proceeds
through Knightsbridge, talking all manner of confident nonsense,
until he reaches the "audacious Ruffians" at the Kensington toll-
gate (which was to be seen until the eighteen-sixties near Hyde
Park Gate). Continuing, he observes, high up to the right of the
road, the brick and stone quoins of Campden House, which had
been built early in the seventeenth century and was then a fashion-

able boarding-school for girls. Rinaldo superbly describes it as "a Nunnery for the Education of all the young Ladies in London, here they remain until they are mariageable, they are then carried by their Mothers Aunts or some Relation to market. Of these markets there are two large ones beside a great many lesser, one is call'd Ranelagh the other Vauxhall."

Rinaldo advances along what is now Kensington High Street until he reaches another toll-gate which formerly stood just before the junction with Earl's Court Road. He then observes "on the right a Building in the Gothic Stile which is the Seat of a Peer who by a lucrative office under the crown call'd a Public Defaulter has acquired an immense fortune, they say many Millions". This is the sort of muddle (Reynolds suggests) that Baretti might have made out of a distant view of Holland House, whose owner, the first Lord Holland, had lined his own pocket while he was Paymaster-General of the Forces.

At Hammersmith, Rinaldo is tempted to visit a dance in the Assembly Rooms—an episode which enables Reynolds to parody the grotesque gallantries in which Baretti continually indulges on his Spanish travels. He may have recalled his own recent visit to the Richmond Assembly—and the abrupt ejection of Rinaldo by "the Captain" carries more than a hint of Baretti's notorious skirmish in the Haymarket.

Turnham Green, the next place on the road, was a stock joke in eighteenth-century society. It figures particularly in a story that illustrates Goldsmith's eagerness to shine in company and his notoriously clumsy attempts to do so. Reynolds' niece Theophila left this account of the incident:

At a dinner at Sir J. R's a gentleman present repeated a "Bon-mot" he had heard in a party where he dined. At the table were some peas which ought to have been green but were turned yellow in boiling. A friend took the dish from the table & giving it to a servant told him to take them to Hammersmith. Why to Hammersmith? demanded the company. Because it is the way to Turnham Green.

Goldsmith was so delighted with the witticism that he desired my aunt, Mrs Reynolds, would give him an opportunity at supper, when some additional guests were expected, to exhibit it as his own. Peas not being in season, my Aunt proposed some yellow pickles as a substitute. Accordingly when we went down to supper & before the company had well taken their seats & Goldsmith standing, he snatched the pickles from the table, & turning to my Uncle's servant, said: "Here Ralph take these pickles to Turn 'em Green." The party in the secret were convulsed with laughter and the others, seeing nothing to laugh at, were astonished at their merriment.[15]

This must have happened between 1770, when Theophila ("Offy") went to live with Sir Joshua in London, and Goldsmith's death in April, 1774. It is possible that it may have inspired Rinaldo's particularly glowing account of the beauties of Turnham Green, "a second Elysium", which resembles Baretti's description of the royal garden at Aranjuéz in his book; Baretti also quotes a "Mr Clark" in a footnote. The ludicrous phrase "beautifully and thickly inhabited by poultry and swine as well as men" is taken directly from Baretti in another context (Vol. IV, p. 94).

Turnham Green in the eighteenth century was actually a desolate and unsavoury waste. A modern public house still bears the name of the Packhorse and Talbot, where Rinaldo's "Calassero" stops to "wet his Whistle". It was a noted inn, at the western edge of the Green, much frequented by travellers on the great west road in Reynolds' day.

Rinaldo continues:

> Returning to my Posado I saw a Lady coming down stairs with her little daughter a very pretty girl about six years old. What is your name my sweet angel said I? My name is Charlotte Chambers answered the little thing, and dropt me one of her best courtesies. You are so pretty said I that I must give you a kiss if you please, and lifting her up in my arms carried her to the coach.

This passage was copied by Reynolds almost word for word from Baretti (Vol. III, p. 235), with the exception that the name of the girl is given by Baretti as Pepina Martinez. The fact that Rinaldo substituted Charlotte Chambers is the best possible proof that the skit was written to amuse William Chambers, for a letter from Chambers to his "dear little girl" shows that in 1771 his daughter Charlotte Augusta was "about six years old".[16] She was probably a favourite of Reynolds, who was very fond of children, and especially—the intelligent bachelor's failing—of little girls. Among Chambers' papers there is a scrap containing the words "Dear Sir Joshua Reynolds" in a childish hand.[17]

IX. THE THAMES FROM RICHMOND HILL

$(27\frac{1}{2}'' \times 35\frac{3}{4}'')$

The episode of the "diuretic whistle" that follows is one of the funniest things in the skit (its frankness probably ensuring that it was not shown to Reynolds' earlier biographers). We note that Rinaldo says he "will get my friend Gardini to prick down the musick that it may be publish'd, for perhaps it may have the same effect upon Christians". Then Rinaldo reaches Kew Bridge, built of wood about 1740, and after a hurried visit to the Queen at Kew—characteristic of Baretti's vanity—resumes the drive in his "Calash" to the Red Lion at Brentford, a famous house whose ancient glories have vanished—Henry VI held a chapter of the Order of the Garter there—but whose name still occurs in the High Street.

Rinaldo properly states that Brentford is "a place renowned in History", and he duly contrives to give as confused an account of it as anything in Baretti's book. The ancient folk-lore which gave rise to the proverb "There cannot be two kings of Brentford" leads Rinaldo to state that if the King of England had not owned "a chateau directly opposite the Town . . . Don John Alderman Wilks would certainly before this have been elected King of Brentford. This Don John is the Idol of the inhabitants of this town, his name is wrote on every door window shutter and dead wall throughout the Town either with letters or Hiroglifick figures."

That charming villain John Wilkes had long been one of Reynolds' radical weaknesses; he had sought him out in one obscure address after another, while Wilkes was daily seeking to avoid arrest; and for Reynolds, as for many others, Brentford was practically synonymous with Wilkes. The town was then notorious for its mud and for its rowdy elections. It was the polling-place for Middlesex, and Wilkes was repeatedly re-elected there in 1768–70, despite the disapproval of Parliament. By 1774 he was Lord Mayor of London and half-way to respectability.

The *Journey from London to Brentford* can be dated with confidence, as we have seen, to the years 1770 or 1771. Whether or not Reynolds ever showed it to Baretti, whose portrait (Plate VIII*b*), taken as he screwed up his eyes to read a little book, was one of his masterpieces of 1774, is something we cannot tell; but it is hardly likely. For from this parody emerges a lively impression of a more mischievous Reynolds than we have known. If the improbable idea still lingers that the friend of Baretti and Chambers, of Goldsmith and Wilkes, went on holiday with any degree of pomposity, we can finally set it aside—in favour of a merry observer of the road to Richmond, who, if he grumbled at the ruffians at the Kensington toll-gates, might conceivably have wetted his whistle at the Packhorse in Turnham Green.

VIII

Page and Monarch

Page and Monarch forth they went,
Forth they went together.

I

THE relationship of master and assistant is subtle and varied. Whatever his *métier*, the master's office or studio will usually require one or two professional helpers of a clerkly disposition; in Reynolds' studio these were represented by the drapery painters Marchi and Toms. Such men are habitually hardworking, poorly paid and long-serving. But the master will also probably be ready to accept amateur students, who are afforded the opportunity of watching him at work and of picking up hints and scraps of advice, which they may or may not be able to turn to good account, according to their ability and diligence. Reynolds, though encouraging to the young, was not a good teacher; he repeatedly stressed the importance of rules, but he was not the man to impart them, because he had never systematically learned them himself, and his own instinctive feeling for character and beauty was not to be communicated. Therefore it is not surprising that the great majority of his pupils—men like Hugh Barron, Thomas Beach, Charles Gill and William Doughty—made no name for themselves. There were two exceptions: George Watson, who became the first President of the Royal Scottish Academy, and James Northcote, R.A.

The whole life of Northcote—a very long one, for he lived from 1746 to 1831—was conditioned by the influence of Sir Joshua. He was born at Plymouth, the son of a watchmaker, and grew up with the dazzling example of his fellow Devonian always before him. But as he was given little education, and as his father discouraged his artistic ambitions, he would no doubt have settled down to the unwelcome drudgery of watchmaking if he had not been able to save ten guineas, by the time he reached his twenty-fifth year, to make a journey to London. He supplied himself with introductions from a Plymouth alderman, Henry Tolcher, and from Dr John Mudge, and in May, 1771, he presented them with trepidation to Sir Joshua at his house in Leicester Fields.

It took Northcote five days to get to London—he had to walk most of the way—and on his arrival he lodged at a grocer's in the Strand. Sir Joshua received him "with kindness, and offered me any assistance in his power". Soon he was writing to his friend William Elford of Plymouth: "I spend all my daytime at Sir Joshua Reynolds's house copying from the pictures he is so good as to lend me. I am now about a landskip by Rysdale.... His house is to me a very paradise; all the family behave with great good-nature to me, and particularly Sir Joshua's two pupils." To his brother he adds that Sir Joshua "is very kind to me, and often invites me to dine with him. And Miss Reynolds is the most good-natured woman I ever met with.... Sir Joshua behaves to me just as he does to his pupils, or rather with more friendship." [1]

Northcote—short, thin, with prominent features and keen eyes (an unkind contemporary remarked that he looked like a rat who had seen a cat)—supported himself by colouring prints of birds at a shilling a sheet, which he did in the early mornings before he went to Reynolds at nine. He found that Reynolds was so busy that he hardly saw him, and that his pupils knew surprisingly little of his methods of working, being summoned to his room only when "he wanted to paint a hand or a piece of drapery from them", and being immediately sent away afterwards. But Reynolds was pleased with Northcote's efforts, and, discovering him "one evening late in the gallery looking with much attention at the pictures", he spoke to him and invited him to live in the house for four or five years and be on the same footing "as his other scholars". "And then, says he, first I shall be of assistance to you and then you to me, and so we shall assist each other...."

This was the fulfilment of Northcote's highest ambition, and he was heartily pleased to be relieved of the anxieties of board and lodging. It came as rather a shock to him to learn that Fanny Reynolds knew nothing of her brother's proposal, considering that "she has the command of the household and the servants as much as he has". He told his brother in confidence that Reynolds and his sister seldom talked together "as we used to do in our family", and that he never instructed her in painting. But he added: "Do not ever mention anything I wrote to you of him to anybody, for I would not have it thought that I find the smallest fault in a man who has been so kind to me and is possessed of so many noble qualities."

The reader notices for the first time a cautionary note that begins to creep into Northcote's correspondence, a faint hint of disillusionment. Despite this critical undercurrent, Northcote's admiration and gratitude kept him loyal to Reynolds for the rest of his life. Nevertheless, Fanny Reynolds' confidences showed him his hero in altered perspective:

> Miss Reynolds said one day it was almost a pity the science had ever been known, it so entirely employed the minds of those who have ever made great painters that they neglected every other thing in this life and very seldom thought of the future; alluding to the neglect of the Church, which is disagreeable to her. She said her brother had lost as much as he had gained, that is all the pleasures of society, which he had sacrificed to gain a name. . . .

Though Northcote let her run on, he entered a caveat to this last assumption: "But he is surely a man of vast capacity, and a great scholar." He could not discover what Reynolds' religious views were, except that he never went to church, which his sister thought "very wrong".

Northcote now had the opportunity for more talk with Reynolds about his painting methods, and he quickly observed that his use of varnishes involved an "inconvenience . . . which is that his pictures crack; sometimes before he has got them out of his hands". He found Leicester Fields a quiet place to paint in, "almost like the country, for I often hear the cock crow and have seen a hen and chickens strut as composedly through the street as they would at Plymouth". Fanny Reynolds even persuaded him to go to church on Sundays, though this was often a working day both for Reynolds and his pupils. He was admitted to the secretarial duties; in December, 1771, he told his brother that he had copied out the President's Fourth Discourse for him to read at the Academy. Perhaps the servants of the house were young Northcote's chief worry; they were more civil to him than when he first arrived, "but still it is almost impossible to get them to do the most trifling (thing) for me more than they are obliged to by their particular office, and not always then except at table with Sir Joshua and then they are servile enough".

By June, 1772, Northcote was already being entrusted with the painting of important accessories in Reynolds' portraits. He painted a large wooden cage and "some very large weeds" in the portrait of Sarah Anne Child, later Countess of Westmorland, which is now at Osterley Park. This is a charming picture of a little girl of eight, daughter of the well-known banker, who is shown inviting a dove, sitting on the branch of a tree, to fly down into the cage and join its mate: the cage (and the weeds) are so well painted that it would be impossible even for the keenest observer to separate them, on grounds of style, from the rest of the picture. One can assume, however, that Reynolds would have been unwilling to undertake sole responsibility for such an elaborate cage, with so many carefully drawn bars.[2] Having found a capable collaborator, he used Northcote more and more during the next few years.

In his anxiety to appease the servants, Northcote painted a portrait of Reynolds' cook "which is thought much like her but rather handsomer". When the picture was placed on the floor, against a chair, for exhibition to his master and Miss Reynolds, Sir Joshua's macaw, "a very sensible bird", who disliked the cook, "flew over to it with the utmost fury and bit at the hands and face, but when he found he could not get hold of it he looked so very cunning, and went to the side and back to examine it . . . Sir Joshua and Miss Reynolds and all laughed very much". Thus encouraged, Northcote proceeded to "a portrait of the cook's sister who is very pretty".

A young painter living in Reynolds' house enjoyed unusual advantages. Reynolds gave him a ticket for Mrs Abington's benefit at the theatre; Goldsmith offered him half a dozen tickets for *She Stoops to Conquer*. He dined with Johnson and Baretti, and talked with Garrick. In 1772 Reynolds was contemplating a multiple picture of Garrick, which would show him as himself, in the centre, surrounded by fifteen other Garricks in the costume of some of the most remarkable characters he had played. Unfortunately nothing came of this interesting idea, though a portrait of Garrick with his wife was in the Academy exhibition of 1773.

2

The average number of sitters, sixty or seventy, that now came to Reynolds in each year was only half what it had been ten years earlier. He found new ideas and fresh faces in the London streets. There is a striking increase in the number of his fancy and genre pictures, of girls with their pet birds or of Cockney urchins, who might be seen with cabbage-nets on a pole, perhaps, or asleep in a wood, or translated miraculously into angels and shepherd-boys, into a youthful St John or an Infant Samuel. A London beggar-man, White, the original of Ugolino, became one of the best known models of the time.

The year 1773 was much interrupted by excursions. After escorting the King round the Academy exhibition in April, Reynolds joined Lord Edgcumbe on board the *Ocean* for the naval review off the Isle of Wight in June, and watched "The King in the Barge" and the King sailing "in the Yatcht". On June 24 the pencilled entry in the notebook is "Rained all day", and on the 25th he forsook the navy for Carisbrooke Castle. He got himself back to London with a careful note of the cost:

Boat		10.	6.
Do.		3.	6.
Play		6.	0.
Bill	3.	13.	6.
Waiter		4.	0.
Ossler			6.
Post Boy		3.	6.
Petersfield		1.	6.
Liphook		1.	4.
Godalming	1.	1.	0.
Ripley	1.	4.	0.
Kingston	1.	1.	0.
London	1.	1.	0.

It was an expensive but perhaps also a convivial journey.

Reynolds soon set out again, on July 6, for Oxford, where, on the 9th, he was one of fifteen who received the honorary degree of D.C.L. Another was Dr James Beattie, whose elaborate allegorical portrait as the champion of Truth he began in the course of the summer. Reynolds then visited Blenheim—where he received a somewhat cool reception because (his sister conjectured) he appeared "in his boots" and not in evening dress—and, after dining with Burke at Beaconsfield, returned to London on the 14th.

Sir Joshua, having obtained an academic blessing from Oxford, was at his most learned in the pictures he painted this year. He wrote to Luke Gardiner in July, 1773, that "the great object of my mind at present" was the picture of Gardiner's fiancée and her two sisters, Lady Townshend and Mrs Beresford, as "The Graces adorning a term of Hymen"—three plump society ladies indefinitely halted in a sequence of classical ballet, now to be seen at the National Gallery. The subject "affords sufficient employment to the figures", he pointed out, "and gives an opportunity of introducing a variety of graceful historical attitudes".[3] It was an opportunity he coveted, and which he found again in the complicated National Gallery group of Lady Cockburn and her writhing children. These and other painstaking allegories of the period are now too much for us; the sentimental simplicity of little Jane Bowles with her dog at the Wallace Collection seems preferable, reminding us that Sir Joshua was, after all, the contemporary of Greuze and the forerunner of Millais.

In a year of honour and dignity, Sir Joshua was touched by a compliment from his native Plympton which gave him a long view of his worldly progress since he had drawn his first rough outlines on the walls of the school-house. In 1772 he had been elected an alderman of Plympton; in September, 1773, he was chosen mayor. Northcote's brother Samuel, writing from Plymouth, professed himself much astonished that Reynolds should wish to have anything to do with the local affairs of Plympton, "looking upon the foul transactions of a dirty borough as things quite foreign to Sir Joshua Reynolds's pursuits". But he had the perspicacity to conjecture: "He perhaps retains somewhat of the ideas he had of a Plympton alderman when he was a boy looking up at them all as persons of dignity." This was perfectly true; and that Reynolds took pleasure in this gesture from Plymp-

X*a*. JOSHUA REYNOLDS. Self-portrait, *circa* 1773

(50″ × 40″)

X*b*. SIR WILLIAM CHAMBERS, R.A. 1780

(50″ × 40″)

ton is one of the most significant things in his life, demonstrating not only his love of Plympton but also the underlying simplicity of his character, which much experience of the world had not shaken from boyish notions of place and power.

The council chamber of the grey Guildhall of Plympton St Maurice, jutting out on pillars over the pavement, has not altered since Reynolds looked up at it respectfully as a schoolboy from the village street, or since he noted on October 4, 1773: "Plimpton to be sworne Mayor." He painted for the council chamber a portrait of himself in his D.C.L. robes, which hung for many years between early portraits by him of Captain Paul Ourry and Commodore Edgcumbe.*

Samuel Northcote pointed out that, in order to become mayor, Sir Joshua was required to receive the Sacrament. This was probably more than he bargained for, though in the same year he busied himself, unsuccessfully, in advocating that St Paul's should be decorated with pictures, "for the sake of the advantage which would accrue to the Arts by establishing a fashion of having Pictures in Churches".[4] It is scarcely a convincing reason for calling him "High Church", as Northcote is said to have done in talking to Hazlitt.

So much was Reynolds a Plympton man that there is some evidence that he might have been willing to represent the borough in Parliament, had opportunity offered. He told Caleb White-foord that he "had no manner of chance", but Whitefoord replied: "I totally differ from you Sir Jos: and I wish you wo^d but try, for if you do [you] will certainly succeed, for I am sure *nobody makes a better Figure upon a Canvas.*"[5]

The D.C.L. robes came in very useful to Sir Joshua—they provided just that touch of academic dignity which he needed for the self-portraits he soon painted for the Uffizi at Florence and for the Royal Academy (Plate X*a*). They probably suggested to him that it was time the Academy had its own official costume, with a special gown for the President, a matter which is touched

---

* They are none of them there to-day. The self-portrait was sold in 1837 when the Corporation found itself impoverished after the passing of the Reform Act. Besides a number of copies of Reynolds' portraits, the Plympton Guildhall now contains a version of "The Age of Innocence" presented by Miss S. Calmady-Hamlyn in 1946.

upon in the following unpublished letters between himself and Sir William Chambers:[6]

Dear Sir,

At the last general Meeting they wished very much that the dress of the President and the Academicians might be shewn to the King, for many reasons, first, to have his Majesty's opinion of it, and in the next place, that it would fix the dress so that no future President or Academician will presume to Change from any whim or fancy of [his] own, and above all that his majesty having seen and approved of them, it would come to them as an order, and be a real honour to the wearer, which they think it would not be without such Sanction and Authority.

I have an Academicians gown finished and the presidents finished on one side, which I will send to you if you approve of this proposal.

I am with the greatest respect

Yours
J. REYNOLDS.

Leicester fields
Jany 28th 1775.

Dear Sir,

From what you told me this morning and from what was said to me on Saturday, I am inclined to believe, we are in the wrong box with respect to the Academy dresses: for my own part however; though I have had no hand either in advising or promoting them, farther than I was desired; I am ready to follow the majority in what ever shall be thought proper: but submit it to your consideration, whether we should proceed; or, by taking advantage of the objections made by some of our members, lay the project aside.

Yours dear Sir most
truely,
Wm CHAMBERS.

Jany 30 1775.

It is doubtful whether the President thought that he was "in the wrong box"; the project was nevertheless "laid aside". After Reynolds' death, Farington revived it. He did not ask for gowns to be worn, suggesting that "a blue coat, with some distinction of collar, cuff and button would be sufficient, and would subject the Members to no real addition of expence".[7] But he was as unsuccessful as Reynolds, and the Royal Academy has never, in fact, had a uniform. That Reynolds was disappointed by Cham-

bers' opposition and that these were opening shots in the long
struggle between them, is more than probable.

3

Even if Sir Joshua's notebooks for the years 1774-6 were not
missing, they might not have helped us to check Northcote's
assertion that, on the day of Goldsmith's death, April 4, 1774,
he did no work. This would have been something quite unusual
for him, but Northcote was in a position to know, and there is
reason to suppose that he spoke the truth and that Reynolds was
deeply moved. Goldsmith had been five years younger than
Reynolds; like him, he carried the marks of smallpox; like him,
again, he was the son of a country clergyman with a large family,
who came to London to try his fortune. Reynolds had known
him intimately throughout his most active years and had shared
all his anxieties and triumphs. The malicious pen of Mrs Thrale
has sought to bedevil this and other friendships of Reynolds; but
she cannot persuade us that Reynolds felt anything but a disinterested love for one whom Northcote described as "a very
unaffected and good-natured" man.

Reynolds was "poor Goldy's" executor and found the task of
settling his confused affairs a heavy one. Using the subscriptions
of his friends as seemed best to him, Reynolds decided that a
monument by Nollekens in Westminster Abbey should com-
memorate Goldsmith's genius, and that a plain tombstone in the
Temple Churchyard should speak—as it does most eloquently—
for the tragedy of his life.

In 1776 Northcote came to the conclusion that, having served
his five years with Sir Joshua, it was high time for him to leave.
He had had to work very hard in Leicester Square, and had found
little opportunity for his own painting. It annoyed him, too, that
Reynolds strongly disapproved of his receiving visitors; "all the
day I must live like a hermit". That Reynolds' busy painting-
rooms should be strictly reserved for himself, his assistants, and
his sitters was probably not an unreasonable requirement; but
there was only one room in which Northcote was allowed to
entertain his friends in private, and that was "such a room as I am
mortified for anybody to see me in".

Probably not all Northcote's visitors met with Reynolds' approval. One of them was that unprincipled genius John Wolcot ("Peter Pindar", the satirist) who encouraged him to "steal a little bit of Sir Joshua" for him. "Has he no old head of merit lying amongst some old spiders?"

Northcote resisted this temptation; but more serious than the restriction on his liberty was the fact that he had found difficulty in making ends meet. He complained in 1776 that he had "had to rub through these five years with next to no money; and all the clothes I now possess is not worth much more than half a crown. . . . As to staying with Sir Joshua he never gave more than a hundred guineas and their board to anyone, and it will be a sad story for me if I cannot get more than that, besides being employed so much more to my liking by painting heads instead of satin gowns and silk curtains, which I hate because anybody could do that." Not everyone could do it as well as Northcote, however; he set a standard in the painting of accessories which his successors found difficulty in living up to.

If Northcote confessed to having some qualms about broaching the question of his departure, these were soon dissipated. Sir Joshua was full of sympathy, told him that he had stayed long enough and that he had been very useful, and finally parted from him on May 12, 1776, with great cordiality, adding with a touch of complacency: "But now to succeed in art you are to remember that something more must be done than that which was needed formerly. Kneller, Lilly, and Hudson will not do now."

4

"I know him thoroughly, and all his faults, I am sure, and yet I almost worship him." These words, from a letter of January 3, 1776, were probably the fairest summary of his relations with Sir Joshua that Northcote was to achieve. Although he left Sir Joshua's studio he always carried with him the memory of his master and of the stirring years in Leicester Square. He not only wrote a Life of Reynolds, first issued in 1813, which, though something of a hotchpotch, is still an important source of information, but he also compiled an autobiography—rather more critical in tone—which was not published until 1898. Nor did he only commit his recollections to paper. Living into the reign of William IV, he found himself almost the sole surviving repository of anecdote concerning Reynolds and his circle. By nature he was a cautious, timid person, accustomed to playing second fiddle. But, at the same time, Northcote had wit and intelligence, and when, during the last thirty years of his life, he realized that he was increasingly regarded as an authority on the great men of his youth, and on the early days of the Royal Academy, the opportunity to shine rather went to his head. He developed a line of conversational reminiscence which particularly delighted William Hazlitt, who preserved its essence in his entertaining but not entirely reliable "Conversations of James Northcote Esq. R.A."

Northcote owed much to Sir Joshua even after he left his employment. He followed his example by studying in Italy for three years, and on his return to London he gradually acquired a reputation as an historical painter. Elected R.A. in 1786, he proved, within the Academy, a loyal supporter of Reynolds, and, outside it, never ceased to praise his genius as a colourist and portrait-painter. But in what he spoke and wrote about Sir Joshua after his death, a note of subdued resentment is sometimes discernible. Much as he had himself benefited from Reynolds' kindness, he now remembered a lack of warmth in Reynolds' attitude towards him; he accused Reynolds of being jealous of talented rivals, of patronizing only those who could not interfere with himself; and in his autobiography he went so far as to conclude that "the principal drawback on his character, besides this selfishness, was a want of that firm and manly courage and honour which is so absolutely necessary to the highest degree of rectitude".

This is a grave charge which Northcote makes no attempt to justify. There is little doubt, however, of the real reason for his dissatisfaction. He felt that Sir Joshua, by insisting on the importance of the grand style and the pre-eminence of history painting, had led him and other young students "up the garden path", and had failed to support them in later years. Towards the end of Reynolds' life, Northcote apparently had some cause for complaint in one specific instance.* James Barry also probably had this grievance in mind when he wrote that, being "disappointed

* *Infra*, p. 224.

in not finding more in poor Sir Joshua", he could not "make a just estimate of the many excellent qualities I might have really found in him"; but Barry admitted that his own "notions of candour and liberality between artists who were friends, were too juvenile, and romantically strained too high for human frailty in the general occurrences of life".[8]

If Barry had always been as philosophical as this he would have spared Reynolds much annoyance and avoided his ultimate expulsion from a professorship at the Academy. The fact remains that Reynolds' teaching tended, in practice, to produce either respectable mediocrities like Northcote or passionate eccentrics like Barry and Haydon. For himself, he was shrewd enough to see that history painting did not show him at his best; and there is no doubt that in his last years his practical enthusiasm for it cooled. But he had not consciously misled his young disciples. He might have anticipated the heart-felt cry of Keats:

> Haydon! forgive me that I cannot speak
> Definitively on these mighty things;
> Forgive me that I have not Eagle's wings—
> That what I want I know not where to seek:
> And think that I would not be over meek
> In rolling out upfollow'd thunderings,
> Even to the steep of Heliconian springs,
> Were I of ample strength for such a freak. . . .

5

Northcote saw the publication of Hazlitt's *Conversations* in 1830 with considerable misgivings. As an old man in his eighty-fourth year, he looked back over more than half a century to the days when he had toiled in Leicester Fields. Balancing the scales to a nicety had been an exacting task, and he did not wish Reynolds' family to feel that he had been ungrateful to the man to whom he owed everything. The following letter to Reynolds' niece Theophila Gwatkin was preserved among her papers and may now be published:[9]

Dear Madam,

I received safely your two packets which I will take great care of and return them to you by the first opportunity. They contain very

precious matterials which will much enrich the memoirs of Sir
Joshua in the next edition and I am greatly obliged by the sight of
them. You mention the conversations said to be mine and although
it is very true in some parts yet he makes me say ilnatured things most
of which I never uttered or even thought of and I cannot endure the
book and have done every thing in my power to prevent the publication but without effect. It was done all from memory and in the first
instance without my knowledge or consent. Amongst a great deal of
other nonsense I am made to say In page 36 that Rapheal [sic] did
not know how to make a picture. Incredible stupidity. Who then I
should be glad to be informed does know how to make a picture If
the painter of the Cartoons and those grand works in the Vatican
did not know.

In page 298 I am made to say that Sir Joshua Reynolds in his
portrait of Mrs Siddons as the Tragic Muse has not done her justice.
That any one should utter such nonsense is certainly very difficult to
believe. I hope nobody will believe it of me.

I have been so angry with the Bookseller who published it that he
has not sent me even a single Copy of the Book for I told him that
I would do every thing in my power to prevent its sale.

Please to present my best compliments to Mr Gwatkin and the
Ladies of your family and believe me to be with great respect
Dear Madam
Your most sincere friend and very much
obliged humble servant
JAMES NORTHCOTE.

P.S. I was not the author of Fresnoy.

Argyll Place,
Septr. 12th 1830.

The pseudonym "Fresnoy", which Northcote disavows in his
postscript, was used by the writer of a series of newspaper articles
attacking Reynolds and the other founder-members of the Royal
Academy between 1769 and 1773. "Fresnoy" seems to have been
connected with the Incorporated Society of Artists, and may, indeed, have been its chaplain, the Reverend James Wills. He must
not be confused with the French seventeenth-century writer Du
Fresnoy whose *Art of Painting*, translated by William Mason, was
furnished with notes by Reynolds on its publication in 1783.[10]

Nothing could have been more tactless or further from Northcote's thoughts, as a timid newcomer in Reynolds' studio, than

to rush into anonymous polemics against his master. We can certainly acquit him of this, and of any deliberate "ilnatured things" in Hazlitt's *Conversations*. The *Conversations* cannot be relied upon for biographical accuracy, but where they touch on Reynolds they usually convey Northcote's warm admiration. He was, after all, faced with the problem implicit in words spoken by Baretti to Reynolds, which Northcote quotes: "You are extravagant and mean, generous and selfish, envious and candid, proud and humble, a genius and a mere ordinary mortal at the same time." [11] But when he heard the voice of Sir Joshua calling "Hither, Page, and stand by me," he did not fail him.

Northcote died less than a year after he had written his letter to Mrs Gwatkin and had made his peace with Reynolds' shade. If it had not been for Reynolds' kindness, he would not be remembered; and he is remembered now not for his own pictures, nor for his careful painting of Miss Child's bird-cage, but because Hazlitt heard him talk. Bald and wizened, in his old blue striped dressing-gown, he talked himself into immortality with his Devonshire accent in his dirty studio in Argyll Place. "Heestoricaul peinter!" we still hear him crying to Haydon, "why yee'll starve with a bundle of straw under yeer head!"

Women, Wine and Snuff

I

THE eighteenth-century rooms arranged with loving care at the Victoria and Albert Museum make us want to put back the clock and live amongst the furniture of Kent and Chippendale and Vile. But the doors in the panelling lead nowhere—just as well perhaps; for below stairs things were less attractive. Sir Joshua's pictures, silver and cabinets imparted a surface elegance which was not to be found in his basement, or in the privy in his back-yard. Drainage was so elementary as to be almost non-existent; when the wind set that way, the smell of London could be noticed three miles outside. It is small wonder that the water, now being piped into the principal houses, was viewed with suspicion; well water and canal water, liable to contamination from cess-pools, were no better, despite the carrier's cry: "Pure water, fair New River Water, none of your pipe sludge." It seemed almost a hygienic duty to drink wine and to take snuff. Sir Joshua Reynolds made free use of both.

He habitually carried a double box containing two kinds of snuff, and he helped himself from his neighbour at table and from every box within sight. His favourite snuff was Hardham's No. 37, recommended by Garrick and bought in Fleet Street.[1]

Finding himself next to Richard Cosway at a Council meeting of the Academy, Reynolds once offered him his snuff-box. Cosway declined it, saying that a pinch of snuff would be bound to make him sneeze for an hour. "I will lay you a guinea that it does no such thing," said Reynolds. He won his bet; Cosway took pinch after pinch but failed to induce a single sneeze.[2] Reynolds, in fact, was ready to bet on the slightest provocation. During one of his visits to Devonshire, in 1770, his notebook recorded a wager of five guineas on a shooting match "with Mr Treby's bullet gun at 100 yards distance", though whether he won that bet is not stated.

Sir Joshua had a strong head for wine and was probably never more than merry, yet it appears that over many years he drank more than was good for him. He paid for this in a diseased liver, "somewhat scirrhous".[3] "Reynolds has taken too much to strong liquor," wrote Johnson disapprovingly to Boswell in 1775, "and seems to delight in his new character."[4]

The merits and dangers of wine were often debated in Johnson's circle. By 1778 Johnson had firmly decided to confine himself to water (and tea). He had temporarily persuaded Boswell to give up drinking; yet Boswell still spoke in favour of wine. "Boswell is a bolder combatant than Sir Joshua," declared Johnson: "he argues for wine without the help of wine; but Sir Joshua with it." Reynolds maintained that to please the company was a sufficient motive for drinking. "I won't argue any more with you, sir," said Johnson, "you are too far gone." "I should have thought so indeed, sir," replied Reynolds, "had I made such a speech as you have now done." "Nay, don't be angry," said Johnson, "I did not mean to offend you."[5]

On the same occasion Reynolds explained that at first he had not enjoyed the taste of wine, but that he had brought himself to drink it, in order to be like other people. "The pleasure of drinking wine is so connected with pleasing your company, that altogether there is something of social goodness in it," he declared. When Boswell pointed out that he and Johnson would not have been well received on their tour of the Highlands if they had refused to drink with their hosts, Johnson said: "Were I to travel again through the islands, I would have Sir Joshua with me to take the bumpers." During another meeting at which the inevitable subject was discussed Reynolds explained that he rose in the morning in good spirits but was exhausted by dinner-time,— "wine puts me in the same state as when I got up; and I am sure that moderate drinking makes people talk better".[6]

After his dinner Reynolds liked to take a nap.[7] He awoke refreshed, ready for the pleasures of society. Reynolds was cautious about the quality of the wine drunk by The Club, as a letter to Bishop Percy shows: "The wine was tasted, at the Turk's Head, the meeting before the last, and was pronounced to be good wine, but not yet fit for drinking . . ."[8] But he did not always expect a convivial conversation to reach the level of talk with Dr Johnson;

having no false conceits, he abandoned himself to smoking-room humour and inedifying drinking-songs with satisfaction. A sheet of paper in his handwriting[9] suggests the character of one of his less intellectual evenings. It is headed "A boire":

Q.   Pray Mr Doctor can you tell
      What will make a sick man well
Q.A. What's your distemper
A.   Holland Dry.
Q.   Oh 'tis a Fever drink or dye
        drink or dye
        drink or dye
    Oh 'tis a Fever drink or dye.

This pleasantry is followed by an elementary love song:

Jenny is my hearts delight
She is so pretty
She doth excell all the girls in the City
She's witty she's pretty agreable small}
                            tall}

Here's pretty Kitty's health
Ch. Drink it up all
    All all all
    All boys all
    Here's pretty Kitty's health
Ch. Drink it up all.

One understands why Johnson felt that Reynolds was the right man "to take the bumpers".

2

> Give me wine and snuff
> Until I cry out "Hold, enough!" . . .

These fragmentary lines by Keats were long accepted as authentic, until it was found that they had been discreetly edited, and that what Keats actually wrote was "Give me women, wine and snuff."

Do we have to make a comparable emendation in Reynolds' case? The scurrilous "Fresnoy", writing at the time of Reynolds' knighthood, did not hesitate to hint at an unprofessional relationship with Kitty Fisher:

> . . . Have you received a frown from salacious Catherine, the tailor's maid, or is the affection of the fair creature alienated from you entirely since her elevation to matrimony—from you, alas! and many others? . . . No, all your friends, your amiable friends, are still about you; and Catherine has sat to you in the most graceful, the most natural, attitudes, and indeed I must do you the justice to say that you have come as near the original as possible.[10]

It would be rash indeed to deduce from such gossip, or from the fact that Reynolds began a song to "Jenny" and ended it by praising "pretty Kitty", that Miss Fisher was his mistress. So many beautiful women, of all shades of reputation, passed through his studio that he himself maintained that "he had grown callous by contact with beauty".[11] He had learned discipline and self-control, and, as Burke said in one of his letters, he kept "that superiority over the rest, which he always had from his genius, sense, and morals".

If we infer that Reynolds' bachelor life was generally proof against the temptation of women, it does not follow that he was sexually inexperienced, especially in his youth. Probably, however, his experience had been unsatisfactory and incomplete; as elementary as his drinking-song. He had a normal attitude towards women—except perhaps that he could not love. Towards the end

of his life he took part in a discussion with Boswell, Malone and
Courtenay that is extremely revealing. Malone maintained

> that a man has the same fondness as a lover for a woman who has
> been for years his own as for the finest woman whom he has never
> possessed. Sir Joshua justly observed that admitting this was setting
> aside two of the strongest principles of human nature: desire of pre-
> ference and novelty, which were given us for wise purposes. He said
> that something else very comfortable, very valuable, came in place
> of fondness where there had been possession; there was then affection,
> friendship. He said the reason why he would never marry was that
> every woman whom he had liked had grown indifferent to him, and
> he had been glad that he did not marry her. He had no reason there-
> fore to suppose that it would not be the same as to any other
> woman.[12]

Earnest consideration of their sex life was not uncommon
among eighteenth-century intellectuals, and we find another
example of it in the papers of Reynolds' married colleague, Sir
William Chambers:

> With regard to the Alternate feelings of the Sexes for each other,
> they all center in the Great Object of Nature, propagation of the
> Species. Health, Youth, Vigor, agility and Extream sensibility are
> necessary to excite the Superlative degree of Joy. When therefore in
> the Contemplation of an object of a different Sex from our own we
> Observe the exterior Mark of these qualitys [sic] it commands our
> approbation and Excites our desire, but if after fruition we find the
> object due unfeeling in the act of enjoyment the ardours of our
> desires abate and after a few repetitions change into disgust. . . .[13]

It appears from the frank statement of Reynolds that he had
more than once contemplated marriage. Why did the women he
liked "grow indifferent to him"? The probable answer is that they
found him lacking in passion, too cool in his affections, and
increasingly hardened in his bachelor ways. But it was characteristic of Sir Joshua to make a virtue out of necessity. Soon after
John Flaxman, the sculptor, had married, he and his wife met
Reynolds in the street. Flaxman stayed to talk to him for a
moment, while his wife walked on. Sir Joshua asked him who
the lady was, and when Flaxman told him, he cried, "What, are
you married?" "Yes." "Then," said Reynolds, "your improvement is at *an end*." [14]

Reynolds disguised his disappointment, which may have been none the less real, for he was an admirer of women and not unattractive to them. It is most probable that his feeling for Angelica Kauffmann, for example, was at one time something warmer than friendship. In Reynolds' day women did not habitually "come and go", as Mr T. S. Eliot has put it, "talking of Michelangelo"—and when this gifted Swiss girl, who had travelled the Continent and studied in Rome, and who was, moreover, as charming as she was talented, arrived in London in June, 1766, it was not surprising that Reynolds should have been excited. His notebook records an appointment with "Angelica" on October 1, and underneath it is the word "Fiori"—perhaps a reminder to give her some flowers. By October 18 she has become "Miss Angel".

He encouraged Angelica warmly throughout the fifteen years of her stay in England. She was one of the two women foundermembers of the Royal Academy—a striking compliment—and was employed to decorate the ceiling of its lecture-room at Somerset House. Angelica's admiration of Reynolds was no less: "I have visited many painters", she soon wrote to her father, "but Mr Reynolds is the finest of them all, a very great master".[15] She said that Reynolds was "more pleased than anyone" that her first portraits were successful, and added that she had painted his own portrait, which had "succeeded wonderfully and will do me great credit".[16]

Angelica's portrait (*Frontispiece*) shows Reynolds seated before a bust of Michelangelo with his left hand on his knee and his right elbow resting on a table covered with books and papers. The latter were obviously carefully chosen to flatter the sitter, for they include a volume of Johnson's *Idler*, to which Reynolds had contributed, and a copy of Goldsmith's *The Traveller* (Angelica would doubtless have chosen *The Deserted Village*, which was dedicated to Reynolds, if that had then been published). As an interpretation of Reynolds' character, the portrait deserves more attention than it has so far received. Unique in suggesting Reynolds' soft and amiable attitude towards women, it affords a convincing glimpse of his conversational manner with a woman whose society he enjoyed. This gentle, almost effeminate side of him is virtually ignored in Reynolds' self-portraits, in which he preferred to emphasize his virility, unless we except the early self-portrait of about 1746 (Plate I). But it is an impression that recurs in the relatively few portraits of him by other hands. It is even discernible in the National Portrait Gallery group of Reynolds, Chambers and Wilton by J. F. Rigaud, while the Swedish artist C. F. von Breda[17] makes him, in the last year of his life, look something of an old woman.

Reynolds appears not to have painted his own portrait of Angelica (Plate VIII*a*) until 1777, ten years after she had painted him. His friendly interest in her did not slacken in the interval, but it is likely that Angelica's portrait of him, painted in 1766 or 1767, shows Reynolds at the last moment at which the thought of matrimony seriously troubled him. He was in his early forties, rich, successful, of an age to be aware of a bachelor's dwindling opportunities and thinning hair. We can almost imagine him wondering, as he looks at Angelica, whether he should propose marriage to this unusual girl, whether he could overcome his distrust of women-painters (founded on the trying experience of living with his neurotic sister), whether he could marry a Roman Catholic, whether the sacrifice of his independence would bring a new happiness to the house in Leicester Fields. . . . Despite his longing for affection, he felt even more strongly the necessity to avoid being emotionally roused, the need to keep himself to himself. As in all his problems, he was acutely aware of pros and cons, and found it hard to decide.

If he had proposed marriage, there is little doubt that Angelica would have accepted him. She had many other admirers—Nathaniel Dance and Henry Fuseli among them—but the prospect of marriage with Reynolds would have dazzled her. As it is, she seems to have withdrawn her affections on Reynolds' account from honest, warm-hearted, handsome Nathaniel Dance. His brother George told Farington all about his brother's disappointment:

> At Rome He became acquainted with *Angelica Kauffman*, and became so enamoured of Her, she encouraging His passion, that when He came to England, whither she also came, it was settled between them that they shd. marry.—But in England she became acquainted with Sir Joshua Reynolds, who showed Her much attention, and it is supposed she looked to Him, expecting that He wd. offer Himself to Her. Her reception of Dance having now

become more cold, & Her intercourse with Sir Joshua being noticed by Him, He remonstrated with Her in such a manner that she complained of His temper and assigned that as a reason for now refusing to marry Him. . . .[18]

The outcome was disastrous for Angelica, who was sufficiently punished for any fickleness she may have shown. By November, 1767, she must have understood that she would never become the wife of Reynolds, for she then abruptly married the so-called Count de Horn, who proved to be not only a bogus Count but also a bigamist. They were soon separated, but she remained tied to him until his death fourteen years later, when she made a safe and happy marriage with an old friend, Antonio Zucchi.

A curious episode of the year 1775 temporarily revived the gossip about Angelica and Reynolds. It was then that Nathaniel Hone, who had known Reynolds in Italy and had since grown jealous and embittered, submitted his picture "The Conjuror" [19] to the Royal Academy. "The Conjuror" was an accomplished piece of work, fully deserving of inclusion in the exhibition, but it was an obvious satire on Reynolds' derivative painting methods, for it showed an old wizard—immediately recognizable as Reynolds' model, White the beggar-man—waving his wand over a collection of engravings bearing such names as Vandyke, Carlo Maratti, Michelangelo and Titian. At the top left-hand corner appeared a view of St Paul's in front of which a number of small naked figures were engaged in painting—presumably an allusion to Sir Joshua's interest in the decoration of the Cathedral. The Academicians did not wish to reject the picture, and would never have done so if they had not received a strong protest from Angelica, who believed that one of these naked figures was intended for herself. Sir William Chambers, deputed to visit Angelica, tried to make her withdraw her objection; Hone himself assured her that she was entirely mistaken. But Angelica remained adamant; and an unpublished draft of a letter to her from Chambers shows clearly that the Council's decision to exclude the picture was reluctantly forced on them by their lady Academician:

Madam,
    I can assure you not only from the Evidence of my own Eyes but from the opinion of five or Six other Gentlemen very well Skilld in the Naked that the figure you and your friends have mistaken for a

Woman is absolutely a man and designed to represent Mr Newton
our Secretary. He sits at the feet of the president and holds his
trumpet while he with five others appointed to paint St Paul's are
all busied in that opperation. The figures are very slight, very small
& bear no resemblance to the original but that which I think
intended for you has nothing more than the face in sight, the rest
being hid behind a point. The Case standing thus, it would have
appeard very Singular in the Council to insist upon what you
insisted. They could not with any degree of propriety have obeyed
your Commands however willing.

They have however Judged it expedient to make the Cursed
picture in question of more consequence than they at first intended
by honouring it with a formal exclusion. . . .[20]

Hone published his denials and even swore an affidavit; having
altered and clothed the naked figures, he showed "The Conjuror"
privately, at an exhibition in St Martin's Lane. Nothing could
shift his personal animosity towards Reynolds, but he found
little support for it among his fellow Academicians. J. T. Smith
recorded Hone's reception by Joseph Nollekens on one occasion:

Well, now, I suppose, you've come to get me to join you in the
Academy tonight, against Sir Joshua, but you're very much mistaken; and I can tell you more, I never will join you in anything you
propose: you're always running your rigs against Sir Joshua; and you
may say what you please, but I have never had any opinion of you
ever since you painted that picture of The Conjuror, as you called it.
I don't wonder they turned it out of the Academy. And pray what
business had you to bring Angelica into it? You know it was your
intention to ridicule her, whatever you or your printed paper and
your affidavits may say; however, you may depend upon it *she* won't
forget it, if Sir Joshua does.[21]

Reynolds did not forget the episode so quickly, however, for, at
the sale of Hone's pictures after his death in 1785, Smith saw him
"most attentively view the picture of the Conjuror for full ten
minutes".[22]

3

His friendship with Angelica brought Reynolds closer to
marriage, so far as the scanty evidence goes, than did his acquaintance with any other woman. Even had Angelica been less

attractive, an alliance between the leading painter and the outstanding woman artist of their time might have tempted the idealist in Sir Joshua. But he did not contemplate marriage lightly, and could not bring himself to take the plunge. In his early days, when he was studying the Apocrypha, he had felt it natural that Edna should weep at her marriage to Tobias; brides wept, he believed, because the future was uncertain for them, "they consider likewise that all when they marry propose happiness to themselves and that how few obtain it".[23]

There were other romantic stories. Gossip connected Sir Joshua with the beautiful Mary Horneck, afterwards Mrs Gwyn, who was equally admired by Goldsmith; Reynolds is said to have fallen on his knees during a sitting and solicited her hand.[24] His niece declared that the woman who made the strongest impression on his mind was Miss Mary Hamilton: "while reading a novel or any work in which the imagination was employed to represent an image of what was beautiful and interesting, the idea of Miss Hamilton was always uppermost in his mind".[25] Such anecdotes help to show that Reynolds was no woman-hater. For the best glimpse of him in his relations with a young woman whom he liked, we must turn, however, to Fanny Burney's diaries.

Reynolds was a warm admirer of *Evelina* and "sat up all night to finish it".[26] His copy of the first edition in three volumes, with Reynolds' signature on the fly-leaf, fetched £950 when it was sold at Sotheby's in the nineteen-twenties. Two other sets, in similar condition, were sold on the same day for only £250 each. This must have been one of the highest tributes ever paid to Reynolds' memory.[27]

After her first meeting with Reynolds at the Thrales' in 1778 Miss Burney noted, in what might be a description of Angelica Kauffmann's portrait: "I like his countenance, and I like his manners, the former I think expressive, soft, and sensible; the latter gentle, unassuming, and engaging." [28] She was equally pleased with Sir Joshua when she timidly visited Leicester Square in January, 1779, painfully conscious of her new celebrity.[29] "So, you were afraid to come among us?" asked Sir Joshua, drawing up a chair; but "his behaviour was exactly what my wishes would have dictated to him," added Fanny, "for my own ease and quietness; for he never once even alluded to my book, but conversed

rationally, gaily and serenely." When Mrs Cholmondeley, a
formidable blue-stocking, pursued Miss Burney, Reynolds pro-
tected her: "Come, come, Mrs Cholmondeley, I won't have her
overpowered here!" "I love Sir Joshua much for this," declared
Fanny, "but Mrs Cholmondeley, turning at him, said, with quickness and vehemence: 'Why, I an't going to kill her! . . .'"

Reynolds, obviously taken by Fanny, exerted himself to be
tactful, polite and flattering. "I think I have met with more
scrupulous delicacy from Sir Joshua than from anybody," she
wrote, "although I have heard more of his approbation than of
almost any other person's."

Soon afterwards they met again at Mrs Cholmondeley's, that
lady proving less formidable in her own house. Sheridan pro-
voked a lively conversation there:

Sir Joshua, I have been telling Miss Burney that she must not suffer
her pen to lie idle—ought she?

Sir Joshua.—No, indeed, ought she not.

Mr Sheridan.—Do you then, Sir Joshua, persuade her. But perhaps
you have begun something? May we ask? Will you answer a question
candidly?

F.B.—I don't know, but as candidly as *Mrs Candour* I think I
certainly shall.

Mr Sheridan.—What then are you about now?

F.B.—Why, twirling my fan, I think!

Mr Sheridan.—No, no; but what are you about at home? However, it is not a fair question, so I won't press it.

Yet he looked very inquisitive; but I was glad to get off without
any downright answer.

Sir Joshua.—Anything in the dialogue way, I think, she must
succeed in; and I am sure invention will not be wanting.

Mr Sheridan.—No, indeed; I think, and say, she should write a
comedy.

Sir Joshua.—I am sure I think so; and hope she will.

I could only answer by incredulous exclamations.

"Consider," continued Sir Joshua, "you have already had all the
applause and fame you can have given you in the closet; but the
acclamation of a theatre will be new to you."

And then he put down his trumpet, and began a violent clapping
of his hands.

I actually shook from head to foot! I felt myself already in Drury
Lane, amidst the hubbub of a first night.

"Oh, no!" cried I, "there may be a noise, but it will be just the reverse." And I returned his salute with a hissing.

Mr Sheridan joined Sir Joshua very warmly.

"Oh sir!" cried I, "you should not run on so—you don't know what mischief you may do!"

Mr Sheridan.—I wish I may—I shall be very glad to be accessory.

Sir Joshua.—She has, certainly, something of a knack at characters; —where she got it, I don't know,—and how she got it, I can't imagine; but she certainly has it. And to throw it away is—

Mr Sheridan.—Oh, she won't,—she will write a comedy,—she has promised me she will!

F.B.—Oh!—if you both run on in this manner, I shall—

I was going to say get under the chair, but Mr Sheridan, inter-rupting me with a laugh, said:

"Set about one? Very well, that's right!"

"Ay," cried Sir Joshua, "that's very right. And you (to Mr Sheridan) would take anything of hers, would you not?—unsight, unseen?"

What a point-blank question! Who but Sir Joshua would have ventured it!

"Yes," answered Mr Sheridan, with quickness, "and make her a bow and my best thanks into the bargain."

Fanny spares us nothing of her own archness and misses nothing of Sir Joshua's charm. Her play *Edwy and Elvira*, when she came to write it, was not a success; but she was already working on her second novel *Cecilia*, which appeared in 1782. At about the time *Cecilia* was published, Sir Joshua suffered a second stroke, which not only alarmed his friends but interrupted his sitting to Gains-borough, thus depriving us of a most interesting portrait, for the appointments were not renewed. Johnson wrote to condole with Reynolds on November 14, 1782, but when Fanny Burney saw him on December 8 she was already able to report: "He looks vastly well, and as if he had never been ill".[30] His illness may have prevented Reynolds' obtaining the first edition of *Cecilia*,* but he read it as soon as he could and joined with Burke in praising it and in reporting the enthusiasm of such blue-stockings as Mrs Montagu and old Mrs Delany, who "had said she would never read any more; however, when we met, she was reading it

* Mr Aubrey Edgcumbe owns Reynolds' *Cecilia* in five volumes, each bearing his signature; it is not the first edition.

already for the third time". Reynolds told Miss Burney that Gibbon had read the whole five volumes in a day—" 'Tis impossible,' cried Mr Burke, 'it cost me three days; and you know I never parted with it from the time I first opened it.' " [31]

This adulation of Fanny Burney was portentous. It preluded the triumph of a monstrous regiment of women novelists. The surprising nature of her experience goes far to excuse Miss Burney for coyness in writing of it. As he guided her discreetly through the ranks of her admirers, she never failed to appreciate the kindness and delicacy of Sir Joshua. It was at the same gathering (December 8, 1782) that Miss Monckton told Dr Johnson:

"Sir, Miss Burney says you like best to sit in a circle."

"Does she?" said he, laughing; "Ay, never mind what she says. Don't you know she is a writer of romances?"

"Yes, that I do, indeed!" said Miss Monckton, and everyone joined in a laugh that put me horribly out of countenance.

"She may write romances and speak truth," said my dear Sir Joshua. . . .

Reynolds' interest in Miss Burney was sufficiently obvious to excite the gossip of the matchmakers, though she was thirty years his junior. Miss Burney eventually took an opportunity of disillusioning them. "But how, my dearest Susy," she wrote to one correspondent, "can you wish any wishes about Sir Joshua and me? A man who has had two shakes of the palsy! What misery should I suffer if I were only his niece, from a terror of a fatal repetition of such a shock! I would not run voluntarily into such a state of perpetual apprehension for the wealth of the East." [32]

As a continually eligible bachelor, Reynolds excited the inevitable curiosity of his friends. He was obviously attracted to women of talent and intelligence, but we find occasional suggestions that he might have been ready to marry for social advantage. Dr Johnson joked about him with Boswell during their Tour of the Hebrides:

I really believe, I could talk myself into building a house upon island Isa, though I should probably never come back again to see it. I could easily persuade Reynolds to do it; and there would be no great sin in persuading him to do it. Sir, he would reason thus: "What will it cost me to be there once in two or three summers?— Why, perhaps five hundred pounds; and what is that, in comparison of having a fine retreat, to which a man can go, or to which he can send a friend?"... Then I would tell him, that he may marry one of the Miss M'Leods, a lady of great family.[33]

But, one way or another, Sir Joshua eluded all matrimonial day-dreams, whether his own or his friends.

4

In steeling himself against sentiment, Reynolds had a warning ever before him, in the person of his sister Fanny, of the danger of brooding over personal troubles and real or imagined injuries. This kind-hearted lady had won the affection of Dr Johnson, who called her his "dearest Dear" and tried to counsel her with never-failing patience, but there is no doubt that she had allowed her failure in love—and her relative failure as a painter—to make her a restless, difficult woman. The pathetic poems in her common-place book[34] show that, while she had had admirers who did not please her, she suffered in the end from an unrequited love which became an obsession:

> From fifteen years to five and twenty
> Of humble servants I had plenty
> And some so rich who fill'd my train
> Enough to make a woman vain.
> The world approved but still my Heart
> Ne'er felt the force of Cupid's Dart.
> A thousand thousand times I've said
> Let me be destitute & beg my Bread
> Would be by far a happier State
> Than splender with the Man I Hate.
> Marrage cannot a medium prove,
> Or I must hate or I must love.
> Exempt from love I'll spend my Days
> In sweet tranquillity and ease,
> Exempt because I ne'er shall find
> A man that's suited to my mind.
> The prudent ones would often say
> The time will come, too sure the Way
> When these romantick foolish schemes
> Will all appear like Idle dreams.
> Tho' then I laugh'd yet now I mourn
> To find alass the tables turn.

Her notebook is filled with scraps of diary information, drafts of letters, and philosophical aphorisms of the sort beloved of the Reynolds' family; one of these, "The first step to be despised is to be pitty'd", is all too relevant. But in the main her book contains melancholy verses on the theme of unhappy love. There are two poems to "Mr S", who appears to have admired her in vain; and there is a poem to a "Mr B" announcing that she herself had fallen in love—presumably this was the

> attraction for a base a treaterous friend
> which Blasted all my blosoms in their prime

to which she recurs again and again:

> . . . Beneath the guise of friendship fair
> Cupid conceal'd his subtle snare
> But soon I felt the smart,
> 'Tis three years since nay more 'tis four
> Since first I felt its cruel power
> Since first I lost my Heart . . .

Miss Reynolds' commonplace book goes far to explain why her brother did not get on with her and eventually had to ask her to give up her housekeeping duties in Leicester Fields. Having disciplined himself to an active and rational existence, he must have found such an abandonment to introspection demoralizing and disturbing.

It was, of course, no easy task to keep house for him. Reynolds took an artist's pleasure in poking about in the shops, but he was not a ready buyer. Thomas Stothard told Haydon that "he remembered Sir Joshua looking at the effect of some people in a pork shop near Newton Market, and imitated his manner, holding his head back, and taking off his glasses to see the effect".[35] It is traditionally related that he was a frequent visitor to a fish shop in Coventry Street and that he used to walk there before breakfast, turn over the fish, choose what he wanted, and go home to report to Miss Reynolds. According to the fishmonger, Miss Reynolds never chose, Sir Joshua never paid, and both were good hands at driving bargains.[36] But fish in the eighteenth century was expensive; and in London it certainly had to be carefully looked at.

Fanny Reynolds' chronic perplexities and irresolution, which have been described by Miss Burney, must have been so irksome that only a saint could have put up with them. Sir Joshua was not a saint—but he needed a housekeeper, and it was not until his niece Mary Palmer was old enough to superintend his household that he finally requested his sister to move elsewhere. This was probably in the late 'seventies, when Mary was about twenty-five. She did not find her uncle any easier to deal with over money matters, and day after day, at breakfast-time, would "ask Him for money to pay the House Bills, without obtaining it from him".[37]

Reynolds provided his sister with a small income after she left him, but she felt herself ostracized from his society and cruelly neglected; Dr Johnson even drafted a letter of protest for her to send to her brother.[38] (The Doctor must have been not a little embarrassed by this domestic quarrel.) No reconciliation was possible between two such opposing temperaments. To his sister's suggestion in 1781 that he might give her his house at Richmond, on condition that he could use it when he wanted it, Reynolds returned a sarcastic answer: "Tho' I am much older than you I hope I am not yet arrived to dotage as you seem to think I am, voluntarily to put myself in the situation of receiving the favour of living in my own house instead of conferring the favour of letting you live in it".[39] He subscribed himself "your most affectionate Brother"; but his sister judged after his death that he was "a gloomy tyrant".[40]

An adverse verdict from this quarter must be suspect; Sir Joshua's relations with his family were, on the whole, good, and might have been better if he could have persuaded himself to go to church on Sundays. He offered to train his nephew Samuel Johnson as an artist (though the offer was refused); he helped another nephew, William Johnson, to obtain a post in the Supreme Court of Judicature at Calcutta; he gave an annuity to his niece Betsey Johnson, who sat to him for the figure of "Fortitude" in the window at New College, Oxford; he tried unsuccessfully to persuade Garrick to perform a play by his nephew Joseph Palmer and eventually obtained for him from the Duke of Rutland his preferment as Dean of Cashel.[41]

His attitude to his Johnson relatives was, admittedly, as variable as April weather. He could not forget that he had lost a considerable sum of money lent to his brother-in-law, the feckless William Johnson, and after Johnson's separation from his sister Elizabeth he received her desperate appeals for help with considerable irritability. At his worst, he no doubt behaved ungenerously to her. His nephew Samuel, writing to his mother from London in 1775, said: "There is no comfort for you from this quarter. Your suppos'd Brother and you could never have had the same parents or be known to one another in your infancy. He desires He may be look'd on as if He did not exist, for He will do nothing for you . . . I never heard of such a man." [42] That Reynolds later repented and did something to assist this impoverished family can hardly exonerate him from callousness on this occasion. His family were aware of a side to his nature that would never have been guessed at by those who knew only the calm dignity of his social appearances. When his control snapped, he could be sharp and aggressive. It was to his credit that, when he had recovered himself, he was ready to make amends.

5

By contrast, Reynolds' regard for his prosperous sister Mary Palmer and her charming daughters, Mary and Theophila, was genial and unclouded. Theophila, the younger, generally known as "Offy", had attracted him from her cradle days, and her earliest letter, written to her Aunt Fanny on a small sheet edged with pink, takes proper account of her Uncle Joshua:

Dear Aunt,
    This is the first letter I ever did write in my life. Pray give my Duty to Uncle. I am your Dutyful Niece
                                                OFFY PALMER. [43]

In 1770, when she was thirteen, Offy made the long coach journey from Torrington to London to stay with her uncle in Leicester Fields. She came timidly into the tall rambling house, to be fascinated by the macaw that perched on visitors' shoulders and the bedraggled studio eagle that lived in the backyard; the house where Dr Johnson growled and made her cry because she put on her second-best frock for him; the house where Goldsmith gave her his poem "The Haunch of Venison",* and made her laugh by

---

* Goldsmith's manuscript of "The Haunch of Venison", written out especially for Offy Palmer in 1771, was sold at Sotheby's in 1929 for £4,800.

burlesquing Garrick's Hamlet with the aid of a tablecloth; the house in which she formed her lasting friendship with Edmund Burke.[44] Reynolds was just then turning his frustrated affections towards children—and among them Offy was his first and best love. Once he had her in his house, he did not let her go, and she stayed with him more or less continually until her marriage in 1781. It is said that she had already suggested the pose of the figure of comedy in his picture of "Garrick between Tragedy and Comedy" which Reynolds had painted ten years earlier, when Offy was only a child of three or four. It is certain that she now sat to him for his portrait of her reading *Clarissa Harlowe* (1771) and for "The Strawberry Girl" (1773).

It meant much to Reynolds to have this little girl in his house, for children had begun to take an important place not only in his bachelor life but also in his life as an artist. He told Northcote that when he wished to learn what real grace was, he studied it in the attitudes of children; he deplored the advent of the dancing-master with his affectations. The success of his portraits of children, which never fail in their grace and variety, was founded on a close observation of their movements from a very early age. He did not forget an occasion when a little girl accompanied him on a tour of the portrait-gallery of a nobleman's house, imitating the attitudes of the figures with a sublime innocence that implied the most telling unconscious criticism. Some lurking remembrance of this incident may have influenced the portraits of Miss Frances Crewe with her basket on her arm, and of Master Crewe as a jolly little Henry VIII.

Children brought out the gentle, protective quality in him; during the last twenty years of his life he painted them more and more frequently. There was a time in the early 'eighties when he painted them in the nude—a century later another bachelor, Lewis Carroll, went through the same phase in his career as a photographer. But in his closing years, when he painted "Heads of Angels", "The Age of Innocence", and Offy's own daughter as "Simplicity", Reynolds used his child-models to represent an abstract ideal of purity that had never been entirely lost to his mind in all the fever of his waxing prosperity. These are master-pieces of all time, but they also reflect the limits of eighteenth-century culture. To modern taste Reynolds' children may seem

too consistently sweet. Even his London street urchins, so tired
that they fell asleep while they posed for him, were idealized by
that radiant vision, their rags and poverty refined away. The
President of the Royal Academy banished his Whig principles
from the painting-room. The representative painter of a class and
society was not disturbed by thoughts of the miserable lives of the
boys who climbed his chimneys. "The greatest portrait painter
of the age was describing the charm and grace and laughter of
happy and careless childhood," two modern historians have
written: "But so deep and distant was the under-world where
children were stolen from the sunshine as soon as they could creep
beneath an engine or watch a trap-door in a mine, that the sleep
of those rulers who admired Sir Joshua's portraits of innocence,
and took pride in their sensibility and tenderness, was never
broken. . . ." [45] So much must be said in criticism of the Age of
Taste; but dispassionately—for Reynolds went "with the great
stream of life".

Reynolds' love for Theophila (Offy) Palmer was perhaps the
most disinterested love of his life. He confessed it in a sprightly
jeu d'esprit:

> When I'm drinking my tea
> I'm thinking of The
> When I'm drinking my Coffee
> I am thinking of Offey
> So whether I'm drinking
> My tea or my Coffee
> I am sure to be thinking
> Of The or my Offey. [46]

When Offy, aged twenty, was spending a few days away from
him, he wrote her a revealing letter: "I never was a great friend to
the efficacy of precept, nor a great professor of love and affection,
and therefore I never told you how much I loved you, for fear
you should grow saucy upon it. I have got a ring and a bracelet
of my own picture; don't you tell your sister that I have given
you your choice." [47]

If Offy was her uncle's favourite niece, it was perhaps primarily
for the reason noted by Fanny Burney: "The eldest Miss Palmer
seems to have a better understanding than Offy; but Offy has the
most pleasing face. . . ." [48] Offy nevertheless had the sense to make

a very happy marriage in 1781 with Robert Lovell Gwatkin, a well-to-do Cornishman. "That you may be as happy as you both deserve is my wish," wrote Reynolds, "and you will be the happiest couple in England. So God bless you." [49] Burke added a thoughtful homily, expressing the wish "that we, who hoped a great deal from Offy Palmer, should see a great deal performed by Mrs Gwatkin".[50]

The charming portrait of Offy in the present volume (Plate XII*a*) has not been reproduced before, at least not in this form. It was originally painted by Sir Joshua in 1776 and engraved by J. R. Smith, but on Offy's marriage in 1781 he repainted it in the lower hair-style of that time, and also altered the dress, both of which were more becoming to the sitter.

The good looks of the nieces were in contrast. Offy had the archness and innocence of a pretty girl; her elder sister Mary had the prominent nose of an intellectual—she was a handsome woman with an air of distinction. Mary lived at Leicester Fields, with few intervals, from 1773 onwards; and when her sister married she remained to take charge of Sir Joshua's household. The portrait of her reproduced here (Plate XII*b*) will be generally unfamiliar; it dates from 1785 and shows her wearing a fashionable hat of that period which suited her very well. As Mary had no children, this portrait descended in the Palmer family. It was sold by Sir Robert Edgcumbe, and in 1915 appeared in the Blakeslee Sale at New York, but its present whereabouts are unknown.[51]

Mary was a woman of considerable intelligence, whose character showed marked similarities to that of Sir Joshua. She had a good deal of his idealism and ambition; she was persevering, determined, clear-headed; but she had also inherited a fair share of the family restlessness and could be touchy when she was crossed. Sir Joshua knew what he was doing when he urged Offy not to tell her sister that he had given her the choice of a ring or a bracelet. With the style, the manners and the lively conversation that made her an admirable hostess, Mary also preserved, it appears, a certain cool and calculating detachment.

The issues before her were plain. It was obvious, as the 'seventies advanced, that Sir Joshua was becoming increasingly exasperated by his sister Fanny and that her days at 47 Leicester Fields were numbered. It was equally clear that Reynolds was unlikely to marry, that he needed someone to look after him, and that the new housekeeper might well become heiress to a considerable fortune. Without in any way depreciating Mary's natural affection for her uncle—she seems indeed to have been devoted to him —it must be recorded that all these surmises were fulfilled in the event. On Sir Joshua's death, Mary became a wealthy woman. In the same year that she received her inheritance, when she was forty-one, she married a hard-drinking, hard-riding Irish peer, the fifth Earl of Inchiquin and first Marquess of Thomond, who was then a widower of nearly seventy.

It would be unchivalrous to draw conclusions, and certainly Mary was fond of the old nobleman whom she called in her will "my ever honor'd dear lamented Husband". But, equally certainly, this was not a romantic love-match. Was there ever a time when, like her less complicated sister Offy, she might have married for love? It appears that there was, for she had a number of admirers including Dr Charles Blagden, the Secretary of the Royal Society:[52] the tragic story of another suitor, still partly shrouded in mystery, makes one of the most curious episodes in the life of Sir Joshua. We might call it the Tale of the Two Gentlemen.

6

Few who admire Reynolds' considerably restored but remarkably life-like portrait of the "Two Gentlemen" (Plate XI) will know much of the extraordinary story that lies behind it. They see a couple of apparently blithe, gifted, amusing young sparks in their twenties—George Huddesford and John Bampfylde. The elder of the two, Huddesford, might be thought something of a cynic—he was a Wykehamist and is showing Bampfylde a print of Reynolds' portrait of the Master of Winchester, Joseph Warton, probably with appropriate comments. Bampfylde looks moodier and more thoughtful; he accepts the print with one hand; with the other he seems to be holding a musical instrument.

Reynolds assessed them both from personal experience, though without the knowledge that he and Bampfylde were about to be confronted in tragic circumstances. He knew Huddesford the better of the two. Huddesford was a wit and satirist, an "eternal undergraduate", the son of the President of Trinity College, Oxford, and himself a former scholar of Winchester and Fellow of New College. He gave up his Fellowship on making an early marriage and spent a few casual years as a pupil of Sir Joshua, exhibiting some pictures at the Academy. In later life he took holy orders, in what spirit can only be conjectured, and retired to a Warwickshire vicarage; but this lies outside the story.

Huddesford's intimacy with Sir Joshua had encouraged him to adopt a somewhat presuming and over-familiar attitude towards his master, which Fanny Burney implies that Reynolds may have found a trifle embarrassing. His satire *Warley*, dedicated to Reynolds as "the first ARTIST in Europe", was published in the autumn of 1778 and disturbed Miss Burney by referring to her as "dear little Burney". She described an awkward passage of conversation at a dinner-party of Sir Joshua's in January, 1779:

"Pray, Sir Joshua," asked Lord Palmerston, "what is this *Warley* that is just come out?"

"Why, I don't know," answered he; "but the reviewers, my lord, speak very well of it."

Mrs Cholmondeley.—Who wrote it?

Sir Joshua.—Mr Huddisford.

Mrs Chol.—O! I don't like it at all, then! Huddisford! What a name!

Sir Joshua attempted a kind of vindication of him: but Lord Palmerston said, drily:

"I think, Sir Joshua, it is dedicated to you."

"Yes, my lord," answered he.

"Oh, your servant! Is it so?" cried Mrs Cholmondeley; "then you need say no more!"

Sir Joshua laughed, and the subject to my great relief, was dropped. . . .[53]

In *Warley* Huddesford flatters Reynolds—and also Sir William Chambers—with a praise that verges on mockery:

May the Produce of Reynolds's Pencil divine,
Be forgotten when Phoebus no longer shall shine! . . .
May wine, brandy, and beer, be his constant potation,
'Till, like Caesar, exciting the world's admiration,
Too great for a country of Prejudice grown,
Some Cassius supplants him or—Conjuror Hone.

154

XI. REV. GEORGE HUDDESFORD and J. C. W. BAMPFYLDE. 1779
$(49\frac{1}{4}'' \times 39\frac{1}{4}'')$

He is even forward in inviting himself to dinner:

> Oh Reynolds, afford to thy Poet some soup,
> Who for thine entertainment has painted this Groupe!
> A drudge to the Muse she has made me look thinner,
> Send a card, my good Sir, and invite me to dinner;
> I'm quite disengaged—you'll not find one in ten,
> Such a Dabster at cutting and coming again;
> Few can beat me, or else I am strangely mistaken,
> At Westphalia Ham, or fat Gammon of Bacon. . . .

Such was Huddesford, a light, frivolous, not untalented youth, tolerated perhaps for his charm. Bampfylde, by contrast, impressed his seniors—notably Gainsborough's friend William Jackson, the Exeter musician—as a natural genius. Born in 1754, the younger son of Sir Richard Bampfylde, he came of an ancient Devonshire family and went up to Cambridge. Jackson knew him when he was living in a farmhouse at Chudleigh, and used to walk over to see Jackson at Exeter early in the morning "with a pocket full of music or poems, to know how he liked them". "Poor fellow," said Jackson, "there did not live a purer creature." Though untutored in music, he had a remarkable gift for improvisation at the harpsichord, and Southey, perhaps generously, has called the few unpretending poems he has left us "some of the most original in our language".[54] But when Bampfylde moved to London, "a change came o'er the spirit of the dream". Introduced to Reynolds' household, either through his sister-in-law Lady Bampfylde, whom Reynolds painted in 1777, or through Huddesford, he fell hopelessly in love with Mary Palmer.

That Mary was at first attracted to this handsome young poet seems probable—she was herself artistic, sensitive, and played a harpsichord which Reynolds bought for her and had tuned by Broadwood's.[55] She was flattered no doubt by the dedication of his "Sixteen Sonnets", "printed by J. Millidge" in 1778: "To Miss Palmer, These Sonnets, which have been honored with her Approbation, Are dedicated By Her Very Sincere And devoted humble servant, JOHN BAMPFYLDE." The poet's despairing passion is evident in his "Stanzas to a Lady":

> In vain from clime to clime I stray
> To chase thy beauteous form away,
> And banish every care;

155

In vain to quit thy charms I try,
Since every thought creates a sigh,
And every wish a tear.

What exactly happened we can only guess. Bampfylde had
arrived on the scene at almost the precise moment when Mary
Palmer was being asked to cast in her lot with Sir Joshua; so that
it is most unlikely that his suit, however desirable, would have
found any support from that quarter. In fact, there is a suggestion
that he became undesirably dissipated—though whether before
or after his disappointment is not clear. He sat to Sir Joshua on
January 28 and February 8, 1779, probably for the completion of
the double-portrait which had been begun some time before and
was commissioned by Huddesford. This was perhaps the last time
he entered Sir Joshua's house. Mary gave him an irrevocable No,
and, as he showed signs of becoming a nuisance, Reynolds instructed his footman not to admit him.

Bampfylde, angry and deranged, thereupon broke some of Sir
Joshua's windows and was arrested.[56] There had lately been an
outbreak of window-smashing in the neighbourhood, to cele-
brate the acquittal of Reynolds' old friend Keppel at his court-
martial, so that this must have seemed to Bampfylde the obvious
thing to do. Like another poet, the sixteenth-century Earl of
Surrey, who broke London windows by shooting at them with
his cross-bow, he might have protested that his aim was to "wake
the sluggards" to repentance and a sense of sin.

On the strength of Southey's recollections of a conversation
with William Jackson, it has hitherto been stated that Bampfylde
was sent to Newgate, which would have seemed a savage punish-
ment for the desperate young man—and little to Sir Joshua's
credit. This is mistaken. At the most, Bampfylde can have spent
only one night in a cell. After working through a dusty bundle of
recognizances at the Middlesex County Record Office, I am able
to say that he came before the local magistrate, where he was
bailed out and bound over to appear at Quarter Sessions.

The recognizance, headed "Westminst. to wit", shows that
"John Bampfylde of Leicesterfield St Martin in the fields Acknowledges himself to be indebted to our Sovereign Lord the King, in
the Sum of £20", and that his friends "George Huddesford of

Kew in the County of Surry" and "Josiah Millidge of Maiden
Lane St Paul Covent Garden Printer"—Bampfylde's publisher—
loyally pledged themselves for £10 each, "Upon Condition
that the said John Bampfylde do personally appear at the next
General Quarter Sessions of the Peace, to be held for the said
City and Liberty, at Guildhall, in King-street, Westminster, then
and there to answer what shall be objected against him by S^r
Joshua Reynolds Knt and in the mean time to be upon his good
behaviour towards our Sovereign Lord the King and all his Subjects, especially towards the said Sr Joshua Reynolds. And not to
depart the Court without leave. Then this Recognizance to be
void, else to remain in full force. Taken and acknowledged the
6th day of March 1779 Before GEO: REED." [57]*

The case was dropped and does not appear among the subsequent indictments. Jackson discovered Bampfylde (who had
apparently been staying hitherto in close proximity to Reynolds'
house) living in poverty in King Street, Holborn, and saw him
established in decent lodgings with an allowance from his mother.
But the shock of his disappointment had a lasting effect on his
mind. Bampfylde became insane and remained so for nearly
twenty years. He recovered his senses only when he was in the
grip of consumption, from which he died in about 1796.

The happy picture of the "Two Gentlemen" is therefore
shadowed by tragedy. Broken romance, broken windows, broken
mind. Was Bampfylde's rustic innocence corrupted by Huddesford? Was the painter who immortalized him in any way to
blame for the blighting of his life? There is no evidence of this,
or that Mary Palmer made anything but a free choice. But she
may sometimes have played reflectively at her harpsichord, or
turned thoughtfully to the dedication of a book of sonnets.

* See Appendix C.

X

King's Principal Portrait Painter

I

A BIOGRAPHER has the privilege and the responsibility of remembering, as Carlyle said, that his subject "did live and look in one way or the other, and a whole world was living and looking along with him". It is this, Carlyle realized, which distinguishes "the poorest historical Fact from all Fiction whatsoever". There would be danger in isolating the personal and domestic side of Sir Joshua if we thought of him in consequence as continually bowing over the hands of Miss Kauffmann or Miss Burney, or patting favourite children on the head, or playing the heavy uncle in a Molière comedy. The truth is that Reynolds' painting and his professional social activity left him very little private life. Both philosophically and artistically, he cultivated a golden mean; and to his multitude of social acquaintances he was invariably tolerant and benign. It is not surprising that his own household should have been aware of a different Sir Joshua, who valued what little leisure he could find, and when the nice balance of compromise was disturbed and ordered progress was threatened, could lose his temper. If poor Bampfylde had broken Johnson's windows, it is possible that the Doctor might have appeared at his door, as on one important occasion, in his shirt, with a poker in his hand, and exclaimed: "What, is it you, you dogs! I'll have a frisk with you." Sir Joshua could not have done that; but then few men have had Dr Johnson's largeness of heart.

Reynolds was better adapted to meet public rather than private challenges. From 1774 onwards, when Gainsborough came from Bath to London and settled at Schomberg House, Sir Joshua continually exerted himself to demonstrate his variety and learning in portraiture. Gainsborough's presence in London provided an undoubted stimulus, but it is important to realize that he and Reynolds were never in their lifetimes quite the close rivals that we tend to assume they were. Long before Gainsborough came to London, Reynolds had established himself as the chosen painter of both Whig and Tory society, to an extent that Gainsborough never attained.

Gainsborough scorned studio assistance; his colours have lasted better than Reynolds'. Yet an impartial study of a series of portraits by both these great artists suggests that the confidence of Reynolds' patrons was not misplaced, and that his considered intellectual, literary approach was more likely to produce a satisfying likeness, better calculated to show the sitter "in the round", than Gainsborough's sparkling poetry. Apart from a few masterpieces, the slim silvery figures of Gainsborough, so delightful to the eye, repeat themselves throughout our picture galleries in a way that makes us doubt their value as assessments of individual character. It is not simply a contrast between Sense and Sensibility, for Reynolds was not devoid of sensibility, but rather that Gainsborough lacked the temperament, training and detachment for formal portraiture. The distinction was felt by a contemporary such as Lady Spencer who told her husband that she could not bear "the idea of anybody having a picture by Sir Joshua of you beside myself", whereas she considered "a daub by Gainsborough would do full well" for his college.[1]

By a "daub" Lady Spencer probably meant something akin to what we would now call an "impressionist sketch", and it was, indeed, in his ethereal Watteau-ish "fancy pictures" and landscapes that Gainsborough's genius found its truest expression. (Reynolds allowed himself the same spontaneous freedom in his dashing sketch of Georgiana, Duchess of Devonshire at Chatsworth; but it is exceptional in his work.) Gay, irresponsible Bohemian that he was, Gainsborough was born to be an English Watteau or an earlier Constable, and we may even regret that he was compelled to earn his living by portrait-painting. He could not give us, as Reynolds did, the authoritative likenesses of the great men of his time; but he gave us what may be still more precious, a haunting lyric poetry. And it is to Reynolds' lasting honour that he left, in his Fourteenth Discourse, an outstandingly generous and perceptive appreciation of Gainsborough's genius. Therein lies the "transcendent merit" of Sir Joshua, as Caleb Whitefoord described it in some lines written at the Bedford Coffee House, Covent Garden, in 1777:

Reynolds th' *Apelles* of our modern Days,
Shines forth superior, tho' in different ways;
Has of *two* Arts attain'd the laurel'd Heights;
Paints with a Pen, and with a Pencil Writes![2]

The years between 1774 and 1780 were rich in varied achievement. They saw the painting of the Crewe and Buccleuch
children; a gesture towards piety with the child-studies of St John
Baptist and the Infant Samuel; the oriental portraits of Wang-y-
Tong and Omai; the famous groups of the Dilettanti Society; the
graceful though derivative allegorical figure of "Theory" for the
ceiling of the Royal Academy at Somerset House, which was
Reynolds' best effort of that kind; and two portraits of his old
friend, Keppel, grown portly now—to mark his triumph at his
trumpery court-martial, and to match (with their sea backgrounds) the famous picture that had made Reynolds' reputation
twenty-five years earlier. But the outstanding work of this period
is undoubtedly the huge group of "The Family of the Duke of
Marlborough" at Blenheim (Plate XIII)—completed in 1777 and
the fruit of several visits there—in which Reynolds for the first
time applied the grand style of history painting to portraiture with
full success. Professor Waterhouse has called this "the most monu-
mental achievement of British portraiture", and, remembering
Sir Joshua's admiration of Vanbrugh, we may imagine him as
summoning all his powers to produce a picture worthy of Vanbrugh's setting. The rough sketch at the Tate Gallery suggests that
he must almost have despaired at the difficulties involved in composing this intricate group of eight figures (not to mention the
three dogs); and the completed canvas, in which the figures are
ordered with such masterly skill, testifies to intense thought and
labour.

After Reynolds' return to London from his final visit to Blenheim in September, 1777, he wrote with his own hand a letter[3] to
a prospective client, Daniel Daulby, which is valuable as giving an
exact account of his methods at this time. His prices had changed
very little since 1764—thirty-five guineas for a head, "As far as
the Knees seventy—and for a whole-length one hundred and
fifty." (He raised them only once more, in 1782, to fifty guineas
for a head, a hundred for a half-length and two hundred for a
whole length.[4]) As to the ordeal that would have confronted Mr

Daulby—though in fact it appears that he never went through it —Sir Joshua was at pains to make it all as easy as possible: "It requires in general three sittings about an hour and half each time but if the sitter chooses it the face could be begun and finished in one day", and he added, "it is divided into seperate times for the convenience and ease of the person who sits, when the face is finished the rest is done without troubling the sitter." He did not hold out to his prospective client much chance of being able to acquire one of his history or "fancy" pictures: "When I paint any picture of invention it is allways engaged before it is half finished."

One is struck by the extent to which he still exercised personal control over his correspondence and business affairs—noting the address of a model, for instance, on the fly-leaf of his notebook for 1779: "Mrs Ruth Child's Rents Tothill Street Westminster to send a penny post letter when I want her for A neck"; or forwarding the claims of young artists, which he was always ready to do, as in the following letter to Warren Hastings recommending Thomas Hickey:

London July 6 1780

Sir

At the distance of so many years, and the very small pretensions I have of claiming the honour of being known to you, tho it might prevent me from troubling you on other subjects, yet in the present instance I should hope you would think me excusable.

Mr Hickey who is the bearer of this, is a very ingenious young Painter who from seeing the success that has attended others who, with certainly not higher pretensions, have made fortunes by their profession in India; wishes to make a trial of his own abilities. It was natural to have recourse to the President of the Academy for recommendation and it would have been as unnatural in him to refuse giving every assistance to a brother Artist. I only mean this as an apology for the liberty I have now taken of recommending any person, however deserving they may be of your Excellency's protection.

I am with the greatest respect,
your most humble
and obedient Servant
JOSHUA REYNOLDS.[5]

Reynolds had known the Governor-General since he had sat to him in 1766; Hastings had been kind to his nephew William

Johnson, and Reynolds did not shun Hastings' company when he returned to England in 1785, to face the charges of impeachment for corruption and cruelty that were brought against him. But his friends Burke and Sheridan led the attack, and Sir Joshua must have suffered yet again for being "all things to all men". On the first day of the trial, Fanny Burney "perceived Sir Joshua Reynolds in the midst of the Committee", i.e. of the managers of the impeachment. "He, at the same moment, saw me also, and not only bowed, but smiled and nodded with his usual good-humour and intimacy, making at the same time a sign to his ear, by which I understood he had no trumpet, whether he had forgotten or lost it I know not. . . ." [6] Miss Burney's enthusiasm for Burke waned as she heard the vehement language with which he castigated Hastings. The trial lasted so long that Reynolds never saw the end of it or knew that Hastings was acquitted, which would probably have pleased him. His sitters, like a doctor's patients, became his friends; when they differed among themselves—as often happened, considering the impartiality with which he painted most of the notable men of his time—he was inclined to mislay his ear-trumpet and, as Goldsmith put it, to be "hard of hearing". Fanny Burney's account of him at the opening of Hastings' trial is not only amusing; it is also of some psychological interest. Was he, perhaps subconsciously, using his deafness to isolate himself from such disagreeable proceedings?

Towards the close of the 'seventies, Reynolds' chief preoccupation was with the great west window of New College Chapel, Oxford—"The Window", as it figures in his notebooks—a gallant but undeniable failure, although Thomas Warton praised it in a poem. His letters of 1777–8 to the Warden of New College show him embracing the project with his usual enthusiasm, agitating first to be allowed one large window instead of several smaller ones, and again to be allowed "a principal predominant space in the Centre".[7] This he proposed to fill with "Christ in the Manger, on the Principle that Correggio has done it in the famous Picture called the Notte, making all the light proceed from Christ, these tricks of the art, as they may be called, seem to be more properly adapted to Glass painting than any other kind. This middle space will be filled with the Virgin, Christ, Joseph, and Angels, the two smaller spaces on each side I shall fill with the shepherds coming to

Worship, and the seven divisions below filled with the figures of Faith Hope Charity and the four Cardinal Virtues, which will make a proper Rustic Base or foundation for the support of the Christian Religion."

Reynolds tinkered during several years with the oil painting of the Nativity, which was used for the window and for which Mrs Sheridan sat as the Virgin. It proved beyond his powers and was never a success, though the Duke of Rutland paid £1,200 for it. The picture was already in poor condition by the time it reached the Duke, and Reynolds tried to reassure him: "In regard to the Nativity, the falling off of the colour must be occasioned by the shaking in the carriage, but as it is now in a state of rest, it will remain as it is for ever." [8] Soon after Reynolds' death, Marchi was called to Belvoir Castle to restore it. He could not line the picture because it was painted on "a floor Cloth Canvass doubled" but he infused "a preparation of paste through the cracks" and thought that it would stay sound for forty years—a supposition that remains unproved because it was destroyed by fire in 1816. [9] The copy of the painting for the window, by Thomas Jervais, the glass-painter, served only to accentuate its weaknesses, and Reynolds was bitterly disappointed in the failure of his "tricks of the art", his dramatic effect of light and shade, which had been calculated rather for a painting on canvas than on transparent glass. The upper part of the window varies in colours from red, yellow and pink to a dark and muddy brown, the latter predominating (even in the sky) and giving the impression of a considerable mess, as of dirty paint-water.

That Sir Joshua enjoyed working on the window is probable. He may have thought of the pleasure that it would have given his father to see him so employed. He introduced portraits of Jervais, who must certainly bear a share of the blame, and himself as the shepherds, contriving to show himself turning his head rather slyly to look back into the chapel, projecting himself for once into a place of worship. The lower lights, for which Offy Palmer and Betsey Johnson were employed as models, are more austere, less ambitious, and in the circumstances more effective. The window is now confronted by Epstein's "Lazarus", which Reynolds might have thought the unkindest cut of all.

Reynolds had hoped to be allowed to paint the King and Queen when he first became President of the Royal Academy, but it appears that he never did so and that the first, and last, time they ever sat for him was in 1779, for the two portraits which were exhibited in the Academy in 1780 and which are now at Burlington House. The portraits are adequate but not outstanding; they accurately reflect the uneasy relationship which persisted between Their Majesties and Sir Joshua. Although George III was painted by several other artists, and although Sir Joshua conducted him through the Academy exhibition year by year with impeccable courtesy, the King's recognition of the President remained formal and grudging.

This may have been partly due to Reynolds' political attitude, but it was probably still more, as Northcote suggested, because of Reynolds' native dignity and independence, "because he was a great man and a philosopher". Although his manners were unfailingly gracious, he could not kow-tow to anyone; he would never have made a courtier. Northcote may have been right when he said: "The King and Queen could not endure the presence of him; he was poison to their sight. . . . Do not suppose he was ignorant of the value of Royal favour. No—Reynolds had a thorough knowledge of the world. He would gladly have possessed it but the price would have cost him too much." [10] As it was, he was liable to say the wrong thing. When the King met him out walking at Richmond and enquired whether it was true that he was to be Mayor of Plympton, Sir Joshua replied in the affirmative, and declared that the honour had given him more pleasure than any other he had received in his life. Then he remembered his knighthood and added hastily: "Except that which your Majesty was graciously pleased to confer upon me."

The belated royal portraits of 1780 helped to ensure that, if Allan Ramsay died, Reynolds would at least be considered for the post of King's Principal Portrait Painter. Although Ramsay's work was unequal, and has been overshadowed by Reynolds' larger achievement, he deserves to be remembered as an interpreter of character, and during Reynolds' early years in London Ramsay's competition and example had undoubtedly proved stimulating. But for many years Ramsay had painted nothing; lacking Sir Joshua's persistence, he was content to supervise the repetition of the royal portraits by his assistants.

Another Court favourite had also lost standing with the years. Rumours had been flying concerning Sir William Chambers. He remained a dominating figure at the Royal Academy, and held forth with vast assurance on its financial affairs; yet his own handling of money matters was now beginning to inspire less confidence. 1780 was the year that saw the completion of Chambers' Somerset House; the year in which the Academy moved to its new apartments there, facing the Strand; and the year in which Reynolds painted his masterly but equivocal portrait of the Treasurer (Plate X*b*). In May, 1780, while his portrait was on view at the Academy exhibition, Chambers suddenly disappeared. It was rumoured that he had misappropriated the funds allowed him for Somerset House and had fled the country. But on May 24 Horace Walpole wrote to William Mason: "The story of Sir William Chambers is odd. He is certainly in Flanders but there is no embezzlement; he has money in his banker's hands, writes to his family, and sends orders to his workmen at Somerset House. . . ." Four days later he added: "Sir William Chambers has reappeared and been at the Royal Academy. His absence is now said to have been an équipée of gallantry." The episode remains mysterious. It may be that Chambers had succumbed to his passions, which we have already seen him analysing with exactitude. The affair did no good service to his reputation, though when the House of Commons enquired into charges of "jobbery" over Somerset House, Chambers was absolved.[11]

It is not surprising that William Mason should have wished to hear news of Chambers, for he was the author of *An Heroic Epistle* to Chambers, a sharply satirical attack on his *Dissertation on Oriental Gardening* which had exposed Sir William to popular ridicule. The fact that Mason was a close friend of Reynolds is another reason for conjecturing that Sir Joshua's relations with Chambers had not improved since the days when they had been in frequent discussion over his house at Richmond.

3

"King at the Academy at ten," runs Sir Joshua's entry in his notebook for April 28, 1780. It was an occasion for pride: he was not only able to show the King the handsome new rooms at Somerset House but also to point out his Majesty's own picture and Queen Charlotte's, which with Reynolds' portraits of Lady Worsley, now at Harewood House, and of Gibbon, Chambers and the Duchess of Devonshire were among the attractions of an exhibition which included six splendid landscapes by Gainsborough and works by Zoffany, Wilson and Fuseli. The exhibition-room had the benefit of a sky-light on the top floor of Somerset House. There the annual dinner was held for ninety people, instead of the sixty-four of the year before. Dr Johnson sat opposite the Archbishop of York and was well satisfied. The Academy received unwonted publicity; visitors climbed the staircase eagerly; more than £3,000 was taken at the door.

Sir Joshua had reason to be pleased with such striking proof that the Academy was now prosperously established. But he did not rest on his laurels and was as busy as ever in May, and even during the No-Popery riots led by Lord George Gordon in June, when Savile House in Leicester Square was gutted and the mob armed themselves from its iron railings; when night was turned into day by the great fires that blazed throughout London. Sir Joshua was anxious for the safety of his friends among the Opposition supporters of the Roman Catholic Relief Bill—Sir George Savile's house was lost; Burke's was saved by its garrison of soldiers. The King acted promptly in ordering the troops to disperse the rioters without the formality of reading the Riot Act. By so doing he preserved many public buildings, including Somerset House where Reynolds spent the morning of June 7 in some trepidation.

During the uncertainty and confusion, his sittings continued. That they were fruitful and propitious, we know from the forceful portrait of Lord Richard Cavendish and the charming group of the three Ladies Waldegrave seated round their work-table carding their silk, both of which appeared in the Academy exhibition of 1781. Amidst the chaos he was painting more safely, too, for these works remain in sound condition. Horace Walpole had commissioned the picture of his beautiful grand-nieces, the Ladies Waldegrave, daughters of the Duchess of Gloucester, and had proposed that they should figure "as the Graces adorning a bust of the Duchess as the Magna Mater". It is significant that Reynolds, who had been happy to present "The Graces adorning a term of Hymen" only six years before, should have rejected Walpole's conception in favour of contemporary costume and a scene of intimate domesticity. This revolt against classicism marked the spirit with which he began the last decade of his life; and one wishes only that it had come earlier.

Sir Joshua's Discourse in December, 1780, was not conspicuously successful, for it concerned sculpture which he knew little about; but he was "fat and well", or so Fanny Burney reported him in 1781, when he painted the sparkling portrait of her father Dr Burney in his crimson robes which is now at the National Portrait Gallery. He saw much of Dr Johnson, and may now have contemplated his supposed picture of Johnson as a portentous baby, one of several playful child-studies done at this time. He was generous to Johnson's unfortunate godson, the painter Mauritius Lowe, and once again received the Doctor's thanks for a "splendid benefaction". "To a hand so liberal in distributing," said Johnson, "I hope nobody will envy the power of acquiring." [12]

But the great event for Sir Joshua in 1781 was his visit to Flanders and Holland in the summer. Though he may have discussed it with Chambers, Sir Joshua's trip was not a prank of gallantry but a serious artistic expedition. His new appreciation of Rubens, in particular, came at a timely moment, enlivening his brush with a sense of drama and enriching the texture of his paint.

Philip Metcalfe, a wealthy brewer about ten years younger than Reynolds, an intimate friend of Johnson and later a Member of Parliament, was Reynolds' companion on this journey: Farington notes Metcalfe's good qualities and his generosity, but mentions that he could be petulant and overbearing.[13] He was clearly very fond of Sir Joshua, who warmly acknowledged his "long and patient attendance, while I was employed in examining the various works which we saw", and added: "Nor is it an inconsiderable advantage to see such works in company with one, who has a general rectitude of taste, and is not a professor of the art." [14] Judging by the long and careful notes taken by Sir Joshua in innumerable churches and galleries during their two months' tour,[15] Metcalfe must have had the patience of Job.

Reynolds made day-to-day entries in his usual sitters' notebook throughout the trip. His jottings in pencil or red crayon—supplemented by entries in ink by another hand—are now very hard to read, and Tom Taylor's free interpretations of them in his biography are often more courageous than probable. Taylor was cavalier also in his treatment of a notebook of the Flemish Tour at the Royal Academy, crossing through many pages with his pen, "which," in the words of Sir Joshua's great-niece Mrs St John, "ought not to have been done".

The pair left London at eight in the morning of July 24, and stayed for two nights at Margate, whence they sailed at four in the afternoon of the 26th. They reached Ostend at midday on the 27th, and, as there were no pictures to be seen there, went straight on to Bruges, arriving at the Hôtel du Commerce at midnight. Reynolds dived into the Cathedral and the Church of Notre Dame the next morning; but they were soon on their way to Ghent. Considering the general failure to appreciate the primitives at this time, Sir Joshua's comment on the Van Eyck "Adoration of the Lamb" in the Cathedral at Ghent may be called enlightened: "It contains a great number of figures in a hard manner, but there is great character of truth and nature in the heads; and the landscape is well coloured."

The travellers stayed one night at Ghent and went on to spend three days at Brussels, where Reynolds received his first clear impression of "the fascinating power of Rubens's pencil" and enjoyed works by Rembrandt and Van Dyck. They saw several private collections, Metcalfe remarking that "Mr Orion was almost the only gentleman who showed his own pictures, that did not pester us by prating about their merit".

The next stop was at Mechlin on August 2—"arrived at 5 at the Stork Inn in the Great Square, no Milk to our Tea", noted Sir Joshua. They hurried on, after seeing more works by Rubens, to Antwerp. Reynolds' impressions of Antwerp were decidedly mixed:

> Saturday August 4. Antwerp—houses—Dirty finery—the Exchange—fine Streets—The polite Bucher* . . .

* Leslie and Taylor: "Banker."

Sunday August 5. Antwerp. No beggars at Antwerp. Stinking streets and all Inns probably. The Horses of Flanders like Rubens, horses nobler stile* than ours.

Monday August 6. Antwerp. The ordinary people very ordinary without one exception.

In his younger days Sir Joshua might have been tempted to a caricature of two dignified gentlemen walking through Antwerp; and it would have required some subtlety to suggest that, while they admired the plan of the beggarless streets and the nobility of the horses, they regretted the smells and the "ordinary" appearance of the natives. Followed by the faithful Metcalfe, Reynolds escaped from the August sunshine into the cool aisles of the Cathedral and the churches. He had probably never entered so many churches since his Italian days. Antwerp provided a rich harvest of works by Rubens and Van Dyck; and in his published account Sir Joshua—with St Paul's always in mind—once again lamented that English painters and sculptors were given so few opportunities to decorate English churches. "How far this circumstance may be the cause that no Protestant country has ever produced a history-painter, may be worthy of consideration. . . . Why religion should not appear pleasing and amiable in its appendages; why the house of God should not appear as well ornamented, and as costly as any private house made for man, no good reason I believe can be assigned."

If Reynolds was a little disappointed with Belgium, he was well pleased with his reception at The Hague, where, he told Burke,[16] "the Greffier has shown us every civility possible—By the attention which has been paid to us by the Greffier, his nephew, and the rest of his family, the attention of the town upon us has been much excited." He compared the place to Bath and appreciated the trees in the squares. "Dutch pictures are a representation of nature," he went on, "just as it is seen in a camera-obscura. After having seen the best of each master, one has no violent desire of seeing any more. They are certainly to be admired, but do not shine much in description. A figure asleep, with another figure tickling his or her nose, which is a common subject with the painters of this school, however admirable their effect, would have no effect in writing." He was impressed by Wouwerman: "Upon the whole,

* Leslie and Taylor: "still."

he is one of the few painters, whose excellence in his way is such as leaves nothing to be wished for."

From the windows of his carriage as it rolled through Holland, Sir Joshua made painterly observations which he transferred to his notebook in red crayon that has become almost illegible—"Milk-pails. Boats through meadow. Trees, but not a trace of its value round houses," we can read; and elsewhere—"cut hedges" and "gravel walk". In printing the diary, Tom Taylor conjectured and emended imaginatively. Writing to Burke, Reynolds described the length and straightness of the roads, the double rows of trees "which, in the perspective, finish in a point", the dykes, and, of course, the canals which made Amsterdam "more like Venice than any other place I ever saw". On the fly-leaf of his notebook Reynolds copied two sentences that read like examples from a conversational phrase-book: "I better like Street as Canal", and "I will make the pleasure to wait on you."

The latter must have been the sentence most in demand, for in each town that he visited Reynolds took pains to search out the best private collections. He spent a week at The Hague and another week at Amsterdam, during which he went for a day's excursion in North Holland. He told Burke that the village of Brock "appeared rather like an enchanted village, such as we read of in the Arabian tales;—not a person to be seen, except a servant here and there. The houses are very low, with a door towards the street, which is not used, and never has been used, except when they go out of it to be married, after which it is again shut up. The streets, if they may be so called, for carriages cannot enter them, are sanded with fine ink-sand; the houses painted from top to bottom, green, red, and all sorts of colours. The little gardens, with little fountains and flower-knots, as neat as possible; and trees cut into all kinds of shapes."

Sir Joshua's vitality, his perpetual curiosity, his undimmed enthusiasm for pictures shine through the records of this continental tour. Perhaps he transmitted some of this zest to later Presidents of the Royal Academy, who have in their turn impressed it on television audiences. At Dusseldorf he found a man after his own heart in Lambert Kraye, the "Resident of the Academy", as he described him. On Thursday, August 30, he noted:

Mr Krahe breakfasted & dined with us—repeated visit to the Gallery with him. Even. Attend him to the Academy—presented them with my discourses—offer me a diploma of their Academy.

N.B. A student may lodge & board for £15, Visit the Gallery gratis, copy the best Pictures & attend the Academy; & at leaving it present a book to the Library.

All this pleased the teacher in Sir Joshua, and he wrote the same day to Burke: "We are very well contented with our visit to Dusseldorp. Rubens reigns here and revels. His pictures of the Fallen Angels, and the Last Judgment, give a higher idea of his genius than any other of his works."

Returning, he passed through Cologne, where he had nothing to say about the Cathedral and was disappointed in Rubens' "St Peter"—"We went from Dusseldorp to Cologne on purpose to see it; but it by no means recompensed us for our journey." Through Aix and Spa, Reynolds came to Liège, and so back to Brussels, Ghent and Ostend. On September 14 the stucco terraces and new-fangled bathing-machines of Margate told him that his journey was over.

4

In the book, now at the Royal Academy, which Reynolds filled with descriptions of the pictures seen during his Flemish tour, the following note occurs: "Rubens's Character. No man understood the language of the painter better than Rubens, he knew it grammatically and was always sure of his hand." This reflection was a starting-point for the sustained eulogy of Rubens which concludes Reynolds' account of his journey as published by Malone in the collected Works. He was aware of his defects—his women "seldom, if ever, possess any degree of elegance: the same may be said of his young men and children: his old men have that sort of dignity which a bushy beard will confer; but he never possessed a poetical conception of character". On the other hand, he recognized that Rubens' pictures had "that peculiar property always attendant on genius, to attract attention, and enforce admiration in spite of all their faults"; he emphasized "the striking brilliancy of his colours, and their lively opposition to each other, the flowing liberty and freedom of his outline, the animated pencil [i.e. brush] with which every object is touched——"

It was largely from Rubens that Reynolds derived the new and lively dramatic sense which characterizes so many of the paintings of his last period. Professor Waterhouse has pointed the contrast between the serenity of the portrait of Lady Spencer and her daughter at Althorp of 1761 (Plate VIa) and the gay vivacity with which that same grave little girl, now a grown woman— Georgiana, Duchess of Devonshire—plays with her own daughter in the famous picture at Chatsworth of 1786 (Plate XVb). Both are masterpieces of intimate domestic portraiture, but the first reflects the piety of an Italian Madonna, the second breathes the gaiety of the baroque. "Georgiana Duchess" was the link between different worlds, which only a great master with untiring ambition could have learned to span with such consummate success.

At the close of the year 1781, Reynolds was re-painting his portrait of Offy Palmer (Plate XIIa) and painting as its companion a new portrait of her husband, R. L. Gwatkin, both of which are still in the family collection. The early months of 1782 saw him occupied with his portraits of William Beckford, the author of *Vathek*, and of young "Beau" Brummell ("Master Brommell" in the notebook) and his brother, now at Ken Wood. But he was as busy with his pen as with his brush, and in March, 1782, completed his notes for his friend William Mason's translation of Du Fresnoy's Latin poem on "The Art of Painting".

The same month was cheerful for Sir Joshua in a political sense. The surrender of Cornwallis at Yorktown had made the fall of Lord North's Tory government inevitable, and the Whigs under Rockingham came back for a brief taste of power after many years. Burke's appointment as a Privy Councillor and as Paymaster-General with a salary of £4,000 a year must have been most welcome news in Leicester Fields. His handsome son Richard became his Deputy and followed his father in the sitters' chair. More than three-quarters of Rockingham's cabinet are known to us from their portraits by Reynolds, the majority being his personal friends—notably Keppel, who now became Viscount Keppel and First Lord of the Admiralty, and John Dunning, who shortly before his death became Lord Ashburton and Chancellor of the Duchy of Lancaster. Reynolds celebrated Judge Dunning's

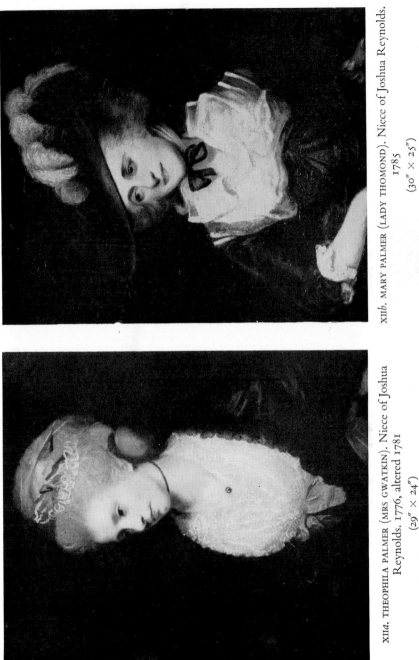

XIIa. THEOPHILA PALMER (MRS GWATKIN). Niece of Joshua Reynolds. 1776, altered 1781
(29″ × 24″)

XIIb. MARY PALMER (LADY THOMOND). Niece of Joshua Reynolds. 1785
(30″ × 25″)

elevation with an unusually attractive conversation-piece, now at the Tate Gallery, in which the Judge, heavy and powerful, faces his sister—whose sympathetic smile is mingled with a touch of awe—across a table holding Sir Joshua's inkstand and before curtains of sealing-wax red.

The Duke of Rutland was appointed Viceroy of Ireland by Rockingham, and Sir Joshua continued to enrich his ill-fated collection. The Duchess sat for him in October and he accepted a commission to paint a posthumous portrait of his gallant brother Lord Robert Manners, who died of wounds received in Rodney's victory over the French in May. The notebook for October 14 shows him accumulating data:

> Lord Robert
> Frock uniform under
>   three years
> Buttonholes
>   embroiderd
>   two & two
> leaning on a Cane
> a sea View
> The hair more
>   dishevelt
>   little powder
>   large Half Length
> The belt.

As he saw his old friends becoming peers of the realm—his fellow-Devonian John Parker of Saltram became Lord Boringdon in 1784—Sir Joshua might have been excused for reflecting that Lord Plympton had yet to be named. Given a prolonged Whig ascendancy, the day-dream might have been turned into reality. Yet one would not have wished to be robbed of "Sir Joshua". It was left to Lord Leighton, P.R.A., to show that the thing could be done.

Rockingham's early death spelled disaster for the Whigs, though Burke returned to his office in the uneasy coalition of Fox and North. The exultations and agonies of 1782 may have left their mark upon Sir Joshua. His second paralytic stroke, already referred to, interrupted sittings to Gainsborough in November. There are many blank pages of the notebook in that month and an appointment for his doctor Sir George Baker soon afterwards. "Your country has been in danger of losing one of its brightest ornaments," wrote Johnson, "and I of losing one of my oldest and kindest friends." But he hoped that Sir Joshua would still live long, "for the honour of the nation", and that he would have "more enjoyment of your elegance, your intelligence, and your benevolence".[17]

Nature had already set a term to that enjoyment, for Dr Johnson himself was failing. Another old friend was removed in January, 1783, G. M. Moser, the first Keeper of the Academy—a man who had no enemies. Sir Joshua wrote his obituary for the *Public Advertiser* of January 30, commemorating his "sincere and ardent piety" and his diligence as a teacher. "By the propriety of his conduct he united the love and respect of his students; he kept order in the Academy, and made himself respected without the austerity or importance of office; all noise and tumult immediately ceased on his appearance. . . ." *

His illness of the previous year affected Sir Joshua's showing in the Academy exhibition of 1783, where he was overshadowed by Gainsborough. But throughout 1783 he enjoyed social life with undiminished zest. The Club flourished, with Fox, Burke and Johnson in frequent attendance; and Reynolds and Johnson exerted themselves to help each other's protégés. Of these perhaps the most interesting was George Crabbe, the poet, who had been introduced to Reynolds by Burke, and whose poem "The Village" was submitted by Sir Joshua for Dr Johnson's judgement. "If you knew how sparing Dr Johnson dealt out his praises," Reynolds told Crabbe, "you would be very well content with what he says." Boswell read the poem, with Johnson's alterations, to

---

* This was no small achievement. Joseph Farington records in his Journal of December 19, 1795, that Joseph Wilton, a later Keeper, "having mentioned to me that the Students in the Plaister Academy continue to behave very rudely; and that they have a practise of throwing the bread, allowed them by the Academy for rubbing out, at each other, so as to waste so much that the Bill for bread sometime amounts to Sixteen Shillings a week; and this relation of Mr Wilton being corroborated by Mr Richards, I moved that 'in future no bread be allowed the Students'. This was unanimously agreed to.—Mr West said independant of every other consideration it would be productive of much good to the Students to deprive them of the use of bread; as they would be induced to pay more attention to their outlines; and would learn to draw more correct, when they had not the perpetual resource of rubbing out."

Reynolds and Mary Palmer in March, 1783, while they drank tea and the rain drummed down in Leicester Fields.[18]

Another and much more awkward protégé of Burke and Reynolds was James Barry, whose remarkable decorations for the Great Room of the Society of Arts in the Adelphi were first shown to the public on the same day as the opening of the Academy exhibition of 1783, and attracted considerable attention. Reynolds nowhere says what he thought of them, but he did remark to Northcote that he "feared he hated Barry"—such an unusual expression, coming from him, showing how seriously his violent and malignant temper had damaged Barry's public and private career. But it is only just to Barry to remember that he eventually made up his quarrel with Sir Joshua, while his paintings in the Adelphi, which still adorn the room for which they were designed, are a larger and far more impressive exercise in the grand style than anything Reynolds achieved. It is tempting to suppose that Reynolds may have been moved by them to embark on the greatest of his allegorical portraits, that of "Mrs Siddons as The Tragic Muse" (Plate XIV*b*), a replica of which is to be seen at Dulwich though the original is at San Marino, California. Certainly he told a correspondent on May 6, a few days after Barry's exhibition had opened, that his portrait of Mrs Siddons was "just began", and it is ironical that Walpole should have been writing in his Academy catalogue at the same time: "Poor Sir Joshua seems to decline since his illness." [19]

The Mrs Siddons is the masterpiece of Reynolds' last decade, the most famous and successful of all his classical portraits. Yet it cannot be held to redeem and justify Sir Joshua's fanciful classical portraits in general. Mrs Siddons, unlike Lady Sarah Bunbury, was a great actress. It was as natural to show her as Melpomene in her classic robe as it was unnatural to make Lady Sarah sacrifice to the Graces or the daughters of Sir William Montgomery "adorn a term of Hymen". This was indeed almost the only possible subject in which Reynolds could properly have applied a classical allegory to illuminate the professional character of his sitter. Like Barry in the Adelphi paintings, he was using the method for one particular and practical purpose, and it is hard to resist the conclusion that his Mrs Siddons was Reynolds' triumphant reply to Barry's sneers at his allegedly mercenary, unidealistic concern for portraiture. After Reynolds' death, Barry spoke generously in his sixth lecture to the Academy: "His portrait of Mrs Siddons is, both for the ideal and executive, the finest picture of the kind, perhaps, in the world—indeed, it is something more than a portrait; and may serve to give an excellent idea of what an enthusiastic mind is apt to conceive of those pictures of confined history for which Apelles was so celebrated by the ancient writers." In this final reconciliation, Barry seems to have recognized that Reynolds, in his prosperity, had not, after all, lost the idealism which he and Blake were serving in bitterness and poverty.

5

Saddened though he was by Dr Johnson's grave illness, Sir Joshua was working at full pressure, and swept back to pre-eminence in the Academy exhibition of 1784. Gainsborough had withdrawn from this exhibition after a quarrel over the hanging of his works, so that Reynolds found little opposition to his lavish display of sixteen portraits, which included, besides Charles James Fox, three actresses in Mrs Siddons, Fanny Kemble and "Perdita" Robinson.

As it was Gainsborough's ambition to be appointed the King's Principal Portrait Painter, his defection from the Academy exhibition of 1784 may have been ill-timed. Having painted all the Royal Family except the Duke of York, and executed many royal commissions besides, he had the right to be considered for the post; but an open break with the Royal Academy was not a good augury for immediate favours. A few days after Gainsborough had opened a rival exhibition of his own works at Schomberg House, Allan Ramsay died on August 10.

What followed is by no means clear. Henry Bate, the protagonist of Gainsborough in the *Morning Post*, at once urged that he should be appointed to succeed Ramsay: "No artist living has so much originality or so strong a claim as far as genius is concerned, on the Patron of Science." [20] But if Edmond Malone was to be believed, Sir Joshua had already been chosen. According to Malone, Reynolds was appointed on the day following Ramsay's death, August 11, 1784, and this would seem to be confirmed by an entry in the Audit Office Enrolments under date March 10, 1785:

> These are to Certify whom it may Concern that by virtue of a Warrant to me Directed from the Earl of Salisbury Lord Chamberlain of His Majesty's Household, I have Sworn and Admitted Sir Joshua Reynolds Kn: into the Place and Quality of Principal Painter in Ordinary to His Majesty in the room of Allan Ramsay Esqr Deceased To have, hold Exercise and Enjoy the said Place together with all Rights, Profits, Privileges and Advantages thereunto belonging in as full and Ample Manner as the said Allan Ramsay did hold and Enjoy or of Right Ought to have held & enjoyed the same Given under my Hand and Seal this 11th Day of August 1784 In the 24th Year of His Majesty's Reign
>
> GEORGE ANNE COOK
Gentleman Usher Daily Waiter.

In the left-hand margin, beside the phrase "in as full and Ample Manner" are written the words "No Fee".[21]

But in actual fact Reynolds did not succeed Ramsay with anything like the smoothness and speed suggested by this entry. Gainsborough's candidature was, after all, formidable. If George Anne Cook did not deliberately perjure himself, he was perhaps following a legal fiction which gave Reynolds' appointment retrospective force, because an unpublished letter to Burke shows that Sir Joshua had to wait a fortnight for the news:

London Aug 24 1784

Dear Sir

Tho I have but a minute to spare I would not neglect letting you know, (*you* who interest yourself so very sincerely in every thing that relate to me) that I receiv'd a Letter yesterday from the Lord Chamberlain appointing me the Kings principal Painter—I beg my Compliments to Mrs Burk—Miss Palmer sat out this Evening for Devonshire.

Yours sincerely
J. REYNOLDS.[22]

Moreover, Reynolds' notebook for Wednesday, September 1, has an entry—written across two pages, as for a great occasion: "$2\frac{1}{2}$ to attend at the Lord Chamberlains office to be sworn Painter to the King."

Northcote said that Sir Joshua expected the appointment to be offered to him without any solicitation on his part, and that it was only with reluctance that he complied with the demands of etiquette and submitted an application. A letter from Johnson to Reynolds of September 2 throws further light on his state of mind at the time:

> I am glad that a little favour from the court has intercepted your furious purposes. I should not in any case have approved such publick violence of resentment, and should have considered any who encouraged it, as rather seeking sport for themselves, than honour for you. Resentment gratifies him who intended an injury, and pains him unjustly who did not intend it. But all this is now superfluous
> ———[23]

Sir Joshua had obviously been angry. He may even have threatened to resign his presidency of the Academy, feeling that the delay in offering him the royal appointment—coupled with knowledge of the hostility of Sir William Chambers and others—made it impossible for him to continue. He was also annoyed because the salary was so small, having been recently reduced, ironically enough, by Burke himself during his period of office. On September 24 he told the Duke of Rutland: "The place which I have the honour of holding, of the King's principal painter, is a place of not so much profit, and of near equal dignity with His Majesty's rat catcher. The salary is £38 per annum, and for every whole length I am to be paid £50, instead of £200 which I have from everybody else. Your Grace sees that this new honour is not likely to elate me very much." On the following day he assured the Bishop of St Asaph: "The Portraits of their Majesties are not likely to be better done now, than they used to be, I should be ruined if I was to paint them myself." [24]

Even the £38 mentioned here is better than the "No Fee" officially noted at the Public Record Office, which is puzzling. The Royal Kalendar of 1786 shows that by then Sir Joshua's salary had been advanced to £50, which put him slightly ahead of "His Majesty's Rat-Killer", F. Schomberg, who, according to the same source, received in 1782 a salary of £48 3s. 4d.*

* The Royal Kalendars for 1784 and 1785 are missing at the Lord Chamberlain's Office. In 1783 the Kalendar shows that Allan Ramsay was paid £50. In 1843 the offices of Principal Portrait Painter and Painter of History and Portraits were combined in that of Painter in Ordinary and Painter of History and Portraits. The office was then held by Sir George Hayter, but there is no mention of a salary.

The chief advantage of Reynolds' new position, beside the accession of dignity, was that it gave him the right to manufacture all the royal portraits that were required for official residences or as presents for foreign potentates—no small matter in the days before enlarged colour photographs. He may not have driven such a thriving trade in these as his predecessor, but he nevertheless found it profitable. The entries in his price-ledgers[25] suggest a fantastic game of cards reminiscent of Lewis Carroll. In November, 1789, Reynolds had in the Academy five Kings and four Queens, and at his house two Kings and one Queen.

He paid Roth, the drapery-painter, only twenty guineas for copying one of these portraits, so that he must have made £30 out of each of them. When Thomas Lawrence succeeded Reynolds as Principal Portrait Painter, after his death, the stock had been reduced to three Kings and three Queens. Lawrence hoped that he would be able to buy these for twenty guineas each, especially "as Sir Joshua had not touched on any of them" and he had to put in hours of work to make them presentable. But he had not reckoned on the hard business head of Mary Palmer, now Lady Inchiquin, who asked considerably more than this. After some haggling, she agreed to accept 150 guineas for the lot.[26]

Sir Joshua's new appointment did not mean that he received any more commissions from His Majesty than before. George III persisted in thinking him a "coarse" painter and disliked the "red trees" of his autumnal backgrounds. Reynolds as "Principal Painter" had to be content with directing the flow of his Kings and Queens, a traffic appropriate to his gambler's instinct. But he was able to add to his court cards by painting the Knave, in the person of the Prince of Wales. He painted him three times, in 1784, 1785 and 1787. The second of these portraits is the head-and-shoulders of the future Regent now in the National Gallery, in which Sir Joshua hints with some dexterity at a developing talent for mischief and dissipation.

XI

The Friend of Johnson

I

NOTHING stands more to Reynolds' credit than the anxious solicitude that he showed for Dr Johnson in the last year of his life. He had so many social commitments that he cannot be blamed for not accepting Johnson's invitation to join yet another "little evening club which we are establishing in Essex-street, in the Strand",[1] especially as James Barry was to be one of the company, but he kept in frequent touch with his old friend throughout the ups-and-downs of his final illness. Recovered from a stroke, Johnson was now afflicted with dropsy and asthma; twice in 1784 he travelled out of town, to Oxford and to his birthplace Lichfield, in the hope of finding improvement. In the midst of his own trouble, he remained as generous as ever, writing to Reynolds on June 1: "I am ashamed to ask for some relief for a poor man, to whom, I hope, I have given what I can be expected to spare. The man importunes me, and the blow goes round. I am going to try another air on Thursday."[2]

As Johnson and Boswell passed through Leicester Square on the way to Oxford that Thursday, Boswell pointed to Reynolds' house and said, "There lives our friend." "Ay, Sir," said the Doctor, "there lives a very great man."[3]

Johnson was back in London before the end of the month. At Reynolds' on June 27, his spirits seemed to rise when the company went upstairs to the drawing-room after dinner, and for once he talked about art, expressing the hope that the Houghton collection and Sir Aston Lever's collection might be bought for the nation, and touching on a question that has often been argued since—"as the nation was much in want of money, whether it would not be better to take a large price from a foreign state?" (In fact, the Houghton collection was sold to the Empress of Russia a few years later for £40,000.) Then Johnson embarked on a heated discussion with young Richard Burke on the difference between intuition and sagacity, at the end of which he said, "Give me your hand, Sir. You were too tedious, and I was too short." And finally he remarked that "he wished much to go to Italy, and that he dreaded passing the winter in England".

Boswell heard this declaration with secret satisfaction, because he had already consulted Reynolds as to how such an expedition could best be financed, and with his agreement had written to invite the co-operation of Lord Chancellor Thurlow. When Johnson learned of their efforts on his behalf he was deeply touched: "This is taking prodigious pains about a man," he said, and added, "God bless you all, for Jesus Christ's sake." On June 30, Johnson, Reynolds and Boswell dined in Leicester Square to discuss the project. "Both Sir Joshua and I were so sanguine in our expectations," recorded Boswell, "that we expatiated with confidence on the liberal provision which we were sure would be made for him, conjecturing whether munificence would be displayed in one large donation, or in an ample increase of his pension." Johnson was so much encouraged that "Sir Joshua and I endeavoured to flatter his imagination with agreeable prospects of happiness in Italy". The old man was under no illusions, however. "Nay, (said he,) I must not expect much of that; when a man goes to Italy merely to feel how he breathes the air, he can enjoy very little."

As so often before, Reynolds sent Johnson home in his coach. Boswell accompanied him to the entry of Bolt Court and bade him an affectionate farewell in the carriage. Johnson "without looking back, sprung away with a kind of pathetick briskness". It was the last time that Boswell ever saw him, for he had to travel to Scotland soon afterwards.[4]

Reynolds was left to negotiate with Thurlow about the ways and means of Johnson's journey to Italy. There was some delay, and Johnson urged him on September 2: "Write, do write to me now and then; we are now old acquaintance, and perhaps few people have lived so much and so long together, with less cause of complaint on either side." Thurlow appears to have broached the matter to the King without success; instead, he offered to advance Johnson five or six hundred pounds on his own account, which might be considered a mortgage of his pension. This Johnson gratefully declined, telling Reynolds, "I do not despair of supporting an English winter." But he was obviously deeply disappointed at his failure to attract the King's attention. "All is not gold that glitters, as we have often been told," he wrote to Sir Joshua from Lichfield on October 2; "and the adage is verified in your place"—an allusion to Reynolds' niggardly salary as Principal Portrait Painter—"and my favour; but if what happens does not make us richer, we must bid it welcome, if it makes us wiser".[5]

Reynolds was not a prolific letter-writer, but there are probably many business letters of his which have never yet come to light. When he might have been writing to Johnson, for example, he was perhaps composing the letter of August 31, 1784, to Bristol Corporation, discovered among unsorted papers in chambers under the Bristol Exchange: "I have the honour to inform you that Lord Ashburton's picture will be sent to-morrow morning by Wiltshire's wagon, which I hope will arrive safe and meet with the approbation of the Corporation. My fee for that size, which is what we call half-length, is 100 guineas."[6] More amusing was a letter written to the Bishop of St Asaph in September, 1784, in which he retailed the alarm of the highly dignified Mrs Siddons at the thought that she might have been tarred and feathered by "the liberty boys" while playing in Dublin: "It was impossible in the midst of her narration which she made very pathetic, to prevent smiling every now and then when the Words tarring & feathering were repeated with such solemnity as if she thought there were no words in the English language that would excite so much horror, this is certainly very excusable in a person that has been so much frightened at it, but I cannot help smiling this minute at the Idea of Mrs Siddons being Tarred & feathered."[7]

In October Reynolds enjoyed one day of high celebration, St Luke's Day, when he was presented with the freedom of the Painters' Company at their Hall in Little Trinity Lane. His notebook shows that he was to be there at eleven in the morning, but it is probable that he stayed to dine. Two years later, Sir Joshua invited Boswell to accompany him to this dinner, telling him that he would call for him "about two o'clock, the black-guards dine at half an hour after".[8] They were "black-guards", perhaps, because they dined so early and upset his working day.

After his return to London in November, Dr Johnson grew

rapidly worse. The last time that Reynolds saw him was with Bennet Langton on November 29, an interview that he described in the illuminating memoir of Johnson which he wrote for Boswell's benefit:

> In his last minutes he received great comfort from the recollection that he hoped he had endeavoured to promote the cause of virtue. During his last illness, when all hope was at an end, he appeared to be quieter and more resigned. His approaching dissolution was always present to his mind. A few days before he died, Mr Langton and myself only present, he said he had been a great sinner, but he hoped he had given no bad example by his writing nor to his friends; that he had some consolation in reflecting that he had never denied Christ, and repeated the text "whoever denies me", &c. We were both very ready to assure him that we were conscious that we were better and wiser from his life and conversation, and that, so far from denying Christ, he had been in this age his greatest champion.
>
> Sometimes a flash of wit escaped him as if involuntary. He was asked how he liked the new man that was hired to watch by him. "Instead of watching," says he, "he sleeps like a dormouse; and when he helps me to bed he is as awkward as a turnspit dog the first time he is put into the wheel." [9]

Boswell tells us that Johnson made three requests of Sir Joshua in his last days—"To forgive him thirty pounds which he had borrowed of him;—to read the Bible;—and never to use his pencil on a Sunday", and that "Sir Joshua readily acquiesced". The sitters' notebooks show that he did not succeed in keeping the last condition, though according to Dr William Scott, later Lord Stowell, he made a half-hearted attempt.

On December 8, Johnson signed his will, appointing Reynolds, Sir John Hawkins, and Dr Scott as his executors, and on the following day, in a codicil, he left Reynolds "my great French Dictionary by Martiniere, and my own copy of my folio English Dictionary, of the last revision", perhaps in a last belated attempt to reform his spelling.[10] He died peacefully on December 13. Sir Joshua's record of his death is one of the few notebook entries that are not concerned with purely personal affairs: "Dr Johnson dyed at 7 in the afternoon."

2

Dr Johnson was buried in Westminster Abbey a week later. Sir John Hawkins had charge of the funeral arrangements and was criticized for providing no organ or choir music, though it is probable that Johnson himself, who was anyway entirely un-musical, would have approved the simplicity of the service. On December 18, Reynolds wrote to Burke:

Dear Sir
  If I thought this Letter was to be paid for, I really believe it would have stopt my writing, as I have not any thing to say worth two-pence. We can scarce expect you would come to town on purpose to attend the Funeral. If you think of doing Dr Johnsons memory that honour, we have fixed on you as the first Pall Bearer with Mr Fox, the Rest are Lord Palmerstone Mr Windham Gen[1] Paoli & Mr Langton. We meet at ten o'clock on Monday in Bolt Court, by eleven we must set out in order to be at the Abbey by twelve.
  I am just come from Lord Palmerstones Dinner it was composed of the Club only, except Dr Warren who is likewise to be of the Club if it so please his Brother Doctor.
  I am with the greatest respect

Yours
J. REYNOLDS.[11]

Burke attended the funeral and acted as a pall-bearer, as did two others named by Sir Joshua, William Windham and Bennet Langton. The remaining pall-bearers were, however, different; they were Sir Joseph Banks, Sir Charles Bunbury and George Colman, all members of The Club. Sir Joshua and General Paoli were among the mourners.[12]

With the death of Johnson, Reynolds lost the greatest single influence of his adult life. It was primarily an influence that moulded his character and writing, but, though Johnson cared little for painting, it is not far-fetched to suppose that his example indirectly affected Reynolds' artistic career, confirming his pre-dilections as a literary and classical painter, and strengthening his determination to achieve a style in portrait that was consistent with biographical truth. Supposing that he had never met Johnson, it is doubtful whether Reynolds would have stood so high as a public man and as a philosophical critic of the arts. To

184

be long familiar with conversation of Johnson's quality, to have continual access to a great mind "always ready for use", were advantages that left their mark on a spirit already ambitious. Reynolds was aware of Johnson's faults, as he was of his own; but what impressed him most was Johnson's practice "of always on every occasion speaking his best". Alike in his painting and in his Discourses, he adopted that principle as his own.

Those critics of Reynolds who had maintained, mistakenly, that Johnson was responsible for a major part of his Discourses, must have looked forward with a certain malicious glee to observing the effect that Johnson's death would have on them. Reynolds' work on his Discourses had always been continual and progressive. It had been his habit to make changes in the original manuscript, from which he addressed the Academy, before its appearance in print. The Twelfth Discourse was delivered on December 10, 1784, three days before Johnson's death, and at a time when Johnson was obviously unable to give it any revision. One might therefore have expected that fewer alterations would have been made than previously; yet in fact there were more changes than usual. If anything the alterations increased after Dr Johnson's death.

The truth is that Reynolds produced the text of his Discourses alone, by dint of enormous pains, but that before they were delivered and again before they were printed he often referred them to Johnson, while he lived, and sometimes to Burke for their advice on points of style. Burke's help was probably not extensive; Reynolds benefited from Burke's gift of theorizing and from occasional remarks thrown out by him in conversation, but Burke's handwriting nowhere appears on the surviving manuscripts. Johnson's handwriting does, however, appear occasionally, making small grammatical improvements, while there are phrases in the earlier discourses which have a Johnsonian ring. The interpolation of a passage quoting Bacon in the Third Discourse may have been due to Johnson's intervention. Yet all the available evidence tends to show that Johnson's share in the discourses was relatively small, and Burke's still smaller, and that the contentions of Horace Walpole and others to the contrary were entirely unjustified.

After Johnson's death, Reynolds' friend Edmond Malone, the

Shakespeare critic, began to look through the Discourses. He not only scrutinized the new ones as they were composed, but he saw through the press the collected edition of 1797, which had the benefit of Reynolds' last corrections. In their final form, therefore, the Discourses owed as much to Malone as to Johnson or Burke, small textual emendations and corrections of spelling making up the majority of the changes.

As a writer no less than as a painter, Reynolds worked from portfolios of notes or sketches. His folders bore such labels as "Analogy", "Method of Study", "Self", "Colouring", "Discourses not used", "Michael Angelo", "The Advantage of Early Habits". When the time for the delivery of a Discourse drew near—it was usually the beginning of December—he paced up and down his room in the middle of the night, writing and re-writing, continually discarding, and struggling to make his meaning plain.

Since his death the Discourses have proved in fifty editions that Reynolds' labour was not in vain. He evolved a literary style that matched his brushwork in clarity and grace, and he is one of the very few great painters who have expressed themselves as successfully in words as on canvas. A measure of the credit must go to Dr Johnson, who "formed my mind" and "brushed off from it a deal of rubbish". But the determination of his pupil to make the best of himself was the decisive factor. Although the neo-classicism of Reynolds is in many ways uncongenial to modern taste, the developing argument of the Discourses remains of permanent significance. His insistence on painting as a liberal and literary art, his attempt to reconcile the "decorum" of Raphael with the "sublimity"—increasingly stressed in the later Discourses—of Michelangelo, reflects the timeless struggle to combine the sensual and intellectual life of man. Genial and rational himself, Reynolds yet fought against the dark impulses common to mankind—the demon (later erased) that crouched by the pillow of his Cardinal Beaufort, the crude sexuality of his "Snake in the Grass"—so that the lesson of his Discourses is the measure of his own moral example, and of his belief that art must be the mediator between man and nature. It is pleasant to find Johnson reading the Discourses and saying "I think I might as well have said that myself" or "Very well, Master Reynolds; very well, indeed".[13]

3

Without Reynolds, the countless admirers of Johnson in the years since his death would scarcely have known what he looked like. There are, of course, portraits by other artists, Opie, Barry and Northcote among them; and there are vivid descriptions in prose; but Dr Johnson lives in the public imagination from Reynolds' portraits, of which he painted at least five that are certainly authentic. As a record of friendship and a tribute to greatness, this series of portraits, too easily taken for granted, stands unsurpassed in English painting.

The five Johnson portraits well represent Reynolds' development from the 'fifties to the 'eighties. We see the Doctor first, in the portrait of 1756 (Plate V*a*), through the eyes of an admiring young stranger, an enigmatic, portentous figure seated at a table with a pen in his hand. It is a direct portrait, a first impression. By the time he came to paint the Knole portrait (Plate V*b*) in 1769, Reynolds was ready to idealize Johnson as a classical philosopher, in the intimate loose robe, with a collar open at the neck, that he gave to Goldsmith, and with a strongly marked profile and gesticulating hands. The third portrait emphasizes the danger of excessive reading by candle-light and recalls the portrait of Baretti painted at about the same time, 1774–5; it shows Johnson screwing up his one good eye to read a book held close to his face. This was too candid for Johnson. When Mrs Piozzi reminded him that Reynolds had shown himself holding a hand to his ear, he replied: "He may paint himself as deaf as he chuses; but I will not be *blinking Sam*."

The fourth portrait, the half-length now at the Tate Gallery, originally intended for the Thrales' Streatham collection, dates from 1778 and is perhaps the best known of the five. The Doctor's characteristic pose has changed little since 1756 but he has grown heavier with the years; the great intellectual head stares straight out of the canvas; the left hand rests on his stomach. The fifth portrait, painted for Dr Taylor of Ashbourne during the last two years of Johnson's life, is a speaking likeness, in which the light is concentrated on the face, the body being left in shadow; this portrait is now in America. And, as a postscript to all these, we have "the Infant Johnson" in the Lansdowne collection.

The attribution is based on slender hearsay evidence, but with his large brooding head and full-blown cheeks, here is no ordinary infant. It pleases us to think of this formidable baby as young Johnson, and the fancy is consistent with the humour of Reynolds.[14]

Such is Reynolds' own artistic record of his friendship, and it is still one of Johnson's best memorials. But no sooner had Johnson died than Reynolds took the lead in campaigning for a public monument to his friend, a preoccupation which became one of his principal interests for the rest of his life. At his death it was still unrealized.

As Johnson was buried in Westminster Abbey, the first intention, natural enough, was that the monument should also be in the Abbey. The Dean and Chapter gave their consent, and in May, 1785, Reynolds told the Duke of Rutland: "We are going to erect a monument to the memory of Dr Johnson; we have all subscribed two guineas each. I will, in consequence of what your Grace has said, take the liberty of putting down your name for that sum." [15] By "We" Reynolds meant the members of the Literary Club, whose support was assured. An attempt to interest the general public by means of advertisements in booksellers' shops met with a poor response. In 1788 The Club decided that their subscription must be raised to five guineas; and Reynolds was deputed to ascertain what fee John Bacon, R.A., would require for a full-length statue.

There was now some doubt as to whether the figure of Johnson lent itself to this form of monument. Malone assured Sir Joseph Banks: "Sir J. R. says that Johnson's limbs were so far from being unsightly that they were uncommonly well formed, & in the most exact & true proportion." Bacon asked six hundred pounds for a statue, but after five years The Club had raised only two hundred. More drastic action was needed. This took the form of a public meeting, held on January 5, 1790, at which Reynolds, Burke, Malone, Metcalfe, Boswell and others were appointed members of a special committee.

So energetic was the new committee that by the beginning of 1791 between £700 and £800 had been collected. Reynolds had now reached the conclusion that St Paul's, and not Westminster Abbey, would be the best place for the statue. Having long been anxious that the Cathedral should be worthily decorated, and hoping for a resulting benefit to his Academicians, he was prepared to take Dr Johnson's statue as a test case. Sir Joseph Banks relayed his arguments to Malone:

> Sᵣ Joshua who preferrs St Paul's says that the honor as well as the interest of the arts are materialy at Stake in the business & will receive a material advantage if we set the example of erecting a monument in a Church which has hitherto Lain Fallow for the harvest of the Chisel, that Westminster is already so stuffd with statuary it would be a deadly sin against taste to increase the squeeze of Tombs there & that St Paul's is the most honorable station for the monument of a Great Man. Burke says waggishly this is Borrowing from Peter to give to Paul but he supports Sᵣ Joshua Fully & Firmly.[16]

The chief argument against St Paul's was that any statue erected there would have to be of such colossal dimensions that the funds collected would be insufficient to pay for it. Sir Joshua overcame this difficulty by promising to make up the balance himself.

Reynolds brought all this up at meetings of the Academy and persuaded the Council to allow him to write to the Dean and Chapter of St Paul's, offering the advice of the Academy on any monuments to be erected and "on whatever affects the beauty and decoration of the building".[17] He also urged the General Assembly, with the support of Benjamin West, to vote a contribution of a hundred guineas towards the monument "of the late Dr Samuel Johnson, Professor of Ancient Literature in the Royal Academy".[18]

It might have been thought that this honourable suggestion would have been allowed to pass, as an exceptional gesture, without serious objection. But Reynolds' old antagonist Sir William Chambers had never been a member of The Club and had always envied Sir Joshua his literary friends. He saw his opportunity, as Treasurer of the Academy, of striking a shrewd blow at Sir Joshua and he wrote a very able letter which was read out to the General Assembly on July 2, 1791:

> To the President and Academicians of the Royal Academy, in General Meeting Assembled.

> Gentlemen,
> Some very particular business obliges me to leave Town, and

prevents my Attendance this Evening at the General Meeting. If nothing more were to be agitated than is mentioned in the summons, my absence, with that of half the Academicians, would be immaterial; there would still be a sufficient number to confer an empty title, but there is reason to apprehend that a proposal is to come forwards, totally foreign to the business and views of the Academy: a proposal, which if it is agreed to, must open a door to all sorts of innovation, must weaken the Academy in its revenues, & disable us from pursueing with proper Spirit and full effect, the true objects of our institution.

Our business is to establish schools for the Education of young Artists; Premiums for their encouragement; Pensions to enable them to pursue their Studys; an Exhibition, wherein they may set their talents to public view; and honorary titles of distinction, to be confer'd on such as are deemed to deserve them. The Royal Academy has it still farther in view, to maintain itself; to reward its Members for services done; to assist the Sick or distressed Artist; to extend its beneficence to the relief of his family; to help the Widows and Children, of such, as leave them unprovided for.—All these, I apprehend, are sufficient objects for any Society to carry in view, without going a stray to hunt for more. We find it very difficult to fulfill even these; our Donations do not by any means equal the necessities of our distressed Suitors, and our travelling Pensions are too few, for so respectable an Establishment as Ours. If therefore we judge it expedient to tap the fund of the Academy, let it flow into these, its proper channels; and let it not be spillt in useless driblets, on things absolutely foreign to the intent and Purpose of our Establishment.

The Proposal I allude to, is that made in the last Meeting of the Council, which is, I apprehend, the true cause of your being Summoned to meet this Evening. It was a Proposal made by the President, to contribute largely out of the Fund of the Royal Academy, towards the Monument of Dr Johnson, about to be erected in St Pauls. To me it seemed, I freely confess, that one might with equal propriety have proposed the Erection of a Triumphal Arch to Lord Heathfield, or a Mausoleum to the inventor of Fire Engines, or a Statue to any other person, whose pursuits, and whose excellence lay totally wide of ours. If Monuments were to be our objects, how could we without Shame and contrition, Vote one to Dr Johnson, while Cipriani,—Moser,—Gainsborough, Cotes,—Wilson;—and so many others of our departed Brother-Academicians, are left unnoticed and forgotten, in the dust.

Let us therefore save our Credit, and spare our repentance, by
Voting no Monument at all.
I have the honour to be with very great Respect
                                        Gentlemen
                              Your most obedient humble Servant
                                        Wm CHAMBERS

Berners Street,
July 2^d 1791.[19]

Despite its narrowness and severity, and although it ignores
Johnson's honorary professorship of the Academy, as well as the
benefit that might accrue to Academicians through the decoration of St Paul's, this is still an excellent and persuasive letter.
It poses very well the eternally recurring clash, common to all
Academies, between the distinguished artist of wide general
culture and extended society, and the stubborn, maybe self-
righteous official. With all its merits, Chambers' letter leaves the
reader more than ever thankful that he was not the first President
of the Academy and that its traditions were established by Sir
Joshua Reynolds. One can imagine Chambers drafting another
good letter opposing the election of Sir Winston Churchill as
Honorary Academician Extraordinary.

Chambers' letter did not deter the Academy from voting a
hundred guineas towards Dr Johnson's statue. But Chambers was
not defeated; his influence at Court gave him another weapon.
The contribution was vetoed by the King; and Chambers thus
had the satisfaction of wounding Sir Joshua in his deepest affections
and robbing him of a small pleasure on which he had set his heart.

Peter Pindar, writing in 1785, had not hesitated to name
Chambers as the chief cause of dissension and the main promoter
of unworthy elections within the Academy:

> Though *thou* 'midst dulness mayst be pleased to shine,
> Reynolds shall ne'er sit cheek by jowl with swine.

4

Although he knew that the project was going forward, and
although he corresponded at length with Dr Samuel Parr about
the wording of the epitaph, Reynolds realized in the last year
of his life, when his health and eyesight were failing, that the

erection of Johnson's statue in St Paul's must still be long delayed. This consideration may have led him to propose to Burke that his friend Giuseppe Bonomi might design a simple obelisk in honour of Johnson which could be erected without delay in the grounds of Burke's house at Beaconsfield. There is no mention of Johnson in the following unpublished letter to Burke, but the date of its composition makes it possible, though not certain, that the obelisk was intended as a memorial to Johnson.

London Jan: 25 1791

Dear Sir,

I have settled everything with Bonomi relating to the Obelisk. I represented to him the shortness and uncertainty of life, I cannot boast indeed that I said any thing new on the subject, except what related to myself, that I wished to *see* it up, and therefore beged it might be done as soon as possible. He promises by May next to finish it. It is necessary it seems that the ground should be opend on the spot; about a month before the foundation is laid, in the mean time, merely from curiosity, it is wished that a little pit be now dug in order to ascertain the nature of the ground, they may stop when they come to a hard sandy soil.

The whole stonecutters business will be prepared in London. The Obelisk will rest on the back of four Cats, they will inevitably appear like four Tigers, which will raise their Characters not a little. The Inscription, if any, must be cut in town; but there is no hurry for it.

I believe you will think it necessary to make a narrow gravel walk from the Wood to the Obelisk and from thence round the ground to the east part of the house.

Mr & Mrs Hassell dine with us on Sunday next it will make them very happy to meet you—possibly you make [may] think it necessary to come to Town a few days before the meeting of Parliament.

I am with the greatest respect

Your most obedient humble
Servant
J. REYNOLDS.

The report is that you are to have a Peerage and a Pension, however I heard from very good authority that the Chancellor said at his own table that such a measure would be very proper and that he would support it whenever it was proposed.

Pray send an impression of your Crest.[20]

The eighteenth-century connoisseur had a fondness for solitary columns in woodland glades. Sir George Beaumont raised just such a cenotaph to Reynolds' memory at Coleorton, and it has been immortalized by Constable. Half-hidden by undergrowth, stained with damp and lichen, these melancholy tokens to ancient friendships still stand throughout the English countryside; they are more moving than city statues. The wood to which Reynolds refers in his letter is presumably "Walk Wood", a favourite haunt of Burke; Johnson had visited him at Beaconsfield and would have known it. But the obelisk has proved as elusive as Burke's peerage —there is no trace of it in modern Beaconsfield; the grounds of Butler's Court have been largely built over; and we do not know that the obelisk was ever erected.[21]

Not until four years after Reynolds' death was Bacon's statue of Johnson placed in St Paul's. According to a tradition in the Bacon family, it was Reynolds who insisted on the classical toga and the bare head, neither of which suited Johnson, and which suggested to John Bailey "a retired gladiator, meditating upon a wasted life".[22] But if we may not congratulate Sir Joshua on his taste in sculpture, we cannot deny his devoted homage to his friend, whose memory he served to the last.

The Silver Spectacles

I

REYNOLDS had reached the point at which a man begins to look back over his life. He had been fortunate in his era, which had given full scope to his energy and ambition. Though he had made his home in London, his life had been governed by the broad acres of England, by the landed gentry, mainly but not exclusively Whig, who had been his first and were his continuing patrons. An enlightened aristocracy had supported the first great school of English painting; their travels had made fashionable the culture of Europe, and Reynolds had furnished an intellectual justification for the Grand Tour; they had commissioned his paintings to hang in the galleries of their country houses as witnesses of their authority. Born into a family of sleepy scholarship, Reynolds had left it to see for himself the masterpieces of the Vatican, to sit at the feet of Dr Johnson. His ambition had supplied the defects of his education. Because he had the gift of detachment, because he could take a general view, he was able to state a theory of art which was valid for his own time—and must still be studied in ours.

Both Sir Joshua and his century have suffered from their prosperity. Neither can be impatiently dismissed. Reynolds mirrored his age—an age of sound prose and rational philosophy, the age of Locke and Hume and Burke. The spirit of eager enterprise, so evident in his own life, saves the eighteenth century from the reproach of decadence and preciosity. The soldiers and sailors whom Reynolds painted were not decadent—they had conquered Canada, subdued India and ruled the seas; some were heroes like General Eliott, the defender of Gibraltar, who became Lord Heathfield and retired to end his days at Turnham Green. And yet the scales were carefully weighted, too delicately balanced to keep their trim. In time, poetry and imagination would have their turn—and enjoy it to excess (until the whole lesson of compromise had to be learned afresh). Beneath the surface elegance, the poor lived in dirt and squalor, while, almost imperceptibly, the Industrial Revolution—with whose early stirrings Reynolds had made such slight acquaintance at the Society of Arts—was undermining the old order. When the storm burst in France, in 1789, Burke and Reynolds, horrified, had second thoughts about their opposition to the "King's Men". They realized that the balance of the constitution demanded a new Conservatism.

A history of the eighteenth century could be written from Reynolds' constant companion, Kearsley's *Pocket Ledger*. In one year (1782) the pocket-book discoursed on earthquakes, calligraphy, sealing-wax, military drill and mushrooms—a gay epitome of an enterprising enquiring century. In 1786 the pocket-book contained the Laws of Cricket—the game that the French nobility never learned to play with their peasants; it also offered a cure for the bite of a mad dog. The account of the "New Tax Upon Male and Female Servants" made less cheerful reading; an unmarried man like Reynolds, who already paid the special bachelor tax, now had to pay twenty-five shillings more than a married man for every male servant and double duty on all female servants. His pocket-book for 1787 included "A Set of Interesting Resolutions", well calculated to appeal to eighteenth-century reasoning. Someone has turned down the page; I like to think it was Sir Joshua. Here are some of the resolutions:

"*To live and to die in the public profession of the religion in which one was born and bred.*" An awkward maxim for Sir Joshua. As Dr Trevelyan has pointed out, the best of the eighteenth-century upper class "aimed at the full and rational enjoyment of this life, rather than at preparation for the next, of which they spoke seldom and then with a cheerful scepticism".

"*To rise early, and as often as possible to go to bed before midnight.*" Reynolds had no need to be ashamed of his practice in this respect, especially if the words "as often as possible" were liberally interpreted.

"*Not to let passion of any sort run away with the understanding.*" This had been one of the chief aims of his life.

"*Not to fall in love on the precipice of threescore, nor expect to be fallen in love with.*" Reynolds had passed sixty, but he would probably have accepted this proposition, despite the tax discrimination against bachelors.

"The possible tenure of existence is of too short possession for the long night that is to succeed: therefore not a moment is to be lost." Here was a maxim after Reynolds' heart. Writing to her cousin in Calcutta in 1786, Mary Palmer said: "My uncle seems more bewitched than ever with his pallet and pencils. He is painting from morning till night, and the truth is, that every picture he does seems better than the former."[1]

2

It was not in Reynolds' nature to be idle, but his persistent activity in his riper years was not due to artistic motives alone. He still wished to earn. Wealthy as he was, he did not feel himself to be entirely secure. Money values had fallen considerably; taxation had increased. The house and its hospitalities, the coach, the menservants and maidservants had still to be paid for. His small salary as King's Painter continued to irk him. In July, 1785, we find him asking the Duke of Rutland, Lord-Lieutenant of Ireland, to use his influence with Pitt to secure him the sinecure post of "Secretary and register to the Order of the Bath", which would have increased his income by £300 a year. "Mr Pitt, I fear, has not much attention to the arts," Reynolds truly remarked; "if he had, he would think it reasonable that a man who had given up so much of his time to the establishment of an Academy, and had attended sixteen years without any emolument whatever, and who unluckily, when made the King's Painter was the first person in that place who had their salary reduced to a fourth part, that he should have some compensation."[2]

The application failed. Meanwhile, Reynolds hurried off on his last visit to the continent. He had come to consider the buying of pictures for his own collection as a lucrative form of investment, and the object of this brief visit was a sale in Brussels of pictures from the dissolved monasteries and religious houses of Germany and Flanders. He thought these pictures "the saddest trash that ever were collected together". But he made several purchases from private collections, including a number of works by Rubens

XIII. THE FAMILY OF GEORGE, 3RD DUKE OF MARLBOROUGH. 1778

(126″ × 113″)

and Van Dyck; according to Northcote, he spent more than a thousand pounds.[3]

Reynolds, indeed, was now something of a dealer in pictures, who sent his own emissaries to auction sales; he acted as agent and adviser for wealthy friends; his collection covered the walls of his home almost to the ceiling. Sir Joshua's flair was not infallible, and some of his amateurish restorations were disastrous, but time has confirmed the accuracy of many of his judgements, notably in the case of works by Poussin and Watteau.*

The Rubens' pictures tended to disappoint him on this second visit to Belgium. He could not think why. Then he remembered that, the first time he saw them, he had held a notebook in his hand: "By the eye passing immediately from the white paper to the picture, the colours derived uncommon richness and warmth. For want of this foil, they afterwards appeared comparatively cold." [4]

3

During the five years that followed the death of Dr Johnson, Reynolds, despite failing eyesight, painted perhaps the finest portraits of his life. The best of these, in marked contrast to some of the highly complicated creations of his middle period, were simple, comparatively direct paintings; his technical mastery was impressive, though his use of bitumen was sometimes disastrous. Outstanding among the portraits of this period are the "Duchess of Devonshire and her Daughter" (Plate XV*b*) and the "Lady Betty Foster", both in the Duke of Devonshire's collection; "Lady Caroline Price" at Bath House; the "Lord Heathfield" in the National Gallery; and the "Joshua Sharpe" at Cowdray Park.

Sharpe, "The Artist's Lawyer", and Heathfield, the gallant soldier, make a particularly effective contrast. Ever since he had first settled in London, Sir Joshua had shown a gift for seeing his sitters as individuals, and for using all the resources of background and accessories to accentuate their character. The experience of thirty years was now evident in his mastery of composition: the

* See *infra*, p. 231.

sturdy figure of Heathfield, holding the great key of his fortress, stands out against a stormy background that epitomizes the long siege of Gibraltar and makes a page of history; Sharpe, seated low down on the canvas, symbolizes the man of thought and learning, his heavy features and black sombre clothes set off by the dark red hangings. These dramatic portraits owe something to the fresh inspiration of Rubens, yet they also suggest a return to the methods which had produced the Greenwich "Keppel" and the "Laurence Sterne", a quarter of a century before. Careful composition has not robbed either portrait of spontaneity.

Nevertheless, Reynolds was by no means entirely concerned, in the last working years of his life, with the portraits that he understood so well. Much of his energy was devoted to history painting, with results that were less happy. His interest in this field of his ambition was revived by Catherine the Great of Russia, who commissioned him in 1786, as he informed the Duke of Rutland, "to paint an historical picture for her, the size, the subject, and everything else left to me". He rejected the idea of painting Queen Elizabeth at Tilbury, and chose instead the subject of "Hercules strangling the serpents in the cradle, as described by Pindar, of which there is a very good translation by Cowley".[5] Northcote tells us that Reynolds thought this would provide an appropriate allusion to the difficulties encountered by the Empress in civilizing her Empire, but we are inclined to regret that he did not accept Horace Walpole's suggestion that he should paint Peter the Great putting on his carpenter's clothes to work in the dockyard at Deptford.

In the result, Reynolds' "Hercules" was hopelessly confused and disorganized, though not without some merit in the figure of Hercules. It was, however, greatly admired by the contemporary school of history painters; and William Hodges, the landscape artist, intended a compliment to its glowing colours when he said that "it looked as if it had been boiled in brandy". A rather surprising feature of the picture was the use of the head of Dr Johnson, from the Knole portrait (Plate V*b*), on the body of the blind seer Tiresias. The Empress paid Reynolds 1,500 guineas, and sent him a gold snuff-box, adorned with her profile in *bas relief*, set in diamonds, as a tribute to the "Hercules" and to his Discourses.[6] She also bought from Reynolds another large, and even less successful work, "The Continence of Scipio", which he completed in 1789. Both pictures are now in the Hermitage collection at Leningrad.

These commissions were highly profitable, but Reynolds' motive was not pecuniary, for he might have earned more from portraits. He accepted the vast canvases as an intellectual challenge, and applied to them the same painful process of trial and error that he used in writing his Discourses. Of the "Hercules" he said: "There are ten under it, some better, some worse." But hard work and persistence, though it produced the Discourses, failed utterly to compensate for lack of planning method in the historical paintings.

In 1786 Alderman John Boydell, the print-seller and publisher of engravings, conceived his ambitious and disastrous project of a series of paintings illustrative of Shakespeare. They were to be published by him in an edition of Shakespeare, and to be housed in a special gallery built for them in Pall Mall. He carried through both his intentions, but spent so much money in doing so that he could not leave the pictures to the nation, as he had hoped, but had to disperse the collection.

Boydell was a brave and patriotic patron who wished to show that English artists were capable of historical and poetic subjects, and to give them the encouragement in this respect that they failed to receive from the nobility or from the Church. When Burke saw Boydell at an Academy dinner in 1789, he sent up a note to Reynolds, who was presiding, next to the Prince of Wales. "This end of the table," he wrote, "in which, as there are many admirers of the art, there are many friends of yours, wish to drink an English Tradesman, who patronizes the art better than the Grand Monarque of France: 'Alderman Boydell, the Commercial Maecenas.'" The toast was drunk with the high approval of the Prince of Wales and with "unanimous approbation".[7] Unfortunately the contributors to Boydell's Shakespeare Gallery, of whom Opie and Northcote were the most prominent, specialized in a stagy, stilted fustian which is best forgotten. Nor were Sir Joshua's paintings in the series much better than theirs.

When Boydell first approached Reynolds for a contribution to his Shakespeare Gallery, Sir Joshua, according to his own account, was reluctant to take part, feeling that he was committed to too many portraits. He "twice refused", in his own words, "to engage in the business". Boydell then told him "that the success of the whole scheme depended upon his name being seen amongst the list of the performers". Sir Joshua, flattered, said that he would do what he could, but that he was doubtful. He warned Boydell that his time was valuable, and that the picture would be extremely expensive. Boydell, having replied that the price was no object, proceeded, in the traditional spirit of a "commercial Maecenas", to lay on the table "Bank bills to the amount of five hundred pounds". Sir Joshua demurred, but took the money, giving an undertaking to return it if the picture was never finished. "Mr Alderman Boydell, for a picture of a Scene in *Macbeth*, not yet begun . . . 500 0 0"—thus runs the entry in his account book.

Pursuing his advantage, Boydell bought a canvas measuring nine feet by twelve and sent it to Sir Joshua, who said that it was "the largest that had ever been in his house".[8] Sir Joshua now embarked on "Macbeth and the Witches", fully determined to give Boydell his money's worth.

The result was the very bad, very queer picture still to be seen at Petworth. "Seen" is hardly the right word, for the canvas is a murky ruin. Through the fog one dimly perceives Macbeth, with his back turned to the spectator, waving his hand and haranguing the witches. There seem to be more than the prescribed number of witches; one is a Calibanesque figure; another a forbidding seeress. Reynolds was lavish with macabre stage properties—a bat, a toad, skulls, a naked imp . . . Northcote loyally declared that "the visionary and awful effect produced" was "certainly without a parallel in the world".

Another picture painted by Reynolds for Boydell hangs near "Macbeth" at Petworth. This is "The Death of Cardinal Beaufort" (*Henry VI*, Part II, Act III, Sc. iii.) which pleased Northcote equally. Here, the secondary figures by the bedside are well observed, but the Cardinal, with his unfortunate resemblance to Robinson Crusoe, is not a success. Sir Joshua paid overmuch attention to Shakespeare's line: "See how the pangs of death do make him grin"; Mason records that the model, a stalwart porter or coal-heaver, "sat grinning for upwards of an hour", showing all his teeth. The result is unconvincing; and the picture as it left Reynolds' studio was even more grotesque than it is to-day, for it included a substantial demon, signifying conscience, crouched like the Cheshire Cat beside the Cardinal's pillow. Some charitable hand has since caused this demon to vanish.

Boydell paid a thousand guineas for the "Macbeth"—the sum fixed by a committee of arbitration after Reynolds' death (Sir Joshua had wanted more); five hundred guineas for "Cardinal Beaufort"; and a hundred guineas for a third picture, "Puck", who is quite a jolly fellow, now at Milton Park. When Boydell was compelled to sell his collection in 1805, the profits realized on the two smaller pictures were swallowed up in the heavy loss on "Macbeth and the Witches", which fetched only 378 guineas.

All this is more important in the history of Reynolds than it is in the history of art. Throughout his life he had aimed at something beyond portraiture. His neo-classical contrivances in his portraits had always had the object of raising them above mere likenesses, by marrying them with the Grand Style. He hoped that his history painting, in the final productive phase, would justify his earlier occasional attempts by yielding a masterpiece. This was not to be. Unlike Velasquez, Reynolds painted no "Surrender of Breda", still less a "Las Meninas". His imagination often failed him when he had to supply a sense of mystery or poetry beyond the immediacy of the sitter and exceeding his biographical gift. There are parallels with Velasquez in his failure to attain the exalted in his few religious pictures. Reynolds' "Holy Family" (1788) at the Tate Gallery has many merits, but the Virgin is a pretty society lady in a charade; one is reminded of the earth-bound Angel in Velasquez's "Christ at the Column". Both are portrait-painters' pictures.

Yet, if the larger imaginative qualities were missing, Reynolds did not fail in sympathy when faced with a sitter who interested him; and here his unerring taste as an interpreter sometimes brought him to the level of poetry. In the late 'eighties he was drawn increasingly to children. He idealized them still, but with none of the archness of his "Infant Academy" at Ken Wood, with more of reverence and wonder. Reynolds was not a religious man, but there is an unspoken prayer in his "Heads of Angels" (1787, Plate XIV*a*)—the five portrait-sketches of Frances Isabella Gordon —and in "The Age of Innocence" (1788). Even in a generation not disposed to sentiment, these studies still hold the visitor to the Tate Gallery by their sincerity.

One child, in particular, he painted with nostalgic affection. She was his great-niece Theophila Gwatkin, daughter of his beloved Offy. In a letter to her father of 1789 he sends his love to "little Ophy", and is anxious to have her in his house: "If my sister is still with you, I wish you would send little Ophy with her to Torrington and Mary will bring her from thence to London where I hope we shall see you & Mrs Gwatkin next summer and then you may take her back if she wishes it and I can spare her." [9] "Little Ophy" may have been the original of "The Age of Innocence"; she certainly sat for "Simplicity" (1789). He had some difficulty with her hands, entwined on her lap; Mary Palmer suggested that he had made them look like a "dish of prawns"; in the end he covered them with flowers.

When a friend made him a present of some fruit or comfiture, Sir Joshua dipped reflectively into one of the containers before writing a wistful note to Bennet Langton: "*I have no children.* I therefore send the present, which I found on my return to town to *your* children . . . I thought it necessary to be able to say I had tasted them, which makes a little deficiency in one of the pottles. . . ." [10]

4

As he grew older, Reynolds cherished his happy memories and the friendship of those survivors who linked him with the golden days of Johnson and Goldsmith. He also appreciated the presence of anyone who could help him to overcome his emotional isolation and loneliness. It is understandable therefore that he should now have seen more of James Boswell; for Boswell was a cheerful companion, and Reynolds, though he had no liking for dissipation, had cultivated the art of tolerance, perhaps too well. He had written an affectionate letter to Boswell long before, and had been able to tell him that Burke thought him "the pleasantest man he ever saw", and to add a sentence that went to the heart of their friendship: "I love the correspondence of *viva voce* over a bottle with a great deal of noise and a great deal of nonsense." [11]

It is small wonder, then, that Boswell's *Journal* in the years after

Johnson's death is full of references to pleasant meetings at the house in Leicester Square. Reynolds and Malone never ceased to urge Boswell to persevere with his great life of their friend; and Boswell's ultimate dedication to Sir Joshua was no more than his help and encouragement deserved. Boswell was often Reynolds' companion when he went about London; he accompanied him to dinners, and to exhibitions of pictures; he was placed in the front row when Reynolds lectured to the Royal Academy. In 1791 Reynolds procured his election as the honorary Secretary for Foreign Correspondence in the Academy. Indeed, the only possible disservice that Sir Joshua did to Boswell was to use too much bitumen on his portrait, now in the National Portrait Gallery.

What did Boswell do for Reynolds in return? He did him a bad turn in one particular instance. We know that he persuaded him to attend a public execution at Newgate in 1785. "It is strange how that hard Scot should have prevailed on the amiable painter to attend so shocking a spectacle," wrote *The Public Advertiser*. Reynolds was determined not to show himself an old fogy, and his subsequent letter to Boswell, in which he attempts to rationalize his experience and to justify what he had seen, makes painful reading.[12] The incident is the more distressing because Reynolds' better instincts lay elsewhere; Northcote tells us that he successfully interceded with Burke to save the life of a thief who had robbed his negro servant.

Reynolds was easily led by this entertaining rogue, as he was by John Wilkes. Cynics have suggested that one of Reynolds' motives in maintaining such close friendship with Boswell, and with Burke, was the thought that one or other might write his biography. Neither of them did, though Boswell toyed with the notion. When he received his honorary appointment at the Academy, a newspaper commented: "Boswell's promotion to the office of Foreign Secretary to the Academy, was entirely a deed of Sir Joshua's, who is now sitting to Boswell for his *picture*, to be done in the *size* and *manner* of *Johnson*."[13] The report was justified to the extent that Boswell made some notes on Reynolds' early life, which have been quoted at the beginning of this book, but he had abandoned the idea, as not properly suited to him, long before his death in 1795.[14]

The suggestion that Reynolds was at all influenced in his relationship either with Boswell or Burke by the prospect that they might write his biography is scarcely worthy of him. While Reynolds lived, however, it may have suited Boswell to keep the project alive, as an aid to his intimacy with Sir Joshua. Mary Palmer saw through Boswell and recognized him as a doubtful friend of her uncle. In a conversation with Farington many years later—she was then Lady Thomond—she accused Boswell of having black-balled Sir Joshua's friend, Philip Metcalfe, when he was proposed as a member of the Literary Club. And she summed up his relationship with Sir Joshua succinctly:

> Sir Joshua liked the company of Boswell but he was disposed to stay late and her Ladyship was often obliged to force him away. With all his pleasant qualities Lady Thomond says she much doubts whether he had any strong feeling of regard for anybody. He was occasionally extremely useful in removing reserve causing mirth in company, but he was only induced to exert himself when he had a desire to shine before somebody.[15]

5

Although Reynolds' friendship with Boswell points to the danger of easy-going tolerance, it was bound up with his loyalty to the memory of Dr Johnson. His deathbed reconciliation with Thomas Gainsborough—"liberal, thoughtless, and dissipated", as he described himself—and his subsequent appreciation of Gainsborough's genius in his Fourteenth Discourse show all his more sterling qualities. The episode remains one of the most moving in the history of British art.

There had been differences between the two within the Academy; inevitably there had been vague jealousies; but Reynolds had never made the mistake of underrating Gainsborough, and had repeatedly praised him in public. In 1782 he bought his fancy picture, "A Girl with Pigs", and wrote Gainsborough a flattering letter about it. "I think myself highly honor'd and much obliged to you for this singular mark of your favour," Gainsborough replied; "I may truly say that I have brought my Piggs to a fine market." [16] In the same year Gainsborough began to paint his portrait of Reynolds, which was never completed owing to Sir

Joshua's illness. Perhaps the sittings were not resumed because Gainsborough looked to Reynolds to offer a return of the compliment; and that, apparently, Reynolds did not do.

Despite their rivalry and their differences of temperament, the two men were attracted to each other by a mutual respect and admiration. Yet Reynolds told Northcote—and he was probably right—"that it was impossible for two painters in the same department of the art to continue long in friendship with each other". Gainsborough, having withdrawn from the Academy, was again upset by Sir Joshua's appointment as King's Principal Painter in 1784—he informed Lord Sandwich that he "was very near being King's Painter only Reynolds's Friends stood in the way".[17]

Thus the two great contemporaries remained separated by a barrier of silence until, in the last days of his life, in the summer of 1788, Gainsborough wrote to Sir Joshua a note which cannot be too often printed:

Dear Sir Joshua

I am just to write what I fear you will not read—after lying in a dying state for 6 months. The extreem affection which I am informd of by a Friend which Sir Josha has expresd induces me to beg a last favor, which is to come once under my Roof and look at my things, my woodman you never saw, if what I ask more is not disagreable to your feeling that I may have the honor to speak to you. I can from a sincere Heart say that I always admired and sincerely loved Sir Joshua Reynolds.

THO GAINSBOROUGH.[18]

It must be noted, in all honesty, that the words "and sincerely loved" were not Gainsborough's first thought; they are added above the line.

Gainsborough died on August 2, 1788, not many days after Reynolds' visit, and Sir Joshua made him the subject of his December Discourse to the Academy which is perhaps his literary masterpiece. "If ever this nation should produce genius sufficient to acquire to us the honourable distinction of an English School," he declared, "the name of Gainsborough will be transmitted to posterity, in the history of the art, among the very first of that rising name." Recognizing that Gainsborough, the romantic, luminous, undisciplined genius, was almost the exact opposite of himself, and of all he had taught, he proved as generous in appreciation as he was discriminating in criticism; and he particularly stressed the attributes that they undoubtedly had in common—a deep love of their art and the ambition to excel.

What he had to say of their last meeting, when Gainsborough showed him "The Woodman" and many other of his pictures, is eagerly read. "I cannot prevail on myself to suppress," said Sir Joshua, "that I was not connected with him by any habits of familiarity: if any little jealousies had subsisted between us, they were forgotten in those moments of sincerity; and he turned towards me as one who was engrossed by the same pursuits, and who deserved his good opinion, by being sensible of his excellence." Gainsborough's "regret at losing life was principally", Reynolds believed, "regret of leaving his art".

At the end of this Discourse, Sir Joshua metaphorically rattles the headmaster's cane as he peers over his spectacles at the students of the Academy. Gainsborough was all very well—he was a genius—but Sir Joshua was determined to warn the younger generation that it would get nowhere by trying to copy Gainsborough (or indeed by trying to copy Reynolds?):

> However we may apologize for the deficiencies of Gainsborough, (I mean particularly his want of precision and finishing,) who so ingeniously contrived to cover his defects by his beauties; and who cultivated that department of art where such defects are more easily excused; you are to remember, that no apology can be made for this deficiency in that style which this Academy teaches, and which ought to be the object of your pursuit. It will be necessary for you, in the first place, never to lose sight of the great rules and principles of the art, as they are collected from the full body of the best general practice, and the most constant and uniform experience; this must be the groundwork of all your studies: afterwards you may profit, as in this case I wish you to profit, by the peculiar experience and personal talents of artists living and dead; you may derive lights, and catch hints, from their practice; but the moment you turn them into models, you fall infinitely below them; you may be corrupted by excellences, not so much belonging to the art, as personal and appropriated to the artist; and become bad copies of good painters, instead of excellent imitators of the great universal truth of things.

With Gainsborough's death, some tensions within the Academy were relaxed; Reynolds and Sir William Chambers temporarily shelved their differences as they carried his coffin to the grave in Kew Churchyard. Sir Joshua—for such is human perversity—may have felt the loss of his rival as much as the loss of a close friend. He can hardly have foreseen that the names of Reynolds and Gainsborough would be linked by posterity in that dog-and-cat relationship which sometimes marks the appearance of complementary genius in the arts (and of which Dickens and Thackeray, Elgar and Delius are conspicuous later examples). But his Fourteenth Discourse shows that the association would not have displeased him: "We have lately lost Mr Gainsborough," he had said, "one of the greatest ornaments of our Academy."

6

Reynolds was left supreme in the field of portrait. Busier than ever, he still enjoyed health and vigour, apart from his chronic deafness. There was, however, an additional disability that now troubled him. For a painter, it involved the most serious of all worries—the threat of blindness.

His eyesight had been a source of annoyance for several years. The well-known self-portrait with spectacles (now at Windsor Castle) was exhibited at the Academy exhibition of 1788, but he had probably been wearing spectacles for some time before—perhaps since January, 1783, when he told his nephew William Johnson that "a violent inflammation in my Eyes" had prevented him from writing.[19] He did not entirely accept the idea of himself as a regular wearer of spectacles, however, for his last self-portrait (Plate XVa) shows him without them—a hearty-looking, bluff old man, in the fashionable high coat-collar of the period and with a candid dab of red on his nose. This may be the picture to which he refers on the fly-leaf of his notebook for 1788: "My own without spectacles to Mr Bartolozzi."

The Royal Academy owns a pair of Sir Joshua's silver spectacles, with small round glasses—probably the pair that is shown in the self-portrait, and in a miniature by William Grimaldi at Burlington House. From these spectacles it appears that Reynolds had now become considerably short-sighted and, if the lenses were adequate, of an equal amount ($-4 \cdot 0$ dioptres) in each eye. This means that to-day he would not have been able to read the large letters of an oculist's test type unaided, though he could have read the small print in a book without spectacles—an observation that has some bearing on his reading habits.*

Sir Joshua's notebook for the early months of 1789 is as crowded as ever. The handwriting has deteriorated, but many familiar names still occupy the daily spaces—among them those of the Prince of Wales, Mr Boswell, Mr Sheridan, Mrs Jordan, Mrs Robinson, and Mrs Billington—whose portrait as Saint Cecilia, echoing Rubens and Guido, may be accounted perhaps the last of his successes (for he needed an actress to justify his classicism). Sir Joshua remained devoted to the clubs; there are notes of engagements at the Devonshire, the Eumelian and the Dilettanti. "Mrs Siddons benefit" is noted, and the meeting of the "Sons of the Clergy" yet again reminded him, as his sister had long ago stopped trying to do, that he had lapsed from his father's ways.

Throughout the season a series of balls celebrated the King's recovery from his insanity. White's gave one, Boodle's another, but perhaps the most ambitious was sponsored by Brooks's on April 21. To it went Sir Joshua with Sir John and Lady D'Oyly and his niece Mary Palmer. The last-named escorted Miss Cocks. It proved a distressing evening for the girls; a letter from Mary to her sister Offy gives us a passing glimpse of Sir Joshua as he endeavours, rather vaguely, to fulfil his avuncular responsibilities:

> . . . About eleven we all went to the Opera house which was decorated to be sure in the most beautiful manner possible, had it been for a small company, but as it was it appeared like an immense body of people shut up in a fine purse, or rather in a Ballon. It was all hung round with blue Silk which drew up in the middle of the Ceiling like the Hood of a Cloak, round by the Boxes the blue silk was intermix'd with buff,† & all trim'd with blue and silver fringe drawn up in festoons with silver cord. The pillars were twined round with scarlet sattin ribbon & the whole lighted with wax candles instead of lamps. Air seem'd quite excluded and every lady appear'd to dread the effects of the heat, & added to this not a tenth part of the company could get seats.
>
> For the first two hours I saw every thing with a disposition to be pleased (but even then White's was in my opinion fifty thousand

* I am most grateful to Mr Rupert Scott for examining and reporting on Sir Joshua's spectacles.

† Blue and buff are the club colours. Sir Joshua had been a member of Brooks's since February 18, 1785.

times superior). After that time nothing could be so unpleasant as every circumstance was to me. Just as Mrs Siddons begun to recite the ode, Miss Cocks who was tired to death with standing beg'd me to go with her & get a seat. Lady D'Oyly did not chuse to move before the ode was ended, so we agreed to go with my Uncle & return to her again. When Miss Cocks got about halfway up the room she fainted away, and it was some time before she recover'd sufficiently to be led into another room, which we managed at last by the help of Lord Cholmondely, who order'd the doors of one of the supper rooms to be open'd. We sat there some time, my Uncle with us, but at last he grew tired & said he would go back & return to us again. When the doors were open'd for supper the Company rush'd in & the tables (of which there were about 20) were instantly fill^d; but no Uncle or Sir John or Lady D'Oyly could we see, & Miss Cocks & I were in the most forlorn state, fearing to stir from that room lest we should miss them. However, we might have set our hearts at rest for they seemed to have quite forgot us.

At last I perceived Mrs Bushe at one of the tables & we run up to her. She invited us to sup with them but I declined it, as I concluded our party would never think of supping till they had found us. When Mrs B. had done we went with her again to the Ball room, where for three hours we watched, sometimes standing still, sometimes walking till I was fatigued beyond any thing I ever felt. At last between three & four we met my Uncle and Sir John. They had all been comfortably at supper concluding we were gone home. It seems when my Uncle attempted to return to us, the waiters refused him admittance, as the door had only been open'd to us at Lord Cholmondly's command, & when supper was announced my Uncle got into another room & had forgot the way to that where he left us.

All these tormenting circumstances made the Evening to me irksome beyond expression, & I was so out of love with Balls that when I came home I believe I should have rejected a ticket for the finest ever was plan'd. So much for Brooks. . . .[20]

The crush had been terrible indeed. Sir Joshua had done his chivalrous best to rescue the ladies. We may even visualize him, almost Pickwickian in his spectacles and fine blue suit, remonstrating with the waiters and hammering on the locked doors of the supper-room. It is true that his talent for compromise soon helped him to sit down to a comfortable meal elsewhere; and we do not know what Mary had to say to him when they got home. Perhaps the events of the evening have some bearing on his commencement soon afterwards of a portrait of Miss Cocks and her niece, which is to be seen in an unfinished state at Ken Wood.

On April 23, Mary enjoyed herself much better at the thanksgiving service in St Paul's, where she "heard the King burst into tears" but was relieved "to see him look so composed". She had her own back on Sir Joshua here, for he failed to obtain a ticket of admission and "was obliged to content himself with seeing the Procession from Somerset House".[21]*

Nothing hinted that Reynolds' painting career was almost at an end. He exhibited twelve pictures at the Academy exhibition—"a miserable exhibition this year; my Uncle is the only support", wrote Mary Palmer.[22] The blow fell on July 13. Against the names of the sitters on that day Reynolds scrawled in his notebook: "prevented by my Eye beginning to be obscured". He felt as if a curtain had fallen over his left eye; the suddenness of the attack suggests a retinal detachment such as often occurs in medium degrees of short sight.[23] What probably lay behind it, however, was a malignant tumour caused by disease of the liver. Reynolds' doctors mistakenly diagnosed "gutta serena", a common result of overwork. No doubt overwork had played its part.

Within ten weeks Sir Joshua had entirely lost the sight of the eye. He never painted seriously again. The sitters named in the notebook on the fateful July 13 were Mrs Garrick, Miss ——, and Lady Beauchamp. Miss —— is believed to have been Miss Russell, the niece of Miss Cocks who had "fainted away" at Brooks's ball.

* Because Reynolds noted "St Pauls" in his diary for April 23, Tom Taylor wrote: "On the 23rd of April I find the President—no doubt in his official character—at the solemn service in St Paul's . . ." (Leslie and Taylor, II, p. 531).

XIII

"Count No Man Happy"

Sir Joshua Reynolds' loss of the sight of one eye, and weakness of the other . . . must afflict him deeply. He is another instance of *dici beatus ante obitum nemo*.

BOSWELL, October, 1789

I

AT first Sir Joshua took the inevitable blindness in his left eye with cheerful fortitude. He was even able to direct the completion of some of the pictures he had on hand, perhaps even to work on them a little himself. One of these was a full-length of Lord Rawdon, the soldier friend of the Prince of Wales who later became Earl of Moira and, later still, Marquis of Hastings. This portrait appeared in the Academy exhibition of 1790—the last in which Reynolds was represented—and is now at Buckingham Palace. Opposite the notebook entry of July 13 which recorded that Sir Joshua's eye was "beginning to be obscured", there is a reminder of Lord Rawdon's costume:—

White Wastcoat single breast
a small blue collar
and small Buttons
Epaulet
White Breeches
double breasted Coat
Buttons at equal distance.

But in general Sir Joshua, anxious not to try his remaining good eye, determined to do no more painting and to read and write with caution. For a man of sixty-six—he celebrated his birthday on July 16—he still had plenty of vigour; enforced idleness was exceedingly irksome to him. He was glad of callers, discovering who were his true friends. As Mary Palmer had gone out of town, Ozias Humphry, whom he had helped a quarter of a century before,* and who himself became blind a few years

* *Supra*, p. 86.

afterwards, made a point of visiting Reynolds at breakfast-time to read the news aloud. The recital was disturbing and exciting, for the papers contained accounts of the events in France following the Fall of the Bastille. By way of showing his appreciation, Sir Joshua caused two of the best pictures in his collection to be brought into the room each morning for Humphry's benefit.

Sir Joshua soon grew restless, however, and thought that he would go down to Burke at Beaconsfield with three other members of The Club, Edmond Malone, John Courtenay and Burke's high-minded Whig admirer William Windham (whose portrait he had painted for the Academy exhibition of 1788). The following letter to Burke is cheerful enough:

London, July 25, 1789.

Dear Sir,

We—that is Mr Malone, Mr Courtney and myself propose to have the pleasure of dining with you on Monday, the day after tomorrow.

I should have given this intelligence yesterday that you might have time to forbid us if you were otherwise engaged. If that should be the case perhaps you may have an opportunity of letting us know by some conveyance on Sunday or Monday morning as I take it for granted we shall not set out till twelve,—

Turn over

Mr Windham has just called, and being made acquainted with our Scheme desires to accompany us, but on condition that we change the day to Tuesday, so on Tuesday unless we hear to the contrary we are to make a noise in Beaconfield. I expect this Evening or on Monday half a Buck from Lord Ossory which I will beg leave to send to you as soon as I receive it.

I am Dear Sir
Yours sincerely
J. REYNOLDS.[1]

Lord and Lady Upper Ossory, old and valued friends of Reynolds, did much to comfort him. Lady Ossory—the correspondent of Horace Walpole—embroidered a waistcoat for Reynolds which was such a beautiful thing that he promised not to take snuff whenever he wore it. "Such a rough beast," he lamented, "with such a delicate waistcoat." Sir Joshua looked forward to visits to this couple at Ampthill, even though—as happened on one occasion—it meant watching amateur theatricals, which he

XIV*a*. "HEADS OF ANGELS" (Frances Isabella Gordon). 1787

$(29\frac{1}{2}'' \times 24\frac{3}{4}'')$

XIV*b*. SARAH SIDDONS AS "THE TRAGIC MUSE". 1784

$(93'' \times 57\frac{1}{2}'')$

doubted whether he could hear. He congratulated himself on still having one eye that could be gratified by "beauty and elegance".[2]

The larder at Leicester Fields often received presents of venison from Lord Ossory. In sending that "half a Buck" to Burke in July, 1789, Sir Joshua was assuring a good dinner for himself at Beaconsfield; and a good dinner was needed to off-set the grave news from France. The members of The Club must have shaken their heads that day over their venison; for Burke, unlike Fox, saw no help for the cause of liberty in the French excesses and was already pondering his famous *Reflections*. Reynolds took his tone from his friend: at a dinner at Holland House, where the talk abounded in revolutionary fervour, he proved cautious and cold.[3]

In August he tried the effect of sea air. At Brighton Philip Metcalfe, who lived luxuriously in a house on the Steine, may have been the attraction; and from Brighton Reynolds made a little tour to Arundel, Chichester, Midhurst and Petworth, carefully recording the distances in his notebook, as he had done all his life. Whether Metcalfe, who had made the same round with Dr Johnson seven years before, was again Sir Joshua's coach companion is not known. Reynolds saw Cowdray House in its Tudor magnificence, so soon to be destroyed by fire, and still had the zest to scribble notes of the pictures there. But, for a man who was suffering—though he did not realize it—from a serious disease of the liver, the shaking of a heavy coach on the notorious Sussex roads can have afforded no relief. In future he undertook few long journeys, travelling only occasionally to places like Beaconsfield or Ampthill to see friends. He spent part of September, 1789, at his house at Richmond.

Mary Palmer kept careful watch over her uncle, arranging the evening card-parties which became his chief relaxation, now that he no longer dared to do much reading. His "strong passion" (as Mary called it) for games of chance had not diminished with time, but it was a guarded passion. Seventy guineas was the most she could remember him winning at a sitting. On the contrary, "He generally left behind him whatever money He had about him."[4]

Like many elderly people, Sir Joshua found increased pleasure in birds. He had always had a fancy for them and, whether they were robins, parrots, or eagles, had shown care in placing them in his pictures. Now, when a pet canary, which perched on his hand, flew out of the window, he walked disconsolately through the Leicester Square garden, searching for it in vain.

Enforced leisure gave Reynolds an opportunity to take a closer look at his own neighbourhood through his remaining eye. What he saw probably did not displease such a true cosmopolitan. The man who had done more than any other Englishman of his time to bring his country into communication with the culture of the Continent now found himself living in "Soho". As a description "Leicester Square" was gradually displacing "Leicester Fields", though Reynolds always used the old form. Indeed, the district had slowly transformed itself from the place of some pretension and relative seclusion to which Reynolds had migrated thirty years before, and must already have assumed something of that "foreign air" noted by J. T. Smith early in the next century, when the adjoining streets and the Square itself were filled with continental émigrés of all kinds, Frenchmen, Germans, Italians—artists, actors, musicians and teachers. Reynolds' attachment to foreigners, especially Italians, is obvious to all who study the early records of the Royal Academy. It was an Italian, Giuseppe Bonomi, a close friend of Angelica Kauffmann, who now brought him as close to downfall as ever he came.

2

Pluckily as Reynolds had accepted his misfortune, its long-term effect on him will not surprise those who have followed the reading of his character attempted here. The highest ideals had driven him from early youth to lead a life of persistent activity. His artistic ambitions were steadily pursued as long as his full faculties remained; inevitably they were never entirely satisfied. His social and literary ambitions, almost equally strong, required similar calculated efforts. While his superb vitality served him, he was able to keep his tenseness almost completely under control, though his family were always aware that it existed; so too, apparently, was the sculptor Ceracchi whose bust of 1778 is at Burlington House. When, as now, the strain was compulsorily relaxed, his emotional loneliness and insecurity—extending perhaps to the basis of his artistic theory—oppressed him. His geniality was often clouded; he became, it must regretfully be admitted, quarrelsome and self-assertive.

The affairs of the Royal Academy were now his principal interest. But its council meetings were no longer items to be fitted into a busy working day spent in the company of the most distinguished men and the most beautiful women in the land. The sessions at Somerset House loomed larger than before; Sir Joshua came to them doggedly, intent on preserving place and dignity.

At the beginning of 1790 a long-standing disagreement within the Academy reached its head. Since the death of Samuel Wale in 1786, the Academy had been without a Professor of Perspective. Reynolds had consistently urged the election of an Italian long settled in practice in London who had been employed by the brothers Adam and who specialized in country houses in the Grecian renaissance style—Giuseppe Bonomi (1739–1808), mentioned as a fashionable architect by Jane Austen in *Sense and Sensibility*.

There were no doubts about Bonomi's technical qualifications; but the high proportion of foreigners admitted to the Academy at its foundation and in its early years had brought an inevitable reaction. The claims of foreigners were now scrutinized jealously; in particular, strong opposition could be expected to their election to offices and professorships. Another reason for objecting to Bonomi was that he enjoyed the patronage of Lord Aylesford, well known to be also a patron and friend of Sir Joshua.

Reynolds understood the prevalent feeling that Bonomi's appointment would be a put-up job. But he denied this. He based his advocacy on the firm belief, probably justified, that Bonomi was the best man available to be Professor of Perspective; and he argued, as he had done all his life, that the Academy should follow the French example in taking a liberal view of the claims of foreign artists resident in England. "The intent of the institution was to raise a School of Arts in this Nation," he emphasized; "if we could accelerate their growth by foreign manure it was our duty to use it." [5]

To be elected Professor of Perspective a candidate had to be a full Academician. Reynolds' campaign was complicated by the fact that Bonomi stood entirely outside the Academy; he was neither an R.A. nor did he belong to the class of Associates which had been originated in 1769. The opposing party were one move ahead in this respect; for they had as their candidate Edward Edwards, an Associate since 1773, a worthy but undistinguished painter of humble origin who had been delivering a course of private lectures on perspective as a stop-gap. It was Reynolds' first concern to put Bonomi on terms with Edwards. This he eventually achieved, after several failures, in November, 1789, though only by the dangerous expedient of giving Bonomi his casting vote.

After twenty years as its President, Sir Joshua realized that the ranks of his loyal supporters in the Academy had thinned. G. M. Moser, for example, was dead; and in 1788 F. M. Newton, the secretary, had retired—Sir Joshua inscribing with his own hand in the minutes of the General Assembly the resolution "That a piece of Plate be presented to Mr Newton, as an acknowledgment of their perfect Satisfaction in the able faithfull and diligent discharge of his duty as Secretrary [sic] to the Royal Academy from the year of its establishment . . ." There had always been a nucleus of opposition to Reynolds centred in Sir William Chambers, but Sir Joshua now had reason to regret the hostility of one of the lesser founder members—an unremarkable sculptor and architect named William Tyler, who had lately built the Freemasons' Tavern.

"Tyler was an odd man," said George III years later in a conversation with Benjamin West; "how came he to be an Academician?" "When the Royal Academy was formed," replied West, "there was not a choice of Artists as at present, & some indifferent artists were admitted."[6] Sir Joshua expressed the same view, furiously and ungrammatically, in his notes on the Bonomi affair: "Men who have been used to lay down the law in Alehouses to Masons & Bricklayers presume to interfere in a higher station where he has crept in by mere accident."[7]

Tyler, however, was very much a reality. For years he had nursed a jealous grudge against the aristocrat of painters in the presidential chair. When the death of Jeremiah Meyer gave Reynolds the chance to procure Bonomi's election as a full Academician, Tyler canvassed the opposition vigorously. He knew that most of the Academicians attached little importance to the Professorship of Perspective and he soon persuaded Sir William

Chambers that no Professor need be appointed at all, but that Edwards should be allowed to go on giving his course of lectures. As Reynolds put it, Chambers "enlisted himselfe under the banner of this resolute partizan Mr Tyler who had courage to dare anything, to brow-beat the President in his Chair".[8]

Chambers had feuded intermittently with the President for so long that his accession to the rebels caused no surprise; Sir Joshua had needed all his poise to keep him at arm's length through the years; the *éminence grise* of the Academy was not the man to show mercy to Reynolds in the hour of trial. If Chambers now saw the shadow of obstinacy and pomposity obscuring the President's familiar charm, Chambers was ready to seize the advantage. There lurked in Chambers a vein of shrewd malicious humour which may give a clue to his behaviour. He once wrote some notes[9] headed with the observation "Wit consists in Contrast". One of his instances was "Giving pain to an Object intently bent on pleasure". Others were "a tall upright man hitting his head against the top of a door or a Watertrough w^h overset upon him or the same Stumbling over a mole hill". Another, and perhaps the most pertinent here, was "rendering an Object ridiculous whilest it is aiming at Importance".

It is probable that the old Reynolds, busy with the daily round of his studio, would have taken the measure of his danger and prudently withdrawn from an untenable position, especially as he had received warning from Chambers of his attitude. That course was impossible for him in his present temper. Half-blind, more vulnerable than he realized, he made his way slowly but determinedly up the staircase of Somerset House to the general meeting on February 10, 1790, which would decide the future of Giuseppe Bonomi.

The door of the meeting room swung open to disclose a scene of alarming import for Sir Joshua. Instead of the members being dotted informally about the room as usual, they were all seated in perfect order and ominous silence. The atmosphere was frigid. A glance showed that the numbers of the regular attenders had been greatly increased by the addition of members who were rarely seen at the Academy.

The President walked straight to his chair and peered round for the specimen drawings required from the candidates for the office of Professor of Perspective. Edwards he knew was unlikely to send any drawings (he had declared he was "past being a boy" but probably understood that his lecturing was better than his drawing). Bonomi had, however, produced two admirable drawings, of Mrs Montagu's saloon in Portman Square and of the library at Lansdowne House. These had been placed in a dark corner at the far end of the room.

Sir Joshua asked the new secretary John Richards to put Bonomi's drawings where they could be seen. There was no response. He repeated his request. With studied rudeness Richards rose and "in a sluggish manner" walked past the drawings to ring the bell for a servant. He then stood with his arms folded in the middle of the room.

This was enough to tell Reynolds that his secretary had joined the opposition. He got up and helped to move the drawings himself. "It shews their rude spirit and gross manners of this cabal," he commented, that they should have made the servant "mount that long flight of steps in order to move two drawings from one side of the room to the other".[10]

Sir Joshua then opened the business of the meeting. They were to choose a successor to Meyer, he said, and he hoped that they would vote for "him who was qualified and willing to accept of the Office of Professor of Perspective which had been vacant so many years, to the great disgrace of the Academy". Edwards, he pointed out, had failed to send in any drawings, and he suggested that the only question before them was to decide on the merit of Bonomi's submissions.

But Reynolds may have been technically at fault in displaying Bonomi's drawings. The sole ostensible purpose of the meeting was to elect an Academician; it was not proper for Associates to advertise their qualifications on such an occasion.

"Who ordered those drawings to be sent to the Academy?" asked Tyler peremptorily.

"I did," replied Sir Joshua; and he was made to repeat his answer.

"I move that they be sent out of the room," said Tyler. "Does anyone second this motion?"

Greatly to his credit, James Barry, whose long-standing quarrel with Reynolds had been reconciled, jumped indignantly to his feet. "No," he cried, "nobody can be found so lost to all shame as to dare to second so infamous a Motion. Drawings that would do honour to the greatest Academy that ever existed in the world...." And he said a lot more, speaking most passionately.

Barry's protest failed. Thomas Banks, the sculptor, seconded Tyler's motion. A forest of hands rose in support. Sir Joshua was refused a further hearing, and the meeting proceeded to vote for the new Academician. Paradoxically, another foreigner was elected, by 22 votes to 8—Henry Fuseli, "a very ingenious Artist", as Reynolds admitted with perfect sincerity, "but no Candidate for the Professor's Chair".[11] In fact the Professorship of Perspective was not filled until the election of Turner in 1807, and Edwards continued his modest but apparently adequate lectures for the rest of his life.

Sir Joshua went home distressed and insulted. The next morning he wrote a very angry letter to the secretary resigning the presidency and his seat as an Academician. "I cannot persuade myself any longer to rank with such beings," he told Bonomi.[12]

3

It could not end there, and it did not. Reflection cooled the tempers of both sides. Reynolds' seven supporters* signed a warm protest at the "unprovoked and unmerited personal insult to the President, from whose performances the Arts have received so much honour, and from whose services the Academy has received so many important benefits". The newspapers were much astonished at the treatment meted out by the Academy to its leader, the most famous and most popular artist of the day. One of them published a supposed conversation in verse between Caleb Whitefoord and Sir Joshua which began:

> *Fine doings*, Sir Joshua, instead of *Fine Arts*;
> Knaves enough in the *pack*, but a strange want of *hearts*,

and also contained the lines:

> So Sir William, the *Swede*, has designed the sad jar,
> We see now the *poll* of which he is the *star*;

* Barry, Opie, Northcote, Rigaud, Nollekens, Zoffany, and Thomas Sandby.

Of this mischievous *browing** let's trace the *first growth*;
That the Artists should be CHAMBER *Council* I'm loth.[13]

The newspaper publicity, coupled with a belated realization on
the part of many Academicians of the seriousness of what had
happened, shook the confidence of the rebels and probably made
some of them a little ashamed. Although they had thought Sir
Joshua mistaken and autocratic, they had not anticipated that he
would resign and few had wished to see him go. Chambers, having
shown his power in one direction, was now ready to exert it in
another. Letters passed between him and Reynolds, in one of
which Chambers was able to convey the King's hope that Sir
Joshua would remain as President. Reynolds was not easily molli-
fied, but he withdrew his first letter of resignation and substituted
another written in more temperate language. Meanwhile he
worked into the night, compiling on numerous folio sheets his
"Justification in the matter of Bonomi and the resignation of the
Presid[ts] Chair".

On March 3 the General Assembly passed a stilted resolution
conveying the thanks of the Academy to Sir Joshua "for the able
and attentive manner, in which he has so many years discharged
his duty as President of the Society".[14] This did not satisfy Sir
Joshua. The resolution had been moved by Tyler and seconded
by Banks, which he thought ridiculous; it was signed only by the
Secretary; and it was "sent to the Ex President in the manner of
a Common Note closed with a Waver and without even an Enve-
lope and presented to the Ex president by the hands of the common arrant boy of the Academy". He proceeded with his
"Justification"; indeed he put that bit into it.[15]

Ten days later events took a much more favourable turn, when
Thomas Sandby and J. S. Copley persuaded the Academy to pass
a vaguely worded motion excusing Sir Joshua of irregularity in
the matter of Bonomi's drawings and recognizing that there had
been a misunderstanding. A committee then called upon Sir
Joshua at his home, inviting him to return as President. He received them cordially and made a graceful acceptance. On March
30, 1790, he resumed his seat in the Chair.

---

* Browbeating; Sir William Chambers, it will be recalled, was a Knight of the
Polar Star of Sweden.

The dénouement left him happier than he had been for some time, fortified by the knowledge that his King and country had shown concern for him and an appreciation of all that he had achieved at the Royal Academy. For posterity the complicated story of the quarrel over Bonomi has one outstanding lesson: it demolishes the legend of Reynolds' invulnerable calm and exposes to the light of day those strains and stresses of his character that he had successfully subdued in a lifetime of cultivated style and application. It enables us to measure his greatness in terms of human weakness. Whether or not he was to blame in the particular instance must depend on the point of view; Boswell believed that he was, and told Farington that this was one of his reasons for not writing his biography.[16]

4

Although he had been restored to the presidency, the remainder of Sir Joshua's life did not pass undisturbed. Some uncertainty of temper was probably the cause of most of the troubles. His unsuspected liver disease had already doomed him; and, though his sturdy constitution kept him temporarily active, he was continually perturbed by indications that he might lose the sight of his other eye. Still dabbling occasionally with his paints and brushes, he could not attempt serious work.

Even at The Club, which he had founded, Sir Joshua encountered opposition and saw his friends blackballed.[17] At the Academy things were not the same as before; there were repeated pinpricks. Frustrated in his attempt to secure a place for a young painter named Maquignon in the exhibition of 1790, he received a rebuke from General John Burgoyne.[18] When he removed a picture of the Duke of Gloucester from the same exhibition, Chambers sent him a stern note: "I am very much Surprised to find a picture taken out of the Exhibition by Your private Order, Contrary to a positive law of the Academy, it is a precedent which may be attended with very ill consequences, and a Stretch of power in You, which it will be difficult to justify." [19]

Small wonder that Sir Joshua felt that, if suspicion had usurped the place of trust, if each little administrative action of his was to be challenged, the time had come to part. And it is one of the most glorious things in his life that, out of the dissensions and anxieties of 1790, he was able to draw the measured periods of his Fifteenth and last Discourse—his farewell to the Royal Academy. Once again, the sense of creative effort steadied and strengthened him; as always, the public occasion called out his best; the never-failing will power, hardening into stoicism, gave him words to round off his life's work with grace and dignity.

The last Discourse was read to two or three hundred people at Somerset House on December 10, 1790. Soon after Sir Joshua had entered the room ominous cracks sounded from the floor-boards, and many of the audience moved nervously towards the door. The chief supporting beam below them had given way: it would have been a supreme irony, if Reynolds had perished in the collapse of Sir William Chambers' masterpiece. But, as no one realized what had happened until afterwards, and Sir Joshua remained in his place, the audience settled down again. Reynolds wore a green eye-shade; his voice was more inaudible than ever. Dr Burney told his daughter Fanny that the young students at the back "diverted themselves with conversation".[20]

"Among men united in the same body, and engaged in the same pursuit, along with permanent friendship occasional differences will arise"—Sir Joshua did not shirk the difficulty; but he made light of it. He spoke his words of reconciliation with quiet detachment: "In these disputes men are naturally too favourable to themselves, and think perhaps too hardly of their antagonists." They must sink their differences, he urged, in zeal "for the perfection of our common art".

He told his audience that he would "remember with pride, affection, and gratitude, the support with which I have almost uniformly been honoured from the commencement of our intercourse". He expressed his "unaffected cordial wishes" for their future concord, and added: "My age, and my infirmities still more than my age, make it probable that this will be the last time I shall have the honour of addressing you from this place." There followed a brief survey of the achievement of the Academy, with a special reference to the success of the annual exhibitions. Sir Joshua spoke of his own Discourses, reviewing the principles on which they had been constructed, and affirming with some confidence that he had "succeeded in establishing the rules and principles of our art on a more firm and lasting foundation". A rational method of study, he emphasized, was what he had always recommended: "The great, I may say the sole use of an Academy is, to put, and for some time to keep, students in that course, that too much indulgence may not be given to peculiarity, and that a young man may not be taught to believe, that what is generally good for others is not good for him."

But, in this last moving testimony of faith, it was with Michelangelo and "the language of the gods" that Sir Joshua was mainly concerned. He himself had "taken another course, one more suited to my abilities, and to the taste of the times in which I live"; but, if he had his life to live again, he would tread in the steps of the master; and he ended: "I should desire that the last words which I should pronounce in this Academy, and from this place, might be the name of—Michael Angelo."

Burke rose to quote some flattering lines from Milton. Friends gathered to add their congratulations. And with Burke, Boswell, Burney and a few others, Sir Joshua passed down the staircase of Somerset House and away from the scene of his many triumphs and of his one humiliation.

5

The leave-taking was more symbolical than real. During the first half of 1791 Sir Joshua experienced a revival of spirits. He moved in society, visited Ampthill and Woburn, and presided at several Academy meetings. He stayed for a time in his house at Richmond, which had been let in the autumn of 1790 to the Comtesse de Balbi,[21] and while he was there wrote some interesting random observations on William Gilpin's Essay on the Picturesque.[22] His sense of fun had not deserted him; by way of showing his detestation of the French Revolution, he composed a rough draft of an "Ironical Discourse", found among his papers, in which he turned all his most deeply felt convictions upside down.[23]

With all this mental activity, there was apparent a wish to put his affairs in order. He thought much about his own large collection of pictures, and offered it to the Royal Academy at a low price, but on the unacceptable condition that it should be housed in the

Lyceum in the Strand. Disappointed here, he exhibited 180 of the pictures at a room in the Haymarket in April, 1791, and arranged for the profits from the shillings charged for admission to be given to his old servant Ralph Kirkley.[24] Some of the attributions were doubtful, but the collection made a brave show, including as it did works by many of the European masters, especially the Flemish and the Dutch. The pictures, with three exceptions, were for sale, and Sir Joshua obviously wished to test their value. In the middle of the room stood Bernini's statue of "Neptune and Glaucus", nearly eight feet high, for which Sir Joshua had paid seven hundred guineas as a speculation a few years before, and which had since been reposing in his coach-house. On the "Neptune" he optimistically placed a price of 1,500 guineas; but the statue found no purchaser.

There were other embarrassments besides Bernini's "Neptune" (which returned to the coach-house and after Reynolds' death went to Lord Yarborough for five hundred pounds). It was at this time that Sir Joshua gave some offence to his old pupil James Northcote and probably earned the rebuke in Northcote's autobiography about his lack of "firm and manly courage and honour".* The offence, however, appears to have been venial and to have consisted in Reynolds' failure to encourage John Boydell, during his year as Lord Mayor of London (1790), to proceed with his proposal that every Lord Mayor should commission a large historical picture to hang somewhere in the City. Boydell told Northcote that Sir Joshua had declared that this was a foolish idea, that aldermen did not understand history painting, that portraits were the thing for them, and that he would do much better to commission Thomas Lawrence, whose work Sir Joshua greatly admired, to paint his own portrait.

On the whole this was sound advice, for a portrait by Lawrence would have proved a greater asset to the City than either a historical painting or a portrait by Northcote. To a struggling history painter, however, Reynolds' attitude naturally came as a blow. Confronted by Northcote in his breakfast-room one morning, Sir Joshua was mild but evasive; we can sympathize with his embarrassment.[25]

Equally annoying to him was Sir William Chambers' successful

* *Supra*, p. 129.

opposition in the summer of 1791 to his suggestion that the Academy should contribute a hundred guineas towards the cost of the statue of Dr Johnson, their former Professor of Ancient Literature.* Here, again, he was at pains to justify himself in writing,—this was the paper in which he discussed the merits of titles, and said, "I go with the great stream of life".[26] As with the case of Bonomi, there is no doubt that his guiding motive was the honour of the Academy and the dignity of its professorships.

6

Despite his worries, despite the feeling he must have had that the tide was flowing against him, Sir Joshua's energy and spirits still sustained him. When he and Edmond Malone were returning in his carriage from a visit to Burke at Beaconsfield, in September, 1791, they got out at the inn at Hayes and walked for five miles along the road, though the day was warm.[27] Reynolds appeared none the worse. Probably they discussed his Discourses, which he was revising for a new edition with Malone's diligent assistance.

This is the last encouraging glimpse of Sir Joshua. Soon afterwards his blind eye became swollen and painful, and he had renewed fears for his other eye. He lost his appetite, suffered from indigestion, and became extremely depressed. At an Academy council meeting on October 14, a letter of his to Chambers was read out, "requesting him to take the Chair, He being too much indisposed, to risque the coldness of the Evening".[28] His doctors, Sir George Baker and Dr Richard Warren, were quite unable to diagnose his illness; they suggested that it was imaginary and that if he could exert himself he would shake it off. Only Dr Charles Blagden, the unsuccessful suitor of Mary Palmer, and no longer a practising physician, insisted that there was a physical cause.

Dr Blagden was one of those present on an autumn evening when Fanny Burney, who had lately escaped—largely at Sir Joshua's instigation—from her servitude in the royal household, paid a visit to her old friend. The change in him shocked her. She found him wearing a bandage over one eye and with the other shaded by a green half-bonnet. "He seemed serious even to sadness,

* See *supra*, pp. 189–91.

though extremely kind. 'I am very glad,' he said, in a meek voice and dejected accent, 'to see you again, and I wish I could see you better! but I have only one eye now,—and hardly that.' " Calling again soon afterwards, she found him still more miserable.[29]

Sir Joshua made his will[30] on November 5, in the expectation that he would "soon be totally deprived of Sight". He appointed Burke, Malone and Philip Metcalfe as his executors, and, apart from specific legacies, left all that he possessed to Mary Palmer, who was nursing him with much patience and devotion. His beloved Offy (Mrs Gwatkin) received ten thousand pounds in three per cent Consols. Burke was given two thousand pounds, and excused repayment of a loan of the same amount. His sister Fanny was to be paid the interest on £2,500 during her lifetime. He gave to the beautiful Mrs Gwyn "her own Picture with a Turban"; there were bequests of pictures to Lord Ossory, Lord Palmerston, Sir George Beaumont and others; one thousand pounds was left to his old servant and factotum Ralph Kirkley. The will had been witnessed by Kirkley before it was realized that, as a legatee, he ought not to sign. Another witness was called in and the document corrected.

By the middle of February, 1792, four doctors after a consultation had come to the conclusion that Sir Joshua was suffering from a disease of the liver, but it was then too late to save him by administering mercury. During the last weeks he took laudanum and dozed, as Burke put it, in "tranquil despondency". Burke was one of the few friends whom he could not refuse to see; but Sir Joshua now knew the full terrors of loneliness, which he had held at bay for so long. Ralph Kirkley rarely left him. "He lay whole nights seemingly without sleep," said Kirkley, "but silent, except that after a long interval in the night He would hastily call out Ralph as if to assure himself that He was not alone." [31]

Although his will contained the sentence "I resign my Soul to God in humble hopes of his Mercy and my Body to the Earth", Boswell was not optimistic about Sir Joshua's spiritual welfare. There had, apparently, been no change of heart, no inclination to regret the painting on Sundays. "I am very sorry that he did not imbibe Christian piety from Johnson", wrote Boswell unctuously to the Bishop of Killaloe, who had recently been appointed Chaplain to the Royal Academy. "No clergyman attends him; no holy rites console his languishing hours. I heartily wish that your Lordship were here." And six months later he was again telling the Bishop that he wished Sir Joshua "in one respect . . . had been such as *we* are. But we must make allowance and hope the best."[32]

The end was tranquil. There was some pain but, in Burke's words, Sir Joshua was "tolerably easy" and "congratulated himself on a happy conclusion of a happy life". The Council minutes of the Royal Academy contain the entry: "On the 23^d of Feb^y 'twixt Eight & Nine in the Evening Died Our worthy President."

7

Modern medical opinion has attributed Sir Joshua's last illness to a malignant tumour of the liver, primary in the left eye. Reynolds' neighbour in Leicester Fields, the great John Hunter, came into the house on February 24 to assist at a post mortem examination which revealed that the liver was greatly enlarged, weighing as much as eleven pounds, and "somewhat scirrhous". In view of the medical knowledge of the time the doctors, though they had not shown much imagination, cannot be blamed for failing to consider tumour as a possible cause of the blindness or for not diagnosing the nature of the later disease of the liver; nor could they have suspected that the two might be connected. Yet if Reynolds had lived in the middle of the twentieth century his life would probably have been prolonged for many years.[33]

Mary Palmer believed that her uncle's old friend and fellow Devonian Sir George Baker had done all that could be done. She presented him with a self-portrait and wrote him a grateful note:

My dear Sir George,
  With this you will receive a testimony of my Esteem & regard, believe me I could not give you a greater than presenting you this portrait, for I am Covetous in the extreme of all that represent Him whose memory must ever be so precious, so rever'd & honour'd by me, it is the only *original* I have to give & *you* are the only person to whom I could give it, accept it then my dear Sir as a proof of my gratitude & the respect & esteem of your
  obliged affec^t friend & humble Servt
  M. PALMER.

Leicester Square.[34]

On the day after Reynolds' death, Burke sat down in his friend's house to compose an obituary notice which, if it erred on the side of eulogy, gave a sincere and heartfelt account of "one of the most memorable men of his time". "He was the first Englishman who added the praise of the elegant arts to the other glories of his country. In taste, in grace, in facility, in happy invention, and in the richness and harmony of colouring, he was equal to the great masters of the renowned ages. In portrait he went beyond them. . . ." Burke properly stressed that Sir Joshua had been a modest, unassuming man, and said with perfect truth that "his talents of every kind, powerful from nature, and not meanly cultivated by letters, his social virtues in all the relations and habitudes of life, rendered him the centre of a very great and unparalleled variety of agreeable societies, which will be dissipated by his death".

When he added that Sir Joshua "had too much merit not to excite some jealousy, too much innocence to provoke any enmity", Burke was on less sure ground. Some enmity as well as jealousy there certainly had been; yet the quarrels were usually short-lived. The sceptical voice of Sir William Chambers—who had tried so long and so consistently to ruffle Sir Joshua's official serenity—was not, however, stilled by his death. As surveyor of Somerset House he found it his duty to object to the request of Sir Joshua's executors that his body should lie in state at the Royal Academy on the evening before the funeral, explaining, perhaps correctly but surely gratuitously, that he had no power to authorize the use of the building for that purpose. Benjamin West, the succeeding President, at once sought an audience of the King, who signified "His Royal Will, that that mark of respect shou'd be shown".[35]

The funeral in St Paul's was the most splendid ever accorded to an English artist.[36] Burke stated that Reynolds had directed that his executors should go to no expense; but he knew of Sir Joshua's wish to be buried in St Paul's, and he rightly assumed that, "being not altogether indifferent to this kind of observances", he would not have disapproved.

At nine o'clock on the morning of March 3, the "peace officers" closed the route from Somerset House to St Paul's to all traffic. At ten o'clock the shops on the route were shut and crowds began

XVa.
JOSHUA REYNOLDS.
Self-portrait. 1788–9
$(29\frac{1}{2}'' \times 24\frac{1}{2}'')$

xvb.
GEORGIANA, DUCHESS OF
DEVONSHIRE, AND HER
DAUGHTER, GEORGIANA,
LATER COUNTESS OF
CARLISLE. 1786
$(44\frac{1}{4}'' \times 55\frac{1}{4}'')$

to gather. An officer's guard of thirty men was posted at the entrance to Somerset House.

At 12.15 the coffin was taken from the Model Academy, which had been hung with black and lighted by wax-lights in silver sconces, and placed on the hearse. The procession moved off at 12.30, with twelve "peace officers", two City Marshals, the Lord Mayor and Sheriffs at its head. The undertaker and his men rode on horseback, escorting the hearse with its plumes of feathers. The ten pall-bearers—all peers and many of them close friends of Sir Joshua—were followed by the chief mourner, Offy's husband R. L. Gwatkin, undergoing the worst ordeal of his uneventful life. Giuseppe Marchi and Ralph Kirkley came next; then the executors, Burke, Malone and Metcalfe. The large body of the members of the Royal Academy had the privilege of following them, in their due order of precedence: Chambers and Wilton; Barry and Boswell; Northcote and Tyler; the innocent but contentious Bonomi—all these and many other characters of the play that was ended, subdued to thoughtfulness in their long black cloaks.★

The last of the ninety-one carriages had not left Somerset House by the time the head of the procession, advancing with solemn dignity, had reached the Cathedral. At the windows and on the pavements of Fleet Street the people of London in great numbers silently saluted the passing of Sir Joshua. The slow-moving procession informed those who knew him only from the print-sellers' shops and the gossip of newspaper paragraphs that this artist had a place in the history of the time. The "long black train", stretching, like little figures in a Callot engraving, from the west door of St Paul's to the choir, awed those who had sat at the free-and-easy table in Leicester Fields.

Sir Joshua lies in the crypt of St Paul's between Barry and Opie, and close to Turner, whom he helped in his student days and whose wish it was to be buried near him.

★ The Academy paid £44 1s. 0d. for the funeral splendours, including £12 9s. 0d. for a "Collation". A further £76 10s. 11d. "for Coaches, Attendants, Gloves, Hat-bands, Cloaks, &c. &c.", was contributed by the members individually (R.A. Council minutes).

XIV

After the Funeral

I

THE obituary notices were almost universally affectionate and laudatory. Praising Reynolds as an artist—especially in portrait—and as a writer, they also agreed in assessing as unique and irreplaceable his gifts as a host. The casual and spontaneous conviviality of his table was not to be imitated. Reynolds' dinner-parties had thrived on the detached curiosity of a deep student of character. Modest and unassertive in conversation, he had provided an atmosphere in which writers, statesmen, and even occasionally artists, could relax and feel at home. Often content to listen through his ear-trumpet, he had always possessed the knack of happy and constructive intervention.

A few years after Sir Joshua's death Malone and Farington could find no one qualified to perform this peculiar service to intellectual society.[1] They thought of Sir Joseph Banks; but Banks tended to be heavy and too exclusively botanical. Burke was excessively eloquent and talkative; he would have dominated any gathering. As for William Windham, they found him too fastidious to encourage the needful variety of character and conversation. The haphazard evenings in Leicester Fields had nourished an intimacy rarely discovered in the great houses of Mayfair and hardly equalled even by the third Lord Holland in Kensington.

The obituarists were followed by an ardent band of poetasters, chorusing the praises of Sir Joshua and invoking limpid tears, well-earned bays, mouldering dust and all the stock-in-trade of funeral oratory.[2] The *Morning Herald* ventured the opinion "That Taste turn'd pale when classic Reynolds fell". The *Gentleman's Magazine* asserted:

> Thine Reynolds was the power, and thine alone,
> To seize the varying forms of every grace. . . .

And one who attended the funeral at St Paul's, recollecting that

Van Dyck had also been buried there, sent an "impromptu" to the *Public Advertiser*:

Alike in genius, and alike in worth,
To their deserts a kindred flame was giv'n,
Their faded forms together rest in earth,
And in one flame their souls unite in heav'n.

Mary Palmer retired to Burke's house at Beaconsfield, to recuperate in the country air and to be comforted by praise of her uncle. Blake's puerile epigrams did not disturb her—they came later.* She was now a wealthy woman, though the full extent of her inheritance is difficult to assess because much of it took the form of works of art; Northcote's figure of £80,000 is however a conservative estimate. Sales of part of Reynolds' collection in 1795, 1796 and 1798, including many canvases of his own painting that had been left on his hands, realized sixteen thousand pounds; and there still remained sufficient to bring in a further twenty-five thousand pounds after Mary's death (excluding, of course, many things retained by the family as heirlooms).

Sir Joshua's judgement of pictures was by no means infallible, but at current mid-twentieth-century estimates his collection would be enormously valuable. To take two outstanding examples: Reynolds owned Poussin's "Nativity" which was sold for 205 guineas in 1795 and fetched £29,000 at Sotheby's in 1956. He also owned Watteau's "The Music Lesson", now in the Wallace collection, which realized twenty pounds in 1795 and could not be bought to-day, supposing it was for sale, for less than £20,000.[3] These were brilliant successes, in a collection that contained a high proportion of overrated rubbish—but then Sir Joshua's understanding of Watteau, as of Vanbrugh, was greatly in advance of his time.

Mary Palmer had become a desirable prize. She was married to the Earl of Inchiquin, (later Marquess of Thomond), recently widowed and already approaching the age of seventy, at Beaconsfield in July, 1792, only a few months after her uncle's death. It was apparently a happy marriage, but there were no children. Having survived a fall from his horse, her hearty husband died in 1808; she

* e.g. O Reader, behold the Philosopher's grave!
He was born quite a Fool, but he died quite a Knave.

lived until 1820, when her possessions, many of them priceless relics of Sir Joshua, were distributed among her family and friends by a fair and exhaustive will. They included "a half-length portrait of my beloved Lord in black, painted by me", which went to the Countess of Orkney, and a hundred pounds for the poor of Great Torrington.[4]

To Sir Joshua's memory Mary remained unswervingly loyal. She watched over Malone's edition of the Discourses. She urged the Academy to present a medal in his honour to his family (which they belatedly did).[5] She assisted a memorial exhibition at the British Institution in 1813, and, although disappointed that some of the pictures had faded,* told her sister Offy: "My heart swells when I contemplate the works of this great Man & the public estimation of them, not but what it is wormwood to many, & I have no doubt but you will see many attempts to depreciate what is not to be equal'd, certainly not excell'd."[6]

Offy—Mrs Gwatkin—outlived most of her generation and at the age of eighty-eight was able to talk to B. R. Haydon with keen spirit and animation when he called on her at Plymouth. She died in 1848 at the age of ninety-one.

The exhibition of 1813 was doubtless wormwood to Blake, who must have been equally pained to see his friend John Flaxman's statue of Reynolds erected in St Paul's during the same year. As a piece of heroic sculpture, the statue is worthy of its setting beneath the dome. As a likeness of Reynolds it is flattering and exaggerates his height, yet Flaxman must be given credit for allowing something of a diffident and slightly wistful expression to appear on the face.

In general, Sir Joshua has fared ill at the hands of sculptors, with the exception of Alfred Drury—and of Ceracchi, whose bust at Burlington House hints at some underlying stress. During the Victorian hey-day of his reputation several statues and busts were commissioned which tend to idealize him out of recognition. J. H. Foley's attempt, at the Tate Gallery, with its poor likeness and expression, is particularly unconvincing. It is ironical to see Sir Joshua paraded in close proximity to Sir William Chambers on the frieze of the Albert Memorial, and to find him reappearing with Chambers, though this time at a more suitable distance,

* See supra, p. 54.

high up on the Cromwell Road front of the Victoria and Albert Museum.

Sir William Chambers lived only four years longer than Sir Joshua. During this time he showed himself more intractable than ever. Even George III began to lose patience with his overbearing adviser. The King told the architect James Wyatt that he wanted to do "many things" at Windsor but that he deferred them "during the life of Sir William Chambers".[7] In 1795 Chambers again tried to dictate to the Academy, demanding special powers as the "agent of his Majesty" and informing the Council that they would be ruined unless they economized, and that they could not afford the annual dinner. The Council resisted him stoutly. William Tyler now turned his energies to "regulating" the accounts, as a result of which Farington was able to say that Chambers had "grossly and falsely . . . misrepresented the situation of the Academy affairs to the King". George III himself observed that "in Sir William's manner of keeping accounts there was always something obscure".[8]

It appears that this arch-intriguer's death in March, 1796, came as a relief to the Academy. They were sick to death of his disruptive manœuvres and in retrospect were fully able to appreciate Sir Joshua's tact and courtesy. Nevertheless, Chambers was a remarkable man, not easy to judge. The Royal Academy owed its existence to him, and when he stopped bullying his colleagues he could be superficially jovial. Between squabbles with Reynolds in the last year of his life, Chambers sat next to him at dinner, obliged by singing a Swedish love-song and was affability itself.[9] Yet it is hardly an exaggeration to say that Chambers caused Sir Joshua more worry than anyone else in his life.

2

The death of Reynolds meant in many ways the end of an era. Inevitably the loss of the first President was felt with peculiar force at the Royal Academy. Two months after Sir Joshua's funeral, on the occasion of the annual exhibition, Boswell, appearing for the first time as Secretary for Foreign Correspondence, voiced the passing disquiet:

This is the first Exhibition at which we have met without seeing

233

in the Chair that excellent and eminent person of whom I cannot speak, and you cannot hear, without emotion. Gentlemen, it was a day of anxiety to us all; not, I am sure, from any apprehension of deficiency in the respectable gentleman who now so worthily presides [Benjamin West]:—But there is a kind of uncertainty attending every change—every new situation—which creates a degree of fear in minds of sensibility. I say it with hesitation and delicacy—we could not be quite sure that there might not appear a little of that variable temper, which is imputed to the public, and which, had we experienced it, we could not but have felt with uneasiness. . . .[10]

Boswell need not have been alarmed. The exhibition was "favoured with great attention", and has been so favoured ever since. Whereas in 1769 it had contained only 136 works, in 1792 there were 780 works on show, of which 650 were by non-members. The receipts had advanced from £700 to £2,600. The Academy was a flourishing society possessing substantial investments, able to provide scholarships and to relieve distress among artists and their families. Its schools had already trained more than five hundred artists, including Lawrence, Hoppner, Flaxman, Turner and Soane. In this achievement the example of Sir Joshua Reynolds, his tireless attention to the Academy's interests, above all the prestige conferred on the exhibitions by his own works, had played an indispensable part for which he will always be honoured.

"The outward and the made must always be exact pictures," W. R. Lethaby has said, "of the minds of the makers." As the years have receded, we have been able to obtain an ever clearer view of Reynolds as a supreme exponent, in theory and in practice, of the art of his time. He has transmitted to us the accomplishment and grace—though not the squalor—of the eighteenth century. Much of his enormous output of painting is still, happily, to be seen in Britain. The motors that crunch their way over gravel drives towards stately houses "open to the public" bring Reynolds' countrymen inevitably to pictures with his name on their frames. They will see wonderfully fine pictures, indifferent pictures, bad pictures—studio replicas of varying quality, execrable copies, and pictures faded, cracked or spoiled by bitumen. They must use imagination as well as judgement. To discover Reynolds' masterpieces—and this cannot be done only in London, though there are rich collections in or near the capital—is an exciting adventure.

Those who discover them will have found good reason to believe that Joshua Reynolds was the greatest portrait-painter that England has ever produced.

The search will bring many surprises. Sir Joshua could be dignified or sentimental, sturdily English or deliberately classical, romantic with Keppel, penetrating with Sterne, theatrical with Mrs Siddons, frivolous with Master Crewe—all according to his mood and to the marked phases of his painting career. Though there was great deliberation, there was also—especially in the unfinished sketches—a remarkable spontaneity and vivacity, a direct simplicity as in the portraits of Lady Betty Foster or Lady Caroline Price, and sometimes a strange foretaste of impressionism.

Even in his failures, Reynolds was never "a little painter". From early youth, as he told Boswell, he had thought the art of painting "beyond all others" and had set himself the highest, indeed impossible, ideals. Striving ceaselessly, always unsatisfied, he never became reconciled to his limitations and too rarely painted for pleasure and poetry, as Gainsborough did. A few canvases, mostly from his last painting years—the hovering brush-work of "Heads of Angels" (Plate XIV*a*)—suggest what was lost in the long battle. Yet that steel spring of his determination had enabled him to sweep away the old wooden portraiture and to impose a new vision on a whole generation. The originality of this achievement, which finally established the English school of painting, remains undimmed by the revulsions of fashion. A man is a part of his time; the eighteenth century was a complacent rationalizing age; the generalizations of Reynolds reflected it. That the British people can still respond in the nineteen-fifties to a painter who draws on the classical tradition and is not ashamed to touch the note of nobility and dignity has been shown by the remarkable success in reproduction of Pietro Annigoni's portrait of Queen Elizabeth II: a popularity in direct succession to that of the eighteenth-century mezzotints.

This is not to compare Joshua Reynolds with Pietro Annigoni, an artist who personally has more in common, perhaps, with Thomas Gainsborough; it hints only at the unexpected reappearance of the Italianate spirit of the early days of the Royal Academy. Reynolds, despite his influences, achieved a portraiture more characteristically English than either. But it was Reynolds' unusual merit to be scarcely less distinguished as a writer than as a painter. He chose his friends from the worlds of literature, philosophy, politics, science, from the ranks of the prosperous Dilettanti, rather than from his professional brethren. It was the fusion in him of the artist and the man of letters that made him an intellectual force to be reckoned with throughout Europe.

Reynolds won his place in history by sustained will-power, by never swerving from the exacting ideals which fired him from early youth. It is hard to say whether his zeal for his art or his longing for worldly success had the greatest driving force; in his mind the two were closely related. His mild geniality and his "smile serene" were no legends, however—they have the authority of numerous witnesses; the friendly affection of Johnson, Goldsmith, Burke and many more is equally certain. Sir Joshua was widely respected and loved.

We have therefore the impression of an ambitious and successful man who made himself generally liked by his agreeable manners. "There is no such thing as complete unity in man," said Benjamin Constant, "and no one is ever completely sincere or completely insincere." Accepting this piece of cynicism as applicable to Sir Joshua, it must be added that the good qualities in him far outshone the bad. He may have been mistaken in some of the opinions in his Discourses, but at the time he uttered them he believed them to be sincere. He was not a hypocrite because, in his middle age, he advocated courses that he himself was not prepared to follow—that sneer derives from Blake. He was not necessarily pompous because Lady Burlington found him so;[11] many others did not. Nor is there any evidence that he was untrustworthy or dishonourable, as Northcote maintained in the posthumous autobiography; his earlier reaction is the more reliable—"I know him thoroughly, and all his faults, I am sure, and yet I almost worship him." The worst that can be proved against Reynolds is that, while he was remarkably generous to distinguished friends like Johnson and Burke, he showed a tendency to be close-fisted in his domestic life, and could be stern towards importunate relatives; even here his mood was not consistent—he was willing to relent.

Reynolds well illustrates, therefore, the classic paradox of a complex character, the selfish and unselfish man. It helps to an understanding of the almost inhuman coolness and calm that Mrs

Thrale found in him when we realize that beneath the surface he was tense and intense, restless and sensitive. The alterations in his paintings, his attempts to cover up faulty drawing, his inconsistent and freakish painting methods, the painful and repeated corrections in his writings, the fact that he often wrote rough drafts of his letters and carefully copied them—all these things indicate the doubt and uncertainty under which he laboured. Reynolds' calm was an imposed calm, a triumph of discipline and deliberate style. When the spell of his remorseless labours was broken, as it was in the last years, some of his hidden irritability came to the surface.

No wonder that, knowing himself as he did, he discouraged his students from relying too much on individual genius. But it is not enough to explain him, in Freudian terms, as ambivalent, as unable to reconcile his introversion with his extroversion, as vacillating between impulsive daring and cautious retreat. There was in him, in fact, a strongly individual genius—not the imperative genius of poetic inspiration that Blake worshipped, but a genius for the detached observation of mankind in its variety and for the assessment of character. Allied to it was a gift for philosophical generalization, for seeing life in general terms and in long perspective. His enquiring mind made him seek the company of men of character wherever they were to be found. Despite the titled names in his engagement books, social snobbery was not really one of his failings; the aim was different. It is Reynolds' curiously tender concern for human values that gives his best pictures their enduring hold.

We might expect, from the apparent lack of passion in his temperament, to find his portraits flat and superficial. Some of the run-of-the-mill products of his studio may answer this description, and these contained no doubt a professional admixture of courteous flattery and "up-grading". But give him a sitter who interests him—whether man, woman, or child—and the difference is obvious. In his moments of candid psychological perception Reynolds reveals his own hidden self and transcends his own unfailing taste.

Certain simple things are worth remembering. Sir Joshua was a gentleman, and had a gentle protective regard for women and for children. For all his high ideals, he was a modest man. He was not a good teacher to his own pupils, but he possessed a grand overriding desire to help the young artist. "If all those whom I have endeavoured to help forward by lending them pictures and telling them their faults," he once wrote to William Roscoe, "should do me the honour of calling themselves my scholars, I should have the greatest school that ever Painter had." [12]

A small party of congenial friends, a glass or two of wine, released his strong natural humour and high spirits. When he scribbled "Here's pretty Kitty's Health" or described the "diuretic notes" of the whistling coach-drivers on the road to Brentford, he touched a vein of uninhibited fun and showed that the roots of his strength were firm in his native soil. Northcote tells us that Sir Joshua, looking out of his coach window, once caught sight of a farrier's sign:

> Horses shod agreeable to Nature,
> And according to Art.

In the pleasure with which he memorized and repeated this admirably worded notice, we sense his delight in the world he lived in.

Seeing Reynolds as his friends saw him, we too begin to love the whole man, whom Wordsworth's lines, inscribed on Sir George Beaumont's Cenotaph to his memory at Coleorton, hail as a friend and an Englishman.

> Ye Lime-trees, ranged before this hallowed Urn,
> Shoot forth with lively power at Spring's return;
> And be not slow a stately growth to rear
> Of pillars, branching off from year to year,
> Till they have learned to frame a darksome aisle;—
> That may recal to mind that awful Pile
> Where Reynolds, 'mid our country's noblest dead,
> In the last sanctity of fame is laid.
>   There, though by right the excelling Painter sleep
> Where Death and Glory a joint sabbath keep,
> Yet not the less his Spirit would hold dear
> Self-hidden praise, and Friendship's private tear:
> Hence, on my patrimonial grounds, have I
> Raised this frail tribute to his memory;
> From youth a zealous follower of the Art
> That he professed; attached to him in heart;
> Admiring, loving, and with grief and pride
> Feeling what England lost when Reynolds died.

APPENDIX A

Reynolds' "Journey from London to Brentford"

FOR comment on this hitherto unpublished parody (in Mrs A. T. Copland-Griffiths' collection) of Baretti's "A Journey from London to Genoa, through England, Portugal, Spain and France", see *supra* Chapter VII, particularly pp. 112–18. It can be dated to 1770–1. The MS., written in Reynolds' hand on foolscap paper, presents few difficulties. On the rare occasions on which I have had to supply or conjecture words or letters, I have placed these within square brackets. I have preserved the original spelling, and, as far as possible, Reynolds' punctuation; the latter is exceedingly haphazard, however, and I have made some small alterations in punctuation and paragraphing in the interest of easy reading. The footnotes to the text are Reynolds' own.

D. H.

A JOURNEY FROM LONDON TO BRENTFORD, THROUGH KNIGHTSBRIDGE, KENSINGTON, HAMMERSMITH, AND TURNHAM GREEN

By
RINALDO

PREFACE

How very few writers of Travels among the great number with which the world swarms, seem to have any conception of the nature and disposition of mankind; and yet surely one of the first things requisite, before a man sets about entertaining the public, is to know what will entertain them; what it is they expect to find, what it is they desire to know. A man of a Studious recluse life sets out to see foreign parts, as the phrase is, and when he returns thinks he has done wonders if he discovers any more expeditious method used in manufactures or an improvement in agriculture, in short their works are stuffed with accounts of the state of Arts, Manufactures and Commerce, the Police of Nations and I know not what, which nobody cares one pin about.

A little commerce with mankind would have soon convinced them that there is a much shorter way to fame, they need only observe the

239

manner a travell'd man makes himself entertaining to a Company and may conclude without much sagacity that the same method used by a writer would succeed equally well, this is not by recounting what he has seen but by relating what has or might have happen'd to himself in his journey, and in this as great latitude is allowed as to Poets but then probability is inviolably to be preserved.

Is anybody so stupid as to think there is any such being existing as Paulita and yet how many good pages in my Travels to Spain did I get rid off by her means. Perhaps my Vanity has as the vulgar proberb says let the Cat out of the Bag, but as I love to be witty sometimes so at other times I love to be ingenuous, and with all frankness now tell you the whole art and mystery I have used, and which every man may practice with equal success.

Many people are of opinion that I might as well have wrote my Travels in my Study as going to Spain for that purpose, which is a malicious insinuation and an absolute falshood.

I defy any man, however fruitful his imagination, to spin such a work out of his own brain without those hints which travelling the road will never fail to furnish a man that has any genius. They are the ansae sapienti datum unde fiat sapientior, that is to say, From a Hint a wise man knows how to make a story, but I defy any man to make a story without the Hints.

I think I may boldly say I have not forgot myself throughout that whole work, and flatter myself that I have agreably entertained my readers by giving them an account of the names of the Inns the Landlords and even the names of the Horses with every other information that I thought would prove entertaining to the public, and to shew that I did not depend for success upon any other conduct, I did not even visit the Escurial the most considerable Palace in Europe, tho I was within a few miles of it. Upon the whole I have made such a spot of work* as I believe the world never saw before, and all of my own invention except the Hints which I before mentiond, and the titles of the Chapters which I acknowledge to have taken from the Rev^d Dr Sterne's Sentimental Journey.

I take this opportunity to thank the Public for their favourable reception of that work. The greediness with which it was sought by all ranks and conditions of people is indeed beyond example and very flattering to the Author.

I cannot avoid mentioning one circumstance of which I was myself an eye-witness. On my return from my Bookseller, (who lives in Russell Street,) the day they were published, from thence all along

* A Devonshire Idiom.

Covent Garden through Kings Street, New Street, St Martin Lane and Cranborn Ally home to Leicester fields where I dwell, the concourse of people was so great that men women and children run out of their houses to enquire the cause of this extraordinary procession, how much further this string extended I can give no account, but in less than two hours the whole edition was bought up.

I now present the public with an account of England with many observations on the customs and manners peculiar to the inhabitants of this great Empire.

LETTER I

The Dog and the Lantern—Rotten Row—Thieves everywhere—A remarkable instance of Hospitality. The dangerous Captain or the adventure of an Assembly room. A Nota Bene, and a Digression. The Diuretic Whistle. The Breeches maker tricks the foolish Brentonians. Another Digression.

THE BEGINNING

In my former letters I have given you a pretty exact account of every thing in London that is worthy the observation of an Inquisitive traveller, during three day[s] abode in that City.

This morning I shall set out for Falmouth and from thence to my native country Spain.

The method of travelling in England is in Calashes drawn by eight horses, no carriage besides has so many except the Kings when he goes in state to meet his Parliament. It is a huge Machine near as big as a house, the grand effect it has upon the road cannot be described, it looks like a first rate man of war with all her sails expanded, or the great Caravan that travels over the Deserts of Arabia, a more magnificent Travelling Machine no Nation under the sun I believe can boast.

The name of the Calasser is Robert Jenkins, I have not been able as yet to inform myself of the names of the horses, but you shall have them in my next.

But to give you the daily account of my journey.

Immediatly on leaving London you pass the Gate and enter Knightsbridge, the Inhabitants of this town have a barbarous amusement, they tye old Lanterns or something of that kind to a poor dogs tail and then hoot and hollow and frighten the animal through the streets.

I relieved one of those poor dumb creatures by giving a boy six pence to set him at liberty and was happy the whole day after from the conscious satisfaction of having relieved a fellow creature from misery.

On the left hand a little beyond Knightsbridge are many pleasant Villas pretty contiguous to each other and looking something like a street or Row of houses & are call'd Rotten Row. I was inquisitive to know why it was calld Rotten as they appear'd to be new houses, I was informed that at Portsmouth there was a place which was call'd Rotten Row from being the repository of old ships unfit for service, and that those houses were built for old whores.

We now entered Kensington so calld from the Kings Palace being near it. This town is tolerably well fortified with two Gates. Certain officers attend these gates night and day to examine the ingress and egress of all travellers, the shameless behaviour of these officers exceeds anything I ever met with in all my travels, I really blush'd for them. In other countrys you slip slily into their hands a piece of mony that your baggage may pass unexamined, but these audacious Ruffians never offer to examine anything, but in the sight of the Gun extend their brawny palms and oblige you to give them a maravedo or two or they will not let you pass the gates.

At the end of this celebrated town is Cambden house which is a Nunnery for the Education of all the young Ladies in London, here they remain until they are mariageable, they are then carried by their Mothers Aunts or some Relation to market. Of these markets there are two large ones beside a great many lesser, one is call'd Ranelagh the other Vauxhall. I had not time to visit them during my abode in London.

Immediatly after we pass'd the last Gate of the town I observed on the right a Building in the Gothic Stile which is the Seat of a Peer who by a lucrative office under the crown call'd a Public Defaulter has acquired an immense fortune, they say many Millions.

Our Carriage moving on but slowly I got out and walk['d] on before. The Sun was hot, I grew very thirsty, being almost choaked with the Dust that flew in great quantities about me. I saw a gentleman sitting near the Road in what they call a Summer house smoking his pipe and looking at the carriages as they pass'd. I address'd myself to him and desired leave to drink from that Vessel which he had before him, he put it towards me, but with a Countenance as if he was afraid to refuse me, however I took a good hearty pull and found it a very salubrious draught, they call it Porter. I offer'd him a maravedo as an acknowledgement, he said he did not sell Porter and would not receive it. The English in General are remarkably hospitable.

At Hammersmith we stopt whilst the horses drank. I would not even lose that little opportunity to get information. I enter into converse with the first person I see, whether Master or man all is one. Chatting with the osstler he informed me that all those Carriages which I saw there belonged to a Company who were dancing in that great room, pointing to it with his finger, he told me that it was a weekly meeting held by subscription and that none but subscribers were admitted. I was resolved however to have a peep at them and take my chance of its furnishing out matter for a Letter.

You know Brother a person is respected as he respects himself, man naturally indolent and cowardly gives to him who claims, without troubling himself to examine his pretensions. Without therefore saying with your leave, or by your leave, I enterd the room, put my glass to my Eye, lookd round with an air that implied a conscious superiority check'd with a familiar smile. Of all the Company two only were dancing in a very lazy and inanimate manner, they call'd this dance a Minuet, tis very inferior to the Fandango or Tonadilla. The rest of the company were as stupidly gazing at them! till on my entering the Room they all turned their eyes on me. I walked round, clapped the faces of the little boys, kissed the girls, shook hands with the maidens, called every old man Father and every old woman mother, asked every body his name, offered snuff to all. By putting on this good humour I thought at least it would procure me a good reception and that they would be much pleased in being thus taken notice of by an Hidalgo.

I leave you to judge how great was my surprise (as soon as the two which were dancing had finished their dance) to observe the whole company lay their heads together with their eyes fixed on me, a buzzing whisper going round all the time, the buzz grew louder, still louder and louder, at last I could [hear], who is he? who let him in? how came he here? at last without any discretion or mitigation of voice my ears were stunn'd with a thousand sounds, hissing hooting and hallowing, out with him, out with him, throw him out of the window, kick him downstairs, tumble him in the Kennel. I cannot say how I looked on the sudden hearing of such an uproar. However I had presence of mind to form the resolution of giving a start amidst their hisses and their cryes; and take to my heels, but before I had power to put my resolve into execution, a person (whom I heard somebody call the Captain) came up to me, put his arm under mine and without speaking a word led me to the door. When we arrived at the stair head, (which is without the door) I was going to turn about to thank him for the friendly office he did me in conducting me safe from that infernal crewe, but he prevented me from making any acknowledgements by clapping both his hands upon my two shoulders and with a vigorous exertion of his foot against my posteriors push'd me forward with all his might. I made but one step to the bottom, however I disapointed the brute for I pitch'd on my legs with a dexterity I will venture to say that would have done honour to a Cat. It was lucky I was not hurt, I wonder how I escaped. I hastened to the Calash & was soon out of harms way, as none attempted to follow me into the streets.

From Hamersmith we soon arrived at the famous plain called Turnham green, from this to that there was no adventure good or bad, except that of a flock of Pigeons flying over our heads, by which I guess'd there might be a Pigeon house somewhere near, and upon enquiry I found that I was right, but I had no time to look into it.*

Our Calassero stopt at the Packhorse to drink a pot of Porter which he calld wetting his Whistle. Meanwhile I took a view of this renownd place. I will not attempt to describe the various beauties of this Scene, it beggars all description, it is a second Elysium, beautifully and thickly inhabited by poultry and swine as well as men. Imagine to yourself a large spacious immane plain of the most beautifull verdure except where it is variegated with numberless paths that lye in various directions and intersecting each other chequer the ground in the most picturesque manner, I wish'd for the fanciful pencil of Zuccerelli to have taken a Sketch of it. There are vast excavations of the earth which I was told were made by art, the Gravel with which the roads are supplied are brought from this place which may be call'd the great Granary of Gravel. These immense Pits are generally filld with undulating water, where you see thousands of Boys swimming whilst the men in various Parties are playing at Cricket and Trap ball.

I cannot express the effect it had on my mind, such a mixture and confusion of amusements by land and by water, here the boys swiming diving ducking through the water as if it was their proper element, then scouting running wheeling after each other, then out of the water then in it, then all for Leap frog jumping over one anothers backs, hallowing and screaming notes of joy and transport whilst the Geese Turkeys and Hogs join in the full chorus, Cackling Gobling and Grunting. I could look and listen forever, I never am tired at the pleasing sight of seeing so many people happy and enjoying themselves after their labour.

Returning to my Posado I saw a Lady coming down stairs with her little daughter a very pretty girl about six years old. What is your name my sweet angel said I? My name is Charlotte Chambers answered the little thing, and dropt me one of her best courtesies. You are so pretty said I that I must give you a kiss if you please, and lifting her up in my arms carried her to the coach.

* N.B. Dr Clark in his account of Turnham Green takes no notice of any Pigeon house and does not seem to have heard that Turnham Green is famous for Pigeons.

About fifty yards from the Packhorse, all carriages stop for a few minutes and their drivers whistle a tune, I enquired what all this meant what was the cause of our stoping and why the Calassero whistled, he answered with an arch leer that they [stopd] that the Horses might p—s and whistled that they might p—s to some tune. It is amazing and appears incredible that those drivers have certain diuretic notes which when a horse hears he cannot contain his urine for affection, this tune I have learnt to whistle and will get my friend Gardini to prick down the musick that it may be publish'd, for perhaps it may have the same effect upon Christians, and as far as I know may be an effectual remedy for the Strangary, tis worth trying, if it should succeed I shall think myself as great a benefactor to mankind as he that found out the Cure for the bite of a Tarantula.

We were now in sight of Kew bridge. Prince Ernest I found had been waiting for me near two hours, as he had been informed that I intended passing that way, he forced me into his superb Carriage (after having ordered the Calash to wait till my return), and carried me immediatly to his Sister the Queen of England who receiv'd me with great cordiality my name being not unknown to her. We beguiled an hour in agreable Chit chat. She was pleased with my loquaciousness and I was pleased with her affability. I then took my leave and returned to the Calash which I found just in the place I left it.

A very little way beyond this Bridge is Brentford a placed [place] renowned in History. From London to this Town is as it were one continued village, when I set out this morning I proposed to count the houses from Highpark corner to Brentford, but soon lost my reckoning because of their number.

A complete account of these houses and their inhabitants would in my opinion prove one of the most entertaining that ever was written: but non omnia possumus omnes, and the desires and schemes of everyman, always go much beyond his powers, tho I could not do all I have done something.

I went into the house of a Breeches maker, I pretended to want a pair. I asked him his name, he told me his name was Peter Clements. I ask'd to see his house and afterwards we would talk about the breeches, he said he did not let lodgings but I might see his house. His Kitchen has a good stock of Copper pans pewter dishes, and earthen plates. His Table linnen, tho coarse was clean, and his beds and bed covering of a decent size a thing not common in Spanish houses. I then told him I would call another time about the breeches and took my leave.

As soon as the Waggon stopt at the Red Lion of Brentford, I got out to take a ramble, but I did not go up the fore street as most travellers would do, but went up a line behind the Inn, because I thought that might afford a description not to be found in any book. There I saw a man beating down Cherries with a Stick whilst a young woman catch'd them in her apron. You see I should not have been able to have informed you of this circumstance, the manner the English gather in their cherries, if I had not gone out of the common street.

Brentford is a very populous City situated on the River Thames, its extent is beyond belief reaching as I say to London in one continued Street with very little interuption. This extensive City was formerly inhabited by two Kings who successively dethroned each other. It is the present politics not to suffer the Brentfordians to declare a King of their own, for which they are much discontented, but to keep them to their obedience.

The King of England has a Chateau directly opposite the Town, here he constantly resides and it is said that if this precaution had not been taken Don John Alderman Wilks would certainly before this have been elected King of Brentford. This Don John is the Idol of the inhabitants of this town, his name is wrote on every door window shutter and dead wall throughout the Town either with letters or Hiroglifick figures.

If the Brentfordians would take my advice they would not concern themselves about the succession or whether they have a King of their own or not, and tis ten to one but the time will come when they will repent, when the King shall serve them as Charles did the Catalans, but the common people and the peasantry espeacially, has no need to trouble themselves about these things, for whoever conquers, they continue still the same.

But the multitude was allways foolish throughout the world and is allways made a tool to carry points that concern them but very little or very remotely nor will they ever be persuaded that with respect to them it matters but very little how & by whom they are govern'd.

Though there are many good houses in this Town that would not disgrace any town in Spain, yet none of these inhabitants can be call'd rich, but there is a general equality amongst them, however to speak my opinion I think most of them have a needy look.

At nine o'clock I returned to my Posado and congratulate myself that I went to bed without a broken head fully resolved to have a good nights sleep, but the hatefull Image of the Captain never would cease to present itself to my imagination, so that I tumbled and toss'd all night and dreamt of nothing but being thrown off Towers stairs and precipices.

I shall now quit the Epistolary stile and make some general observations as they come into my head.

The Copper coin of this nation is a farthing and a halfpenny a sixpence & halfcrown in silver, in Gold a five shillings & threepence half Guinea and a Guinea. Of the former of these I have had many in my possession but the two last are very difficult to procure because no coin is so scarce.

I cannot say much in favour of the courtesy of the inhabitants, no man pulls off his hat, nor does any she drop me a courtesy.

No waggoner, pedlar, no rustick do I see at his victuals in the Inns which I enter, will beg me to partake of his meal tho he catches my eye fixed on him whilst he is eating, and tho I express the usual wish that much good it may do him.

APPENDIX B

Reynolds' Painting Technique

By
HORACE A. BUTTERY

THE technical development of Sir Joshua Reynolds' art may be conveniently divided into approximately three phases: (i) After leaving his master Hudson and before going to Italy in 1749. (ii) After his return from Italy in 1753 until the late 1760's. (iii) From the 1770's until his death.

Before Reynolds went to Italy his method of painting was reasonably "direct", much in the manner of his master Hudson. Already he was painting with greater freedom and inventiveness than his master. It is clear that Van Dyck and his grand manner compositions soon influenced Reynolds. This influence can be seen in the small family group in the possession of the Earl of St Germans.

Reynolds' visit to Italy greatly changed his outlook, and on his return in 1753 he tried to produce the effects of Tintoretto and Titian by using transparent glazes over a monochrome underpainting. For sixteen years he persisted in using this method. His palette was limited to a few colours, principally blue-black, white, ochre and carmine. Unfortunately the carmine he used for his flesh tone effects was not permanent; and during this phase, until the late 'sixties, he did not use vermilion mixed with white for his flesh tones. His method at this period was to paint the portrait first in monochrome, using blue-black and white; this included the drapery that was later to be crimson or "pink". Blue coats and dresses were painted "direct".

Once his "lay-in" was completed, he proceeded to produce his flesh tones by glazing over the by now dry underpainting with carmine and naples yellow. His crimson draperies were also produced by glazing with carmine over the blue-black and white underpainting (in an attempt to emulate Tintoretto and Titian).

Even at this early date he had also discovered that bitumen produced a beautiful warm tone. Fortunately he used it sparingly, mainly in the darks of trees and draperies.

Owing to his carmine being a fugitive colour, these portraits of the later 'fifties and 'sixties appear to-day faded and cold. This coldness is

248

frequently increased by injudicious cleaning and lack of understanding of Reynolds' methods at this date.

Perhaps the most instructive picture to show how Reynolds worked at this period is the unfinished double portrait of Burke and Lord Rockingham in the FitzWilliam Museum, Cambridge. There, clearly visible in the head of Burke, is the blue-black and white "lay-in" almost unglazed. The crimson curtain, the chair with its brass studs, and some other accessories are completed, and the curtain and chair glazed with carmine. These completed details show that Reynolds had an assistant working to his methods, who finished the less important details, leaving the portraits unfinished, awaiting the surface flesh glazes to be applied by the Master himself.

In the 'sixties Reynolds aimed at more solid modelling and stronger chiaroscuro, using similar methods; and it was not until the 'seventies that he began to abandon the method of blue-black and white underpainting. He then began to include vermilion in his palette for flesh tones; and the rich clear tone of bitumen becomes more apparent, and also unfortunately more detrimental to the paint surface.

He frequently tends to build up his heads with a thick white priming, so thick that it often gives the effect of impasto, which he required. Over this priming, or false impasto, he modelled with glazes which became more varied and subtle. Waxes were mixed with pigment, quick driers used, and these in turn were glazed with tinted varnish.

His two visits to Flanders and the richness of Rubens' colour and transparent flesh painting doubtless influenced Reynolds, but unfortunately, again, his changed methods were unable to produce these lasting effects. Occasionally, however, in this phase he painted portraits as near to "direct" painting as he could achieve. A very beautiful example of this type of painting is the portrait of Lady Caroline Price.

Perhaps the best preserved of all his works of his third phase, and which until just before the 1939–45 war was still un-lined, is the beautiful portrait of Georgiana, Duchess of Devonshire, and her Baby (Plate XVb). The condition of this picture is as near perfect as can be, but has, owing to Reynolds' methods, darkened in tone. The beautiful and delicate modelling of the head produced by glazes over a white priming, the subtle glazed modelling of the arm are undamaged. The forms of the drapery in the black dress, the curls of the hair are all produced by glazing. In the head there is little real impasto. The area where paint is heaviest is in the child's dress; there white paint appears to have been applied heavily as an underpaint, and the drapery forms produced by glazes afterwards.

In his last years Reynolds became more and more careless of methods and mediums. The use of bitumen becomes all-pervading, to such an extent that in the picture "The Infant Academy" at the Iveagh Bequest, Kenwood, it produced the effect of "running sores".

Two other examples of Reynolds sacrificing permanency for immediate effect are the whole length portraits of Queen Charlotte and George III in the Royal Academy. The head of the Queen is in fact a medallion built up with whitening, white paint and bituminous medium (still not set hard). This *bas-relief* helps to produce an effect of modelling, which he completed with glazes. There is almost no genuine impasto on this head.

Reynolds was the most experimental painter of the eighteenth-century portraitists. Once he had returned from Italy his aim was to produce by various methods a genuine richness of effect. Owing to the use of fugitive colours and faulty mediums, in the majority of cases, these effects were short lived. It is impossible for us to-day to assess what his portraits looked like when they left his easel. Reynolds can never be considered a "direct painter" such as Romney, and by comparison Reynolds' portraits must have altered in tone. Nevertheless, his early works retain great beauty, elegance and charm by their silvery tones and faded carmines (probably now lighter in tone than when painted); and his later works great impressiveness and richness (probably now darker in tone than when painted).

The cleaning of any portrait by Reynolds will always present great difficulty, owing to his experimental methods and the changed tonality of the picture: facts that many earlier restorers failed to appreciate.

These notes are the result of study and physical contact with Reynolds' portraits. More comprehensive and more technical contemporary records of Reynolds' methods of painting, by Charles Robert Leslie, William Mason the poet, Sir William Beechey, James Northcote, Benjamin Robert Haydon, and Reynolds himself, are available to students. All give proof of Reynolds' evanescent colours and faulty mediums.

APPENDIX C

The Recognizance in John Bampfylde's Case

(Middlesex County Records. Ref. SR (W). 3368. Recog. 36)

Westminst. John Bampfylde of Leicesterfield St Martin in the fields
to wit.   Acknowledges himself to be indebted to our Sovereign
Lord the King, in the Sum of £.20.

George Huddesford of Kew in the County of Surry
Acknowledges himself to be indebted to our Sovereign
Lord the King, in the Sum of £.10.

Josiah Millidge of Maiden Lane St Paul Covent Garden
Printer Acknowledges himself to be indebted to our
Sovereign Lord the King, in the Sum of £.10.

Upon Condition that the said John Bampfylde do personally appear at the next General Quarter Sessions of the
Peace, to be held for the said City and Liberty, at Guildhall, in King-street, Westminster, then and there to
answer what shall be objected against him by Sr Joshua
Reynolds Knt and in the mean time to be upon his good
behaviour towards our Sovereign Lord the King and all
his Subjects, especially towards the said Sr Joshua
Reynolds.

And not to depart the Court without leave. Then this
Recognizance to be void, else to remain in full force.
Taken and acknowledged the 6th day of March 1779
Before GEO: REED.

SELECT BIBLIOGRAPHY

(See also under *Notes and References*)

A Journey from London to Genoa, through England, Portugal, Spain and France. By Joseph Baretti. 4 vols. London, 1770.

An Inquiry into the Rise and Establishment of the Royal Academy of Arts. By Robert Strange. London, 1775.

Seven Discourses Delivered in the Royal Academy by the President. London, 1778.

The Works of Sir Joshua Reynolds. Ed. with a memoir by Edmond Malone. 2 vols. London, 1797.

—— 2nd edition. 3 vols. London, 1798.

—— 5th edition. With an additional memoir by Joseph Farington. 3 vols. London, 1819.

Anecdotes of Painters. By Edward Edwards. London, 1808.

The Life of Sir Joshua Reynolds. By James Northcote. 2nd edition revised and augmented. London, 1818.

Diary and Letters of Madame d'Arblay. Ed. by her Niece. 7 vols. London, 1854.

Sir Joshua Reynolds, and his Works. Gleanings from his diary, unpublished manuscripts, and from other sources. By W. Cotton. Edited by J. Burnet. London, 1856.

Sir Joshua Reynolds' Notes and Observations on Pictures, etc. Edited by W. Cotton. London, 1859.

Life and Times of Sir Joshua Reynolds. By Charles Robert Leslie and Tom Taylor. 2 vols. London, 1865.

Sir Joshua Reynolds of Plympton. By James Hine, F.R.I.B.A., Plymouth, 1887.

Sir Joshua Reynolds. By Claude Phillips. London, 1894.

Memorials of an Eighteenth Century Painter. (James Northcote). By Stephen Gwynn. London, 1898.

A History of the Works of Sir Joshua Reynolds. By A. Graves and W. V. Cronin. 4 vols. London, 1899–1901.

Sir Joshua Reynolds. By Sir Walter Armstrong. London, 1900.

The Parentage and Kinsfolk of Sir Joshua Reynolds, P.R.A. By Sir Robert Edgcumbe. London, 1901.

London in the Eighteenth Century. By Sir Walter Besant. London, 1902.

Sir Joshua Reynolds: His Life and Art. By Lord Ronald Sutherland Gower. London, 1902.

Sir Joshua Reynolds. By A. L. Baldry. London, 1903. (Newnes Art Library.)

Sir Joshua Reynolds. By William B. Boulton. London, 1905.

Discourses by Sir Joshua Reynolds, Kt. With Introductions and Notes by Roger Fry. London, 1905.

A History of the Borough of Plympton Erle. By J. Brooking Rowe. Exeter, 1906.

Giuseppe Baretti. By Lacy Collison-Morley. London, 1909.

Thomas Gainsborough. By William T. Whitley. London, 1915.

The Farington Diary. By Joseph Farington, R.A. Ed. James Greig. 8 vols. London, 1922–28.

London's Open-Air Statuary. By Lord Edward Gleichen. London, 1928.
Artists and Their Friends in England, 1700-1799. By William T. Whitley. 2 vols. London, 1928.
Letters of Sir Joshua Reynolds. Collected and Edited by Frederick W. Hilles. Cambridge, 1929.
Private Papers of James Boswell from Malahide Castle. Ed. Geoffrey Scott and Frederick A. Pottle. 19 vols. New York, 1929-36.
Sir Joshua's Nephew. Ed. Susan M. Radcliffe. London, 1930.
Sir Joshua Reynolds. By John Steegmann. London, 1933. (Duckworth's Great Lives).
Boswell's Life of Johnson. Ed. George Birkbeck Hill. Revised and enlarged edition by L. F. Powell. 6 vols. Oxford, 1934-50.
Alterations in the Discourses of Sir Joshua Reynolds. By Lauder Greenway. New York, 1936.
The Literary Career of Sir Joshua Reynolds. By Frederick Whiley Hilles. Cambridge, 1936.
Edmund Burke and His Literary Friends. By Donald Cross Bryant. St. Louis, 1939.
Edmund Burke: A Life. By Sir Philip Magnus. London, 1939.
Reynolds. By Ellis K. Waterhouse. London, 1941.
British Portrait Painters. By John Russell. London, 1944.
National Gallery Catalogues: the British School. By Martin Davies. London, 1946.
A Century of British Painters. By Richard and Samuel Redgrave. London, 1947.
Conversations of James Northcote Esq. R.A. By William Hazlitt. Ed. Frank Swinnerton. London, 1949.
Nollekens and His Times. By J. T. Smith. Ed. G. W. Stonier. London, 1949.
Edmund Burke: Six Essays. By Thomas W. Copeland. London, 1950.
The Autobiography and Journals of Benjamin Robert Haydon. Ed. Malcolm Elwin. London, 1950.
The Royal Academy. By Sir Walter R. M. Lamb. Revised edition. London, 1951.
The Letters of Samuel Johnson. Ed. R. W. Chapman. 3 vols. Oxford, 1952.
Portraits by Sir Joshua Reynolds. Prepared for the Press with Introductions and Notes by Frederick W. Hilles. London, 1952.
Johnson's England. Ed. A. S. Turberville. 2 vols. Reprinted with corrections. Oxford, 1952.
Painting in Britain 1530 to 1790. By Ellis Waterhouse. London, 1953.
Angelica. By Adeline Hartcup. London, 1954.
The Analysis of Beauty. By William Hogarth. Ed. Joseph Burke. Oxford, 1955.
The Last Illness of Sir Joshua Reynolds. By Ernest E. Irons, M.D. Chicago, n.d.

There are several other biographies, books of reproductions with short forewords, etc. Engravings from Reynolds' pictures were published in three volumes by Hodgson and Graves, London, n.d. (all by S. W. Reynolds), and in a further three volumes by Henry Graves and Company, 1865. Catalogues of two Reynolds' exhibitions may be mentioned, that of 1883-4 at the Grosvenor Gallery, London, with notes by F. G. Stephens, and that of 1937 at 45 Park Lane, London, with notes by E. K. Waterhouse.

NOTES AND REFERENCES

B = *Boswell's Life of Johnson*, edited by George Birkbeck Hill, revised and enlarged edition by L. F. Powell. 6 vols. Oxford, 1934–50.

F = *The Farington Diary*, by Joseph Farington, R.A., edited by James Greig. 8 vols. London, 1922–8. (Typescripts of the Diary, including portions unpublished, are at Windsor Castle and in the B.M. Print Room.)

HL = *Letters of Sir Joshua Reynolds*, collected and edited by F. W. Hilles. Cambridge, 1929.

HLC = *The Literary Career of Sir Joshua Reynolds*, by F. W. Hilles. Cambridge, 1936.

HP = *Portraits by Sir Joshua Reynolds*, prepared for the Press with Introductions and Notes by F. W. Hilles. London, 1952.

W = *Artists and their Friends in England 1700–1799*, by William T. Whitley. 2 vols. London, 1928. (The Whitley Papers, on which his book is based, are in the B.M. Print Room.)

INTRODUCTION: A MAN AND HIS TIME

1. HP, p. 22.

CHAPTER 1: PLYMPTON

1. For the history of Plympton, etc., see William Cotton's *Gleanings* (1856), J. Brooking Rowe's *A History of the Borough of Plympton Erle* (1906), and James Hine's *Sir Joshua Reynolds of Plympton* (1887).

2. HLC, p. 2.

3. *Devon and Cornwall Notes and Queries*, Vol. VII, pp. 49–54 (1912–13). (I learn that Mr W. R. Hooper, part-author of a history of Great Torrington, inclines to Mr Murray's view.)

4. HLC, Chap. I, contains the best short account of Reynolds' father and of his famous son's education.

5. HL, pp. 184–5.

6. Mary Palmer's *A Devonshire Dialogue* (London, 1839, p. 15).

7. HLC, pp. 206–8.

8. HL, p. 65. With other books of his, Reynolds' Bible, containing his signature, is now in the possession of Mrs A. T. Copland-Griffiths. It has notes and corrections in his hand.

9. HL, p. 25.

10. F, October 10, 1809.

11. HP, p. 20.

12. See a letter from Mr Bulteel's great-grandson, Lord Mildmay of Flete, in *The Times* of July 21, 1923.

CHAPTER II: THE YEARS OF PREPARATION

1. See a report by Laurence Gomme drawn up for the Records and Museums Sub-Committee of the London County Council, January 29, 1915, preserved at County Hall.
2. *Lord M.* by David Cecil (1954, p. 89).
3. See J. T. Smith, *Nollekens and His Times* (1949, pp. 18–19).
4. William Cotton's *Gleanings*, p. 214.
5. F, February 20, 1807.
6. HL, pp. 4–6 and 9–13; W, I, p. 142 *et seq.*
7. I am indebted to an anonymous article in *Walpole Society*, Vol. VI, pp. 105–6.
8. P.R.O. Ad. 1/383. For Keppel see *The Life of Augustus Viscount Keppel* by Thomas Keppel (1842), Vol. I, p. 145 *et seq.* and *passim.*
9. National Maritime Museum, Greenwich.
10. For the voyage, see HL, pp. 4–13, and the *Life of Keppel.*
11. Article by Sir Charles Holmes, *Burl. Mag.*, May, 1930.
12. HL, p. 5.
13. See an article by John Steegmann, "Portraits of Reynolds", *Burl. Mag.*, February, 1942.
14. *The Parentage and Kinsfolk of Sir Joshua Reynolds*, by Sir Robert Edgcumbe (1901), pp. 17–18.
15. HP, p. 19.
16. HLC, p. 9.

CHAPTER III: ITALY

1. See *The Book of Italian Travel (1580–1900)* by H. Neville Maugham (1903) and Dr G. M. Trevelyan's British Academy lecture, "Englishmen and Italians" (1919).
2. These quotations are from a notebook in Mrs A. T. Copland-Griffiths' possession, of which there is a photographic copy in the British Museum.
3. Metropolitan Museum of Art, New York; HLC, p. 10.
4. HLC, pp. 9–11 and Appendix.
5. W, II, p. 313.
6. HL, pp. 7–8.
7. See *Burl. Mag.*, February, 1942, "Three Phases of Reynolds's Method", by Charles Mitchell, and articles by E. Wind published by the Warburg Institute, 1930–1 and 1938.
8. *Anecdotes of Painting in England*, by Horace Walpole, (1849), Vol. I, p. xvii (footnote).
9. Sir Robert Edgcumbe, *op. cit.*, p. 18.
10. HL, p. 18.
11. *Diary and Letters of Madame d'Arblay*, edited by her niece (1854). December 28, 1782.
12. See Catalogue of the exhibition "Artists in 17th Century Rome", Wildenstein Gallery, London, June, 1955. Mola's caricature is now in the Witt Collection, Courtauld Institute.
13. Soane Museum notebook.
14. Ibid.
15. B.M. notebook.

16. Soane Museum notebook.
17. They are published in full in the first volume of Leslie and Taylor's biography (pp. 67–84 and Appendix).
18. Chambers Papers, R.I.B.A. Library.

CHAPTER IV: REYNOLDS CONQUERS LONDON

1. Mrs Copland-Griffiths' collection.
2. Ibid.
3. B, I, p. 165.
4. County Hall records.
5. See the interesting notes by C. K. Adams and Martin Davies in National Portrait Gallery archives.
6. F, March 15, 1808.
7. Ibid.
8. *Conversations with James Ward*, ed. Ernest Fletcher (1901).
9. W, I, p. 197.
10. National Portrait Gallery archives (Letter of October 15, 1761).
11. Ibid. Ref. 4666 (Letter of April 27, 1813).
12. Mrs Copland-Griffiths' collection.
13. The notebook for 1755 is in the Cottonian Collection, Plymouth. The remainder of the notebooks are at the Royal Academy, Burlington House. The missing notebooks are those for 1756, 1763, 1774–6 (inclusive), 1778, 1783 and 1785.
14. MS. note by Constable in the Earl of Plymouth's Collection of MSS.
15. HLC, pp. 12–13.
16. HP, p. 66.
17. B, I, p. 246 *et seq.*
18. HP, p. 66 *et seq.*
19. B, I, pp. 1 and 245; III, p. 5; V, p. 102.
20. B, VI, Supplementary "Table of Anonymous Persons".
21. Royal Society of Arts records.
22. Torrington burial register.
23. Mrs Copland-Griffiths' collection.
24. HL, p. 92.
25. *The Analysis of Beauty*, ed. Joseph Burke (1955), p. 10.
26. Ibid., p. 16.
27. Mrs Copland-Griffiths' collection.
28. HLC, p. 15 *et seq.*

CHAPTER V: LEICESTER FIELDS

1. For Leicester Square and Reynolds' house there, see an engraving (1754) in Stow's *Survey of London*; *The Story of Leicester Square* by John Hollingshead (1892); Supplement to *The Architect and Building News*, May 7, 1937; *Two Centuries of Soho*, by the Clergy of St Anne's, Soho (1898, p. 129); a report on the house by the Librarian of the City of Westminster, dated February, 1937, notes by W. Dathy Quirke made at the same time, and a collection of photographs, all at County Hall; the Lives of Reynolds, by Northcote and Leslie and Taylor; and material at Westminster Public Library, Archives Department, including drawings by J. P. Elmslie.

2. Illustrated in James Paine's *Plans, Elevations, and Sections of Noblemen and Gentlemen's Houses 1767–83*, Vol. II, plate XCVII.

3. *Conversations of James Northcote Esq., R.A.*, by William Hazlitt (1949, p. 20).

4. W. P. Frith, *My Autobiography and Reminiscences*, Vol. III (1888), p. 124.

5. Letter to W. Jackson at Burlington House.

6. F, January 28, 1799.

7. J. T. Smith, *Nollekens and his Times* (1949, p. 194).

8. Most of the furniture and appurtenances of Reynolds' home mentioned in this chapter—with the exception of the mopstick—can be seen in Mrs A. T. Copland-Griffiths' collection or at the Royal Academy, Burlington House.

9. HL, p. 15.

10. HLC, pp. 23–4.

11. In Professor F. W. Hilles' collection. See HLC, pp. 27–32.

12. B, I, p. 374.

13. Ibid., pp. 377–9.

14. B, IV, p. 322.

15. B, I, p. 145; HP, p. 61.

16. HP, p. 61.

17. B, I, p. 477 *et seq*.

18. HP, pp. 86–8.

19. HP, pp. 40–54.

20. B, III, p. 192.

21. See *Edmund Burke: Six Essays*, by Thomas W. Copeland (1950, pp. 84–5).

22. *Diary and Letters of Madame d'Arblay*, Vol. II, June 1782, pp. 113 *et seq*., and Vol. V, p. 92.

23. B, II, pp. 222–3.

24. W. T. Whitley, *Thomas Gainsborough* (1915, p. 75).

25. Reproduced in *Reynolds*, by Ellis K. Waterhouse (1941, plate 134).

26. F, April 17, 1794.

27. HL, pp. 13–14.

CHAPTER VI: THE ROYAL ACADEMY

1. W, I, pp. 215–17.

2. R.I.B.A. Library: letters to Milbanke of February 21, 1776, and September 22, 1788.

3. HL, p. 15.

4. See *The Life, Studies and Works of Benjamin West Esq.*, by John Galt (1820, pp. 40–1).

5. F, December 12, 1804.

6. John Galt, *op. cit.*, pp. 41–4.

7. HL, p. 22.

8. Sir John Hawkins, *Johnson's Works* (1787), Chap. XI, p. 215.

9. See W, I, Chap. XV, for some of this.

10. W, I, p. 254.

11. F, December 22, 1799; Leslie and Taylor, II, p. 611.

12. F, December 10, 1804.

13. Letter of January, 1770, in the archives of the Upsala University, quoted in an important unpublished thesis on Chambers by Mrs H. M. Martienssen at the Courtauld Institute. For further information on Chambers see Thomas Hardwick's memoir prefaced to Joseph Gwilt's edition of Chambers' *Treatise on Civil*

Architecture (1825); Austin Dobson's essay *Chambers the Architect* in *Old Kensington Palace and other Papers* (O.U.P. World's Classics edition, 1926); and a short study by Trystan Edwards in the Masters of Architecture series.

14. F, December 22, 1799.

15. HLC, pp. 34-5.

16. From a sheet of the fair copy preserved in Sir John Herschel's book of Reynolds' drawings deposited with the Royal Academy.

17. Ibid.

18. William Blake's notes on the Discourses can be read at the British Museum. They are written into a copy of Vol. I of the second edition of Edmond Malone's *The Works of Sir Joshua Reynolds, Knight* (London, 1798). See also Alexander Gilchrist's *Life of Blake* (1863).

19. HLC, p. 49.

20. HP, p. 104.

21. See *The Inquiry into the Rise and Establishment of the Royal Academy of Arts*, by Robert Strange (1775).

CHAPTER VII: THE ROAD TO RICHMOND

1. HL, pp. 79-80; Leslie and Taylor (1865), Vol. II, p. 542.

2. W, II, p. 287.

3. Historical MSS. Commission. Charlemont MSS, Vol. I, pp. 304-5. The rough drafts of Chambers' discourses are in the R.I.B.A. Library.

4. B.M. Add. MSS. 41133.

5. Court Rolls of the Manor of Richmond, p. 1972 (August 12, 1772).

6. B.M. Add. MSS. 41133.

7. Ibid.

8. Ibid., f. 856.

9. *Recollections of the Table talk of Samuel Rogers* (1856, p. 86).

10. Petersham Vestry Books.

11. HL, p. 241.

12. HP, p. 5 and pp. 166-7.

13. HP, p. 89 *et seq.*, and p. 123 *et seq.*

14. See *Giuseppe Baretti*, by Lacy Collison-Morley (1909).

15. From a copy of a letter by Theophila Gwatkin (*née* Palmer) in Mrs A. T. Copland-Griffiths' collection.

16. B.M. Add MSS. 41135 (letter of April 15, 1774).

17. R.I.B.A. Library.

CHAPTER VIII: PAGE AND MONARCH

1. For Northcote, see *Memorials of an Eighteenth Century Painter*, by Stephen Gwynn (1898), also W, II, p. 279 *et seq.*, and the Whitley Papers in the B.M. Print Room, where Whitley has collected Northcote's letters from various sources. Northcote's Life of Reynolds (2 vols., 2nd ed., 1818) contains much personal reminiscence. His "Conversations" with Hàzlitt are available in an edition of 1949, and he also figures in *Conversations with James Ward*, ed. Ernest Fletcher (1901).

2. The picture is reproduced in Waterhouse, *Reynolds* (1941, plate 147). See a note by Martin Davies in National Portrait Gallery archives.

3. HL, pp. 35-6.

4. HL, p. 37.

5. Whitefoord Papers. B.M. Add. MSS. 36596, f. 229. See also William Cotton, *Gleanings* (1856, p. 255).

6. B.M. Add MSS. 41135, ff. 586 and 59.

7. F, November 25, 1793.

8. *The Works of James Barry, Esq.* (1809), Vol. II, pp. 538–40.

9. Mrs A. T. Copland-Griffiths' collection. The references to Hazlitt's *Conversations* will be found, in the edition published in 1949 by Frederick Muller, on p. 24 and p. 201. The letter is addressed "To Mrs Gwatkin, Stoke Green-house, Baylis near Colnbrook, Bucks", and postmarked September 13, 1830.

10. See W, I, pp. 251–3, 289–91, 292, 373; and W, II, pp. 272–9.

11. Hazlitt's *Conversations of James Northcote* (1949 edn., p. 80).

CHAPTER IX: WOMEN, WINE AND SNUFF

1. William Cotton, *op. cit.* (1856), pp. 92–3.

2. F, January 16, 1796.

3. According to the post mortem. See Dr Ernest E. Irons, *The Last Illness of Sir Joshua Reynolds.*

4. B, III, p. 329 (footnote).

5. B, III, pp. 328–9; April 28, 1778.

6. B, III, p. 41; April 12, 1776.

7. William Cotton, *op. cit.* (1856), pp. 90–1.

8. HL, p. 99. February 12, 1783.

9. Mrs A. T. Copland-Griffiths' collection.

10. W, I, p. 252.

11. Leslie and Taylor, I, p. 430.

12. *The Journal of James Boswell 1786–1789: Private Papers of James Boswell from Malahide Castle,* ed. Geoffrey Scott and Frederick A. Pottle, Vol. XVII. March 29, 1788.

13. R.I.B.A. Library. Undated fragment.

14. F, October 18, 1803.

15. See Adeline Hartcup, *Angelica* (1954), p. 40.

16. Ibid., p. 42.

17. Repr. in *Burl. Mag.,* February, 1942.

18. F, January 6, 1808.

19. Mr J. Maher's collection. Exh. R.A. 1951–2, and Ken Wood, 1955.

20. R.I.B.A. Library.

21. J. T. Smith, *Nollekens and his Times* (1949, p. 70).

22. Ibid., p. 75.

23. HLC, p. 207.

24. W, I, p. 149.

25. F, May 9, 1806.

26. *Diary and Letters of Madame d'Arblay,* edited by her niece (1854), Vol. I, p. 53 (August, 1778).

27. Letter from Aubrey Edgcumbe to the author.

28. *Op. cit.,* Vol. I, p. 88 *et seq.* (September, 1778).

29. Ibid., January, 1779.

30. Ibid., Vol. II, p. 153 *et seq.* (December 8, 1782).

31. Ibid.

32. Ibid., Vol. II, p. 177 *et seq.* (December 28, 1782).

33. B, V, p. 286.

34. Mrs A. T. Copland-Griffiths' collection.
35. *The Autobiography and Journals of Benjamin Robert Haydon*, ed. Malcolm Elwin (1950), p. 412.
36. *Old and New London* (Thornbury and Walford), Vol. IV, (1897), by Edward Walford, p. 235.
37. F, March 15, 1808.
38. *The Letters of Samuel Johnson*, ed. R. W. Chapman (1952), Vol. III, p. 270.
39. HL, pp. 79–80.
40. F, January 17, 1799.
41. *Sir Joshua's Nephew*, ed. Susan M. Radcliffe (1930), pp. xii–xiii, etc.; HL, p. 162.
42. Susan M. Radcliffe, *op. cit.*, p. 123.
43. Mrs A. T. Copland-Griffiths' collection.
44. See Malcolm Elwin, *op. cit.*, Haydon's Journals, p. 634.
45. *The Town Labourer: 1760–1832*, by J. L. Hammond and Barbara Hammond (1920), p. 193.
46. From a version written in a vellum-bound book formerly belonging to Sir Joshua by Offy's grandson J. R. Gwatkin, who may have heard it from his grandmother (Mrs A. T. Copland-Griffiths' collection). A more finished version appears in Leslie and Taylor, Vol. I, p. 5 (footnote).
47. HL, p. 54.
48. *Diary and Letters of Madame d'Arblay, op. cit.*, Vol. I, September, 1778.
49. HL, p. 78.
50. Leslie and Taylor, Vol. II, pp. 318–19.
51. Mrs A. T. Copland-Griffiths owns another version of the portrait, perhaps a copy by Frances Reynolds.
52. See W, II, pp. 157–61, for information about Mary Palmer.
53. *Diary and Letters of Madame d'Arblay, op. cit.*, Vol. I, January, 1779.
54. For Bampfylde see W, II, pp. 157–61; *Devon and Cornwall Notes and Queries*, Vol. VII, pp. 219–22; a letter from Southey to Sir Egerton Brydges in "Autobiography" of Sir E. B. (1834, pp. 257–61); Southey's *Specimens of the Later English Poets*, Vol. III (1807), p. 434 et seq.; Routledge's British Poets (1853); and D.N.B. entry.
55. W, II, p. 159.
56. W, II, p. 158; "Autobiography" of Sir Egerton Brydges, etc.
57. Middlesex County Records. Ref.: SR (W). 3368. Recog. 36.

CHAPTER X: KING'S PRINCIPAL PORTRAIT PAINTER

1. Letter of 24 May, 1787 (Althorp MSS.).
2. B.M. Add. MSS. 36596, f. 208.
3. Fitzwilliam Museum, Cambridge; HL, p. 56.
4. Ellis K. Waterhouse: *Reynolds* (1941, p. 14).
5. B.M. Add. MSS. 39871, f. 6.
6. *Diary and Letters of Madame d'Arblay, op. cit.* February 13, 1788.
7. HL, pp. 58–61.
8. Ibid., p. 111. September 24, 1784.
9. F, October 3, 1796.
10. W, I, pp. 255–6.
11. Whitley Papers, B.M. Print Room.
12. *Letters of Samuel Johnson* (1952), ed. R. W. Chapman, Vol. II, p. 732. June 23, 1781.

13. F, November 3, 1799; February 6, 1804.
14. Edmond Malone's edition of Reynolds' *Works* (1819, Vol. II, p. 248).
15. Ibid., pp. 247–427.
16. Reynolds' letters written to Burke on this continental tour are in HL, pp. 80–8.
17. B, IV, pp. 161–2.
18. HL, pp. 100–1; B, IV, p. 510.
19. HL, p. 103; W, II, p. 6.
20. W. T. Whitley, *Thomas Gainsborough* (1915, p. 231).
21. Public Records Office. See also Malone, *Works* of Sir Joshua Reynolds (1819, Vol. I, p. lxxiv).
22. Wentworth Woodhouse Collection, Central Library, Sheffield.
23. B, IV, pp. 366–7.
24. HL, pp. 112–13.
25. Fitzwilliam Museum, Cambridge.
26. F, April 16 and 17, 1794.

CHAPTER XI: THE FRIEND OF JOHNSON

1. B, IV, p. 253.
2. Ibid., p. 283.
3. *The Private Papers of James Boswell*, ed. Geoffrey Scott and Frederick A. Pottle (1928–34), Vol. VI, p. 56.
4. B, IV, pp. 334–9.
5. Ibid., pp. 367–8.
6. Published in *The Times*, January 26, 1938.
7. HL, p. 114.
8. HL, pp. 167–8.
9. HP, pp. 80–1.
10. B, IV, pp. 402–14.
11. Wentworth Woodhouse Collection, Central Library, Sheffield.
12. B, IV, pp. 419–20.
13. See HL, especially Chap. VIII, and *Alterations in the Discourses of Sir Joshua Reynolds*, by Lauder Greenway (New York, 1936).
14. B, IV, p. 447 *et seq.* (Appendix H).
15. HL, p. 123.
16. B, IV, p. 468.
17. R.A. General Assembly Minutes, May 5, 1791.
18. R.A. Council Minutes, June 25, 1791, and General Assembly Minutes, July 2, 1791.
19. R.A. General Assembly Minutes, July 2, 1791. A draft reply to Chambers' objections, in Reynolds' hand, is printed in Leslie and Taylor's biography (1865, Vol. II, pp. 610–15).
20. Wentworth Woodhouse Collection, Central Library, Sheffield.
21. With the help of Mr N. de Bazille Corbin, Agent for the Eastern Area of the National Trust, and his secretary, I have investigated a suggestion that the projected obelisk might be identical with the pyramidal mausoleum completed by Bonomi in 1794 for John, second Earl of Buckinghamshire, at Blickling Hall, Norfolk (now owned by the National Trust); but I think this possibility can be ruled out. For one thing, the dates do not appear to agree. According to the Report of the Historical MSS Commission, 1905, Lord Buckinghamshire himself

designed his mausoleum but did not finish it before his death in 1793. Again, the design does not correspond with the description in Reynolds' letter, but is in the form of a plain and lofty pyramid, with the earl's arms and supporters over the entrance and an elaborate inscription at the rear. Besides Lord Buckinghamshire's tomb, it contains those of his two wives. On the other hand, we know that Reynolds visited Burke at Beaconsfield in January, 1791 (HL, p. 208), and Mr J. M. McColl, who has studied the history and topography of Beaconsfield, believes that the reference to "a narrow gravel walk from the Wood to the Obelisk" makes it virtually certain that a site in the grounds of Butler's Court was intended. The purpose of the obelisk remains a matter for conjecture.

22. *Johnson's England*, ed. A. S. Turberville (1933, p. 91); John Bailey, *Johnson and his Circle* (1913, p. 1). The long history of Johnson's monument is best recorded in B, IV, Appendix I.

CHAPTER XII: THE SILVER SPECTACLES

1. Quoted in Leslie and Taylor's biography, Vol. II, p. 482.
2. HL, pp. 131-3.
3. Ibid., pp. 134-5.
4. Malone, *Works*, I, p. lxxii *et seq.*
5. HL, p. 149.
6. B, III, p. 370.
7. Joseph Farington in Malone's *Works* (1819 edn., p. cxcvii).
8. HP, Appendix III, contains the best account of Reynolds' relations with Boydell.
9. HL, pp. 189-90.
10. Ibid., p. 179 (August 31, 1787).
11. HP, p. 16 (1 October, 1782).
12. HL, pp. 127-8.
13. From an unidentified cutting in the Royal Academy Library.
14. HP, Chap. II.
15. F, September 28, 1806.
16. HL, p. 249, and W. T. Whitley, *Thomas Gainsborough* (1915, p. 186).
17. Gainsborough's letter to Lord Sandwich, dated November 29, 1784, was published in *The Times* of January 27, 1955.
18. Royal Academy Library.
19. HL, p. 97.
20. Mary Palmer's letter, dated April 27, 1789, is now in the possession of Brooks's Club. I have introduced the paragraphing and some additional punctuation.
21. Ibid.
22. Ibid.
23. Letter to the author from Mr Rupert Scott. See also Dr Ernest E. Irons, *The Last Illness of Sir Joshua Reynolds* (Chicago, n.d.).

CHAPTER XIII: "COUNT NO MAN HAPPY"

1. Wentworth Woodhouse Collection, Central Library, Sheffield.
2. HL, pp. 208-10.
3. Leslie and Taylor, II, p. 544 (Miss Fox's recollection).
4. F, February 19, 1795.

5. From Reynolds' unpublished *Apologia* in the Bonomi affair, painstakingly reconstructed by Professor Hilles; HLC, Appendix III (p. 270). Joseph Farington's account of the affair in his *Memoir*, bound up with Malone's *Works* (1819 edition), is a useful corrective in certain respects.

6. F, January 8, 1804.

7. HLC, Appendix III (p. 276).

8. Ibid., p. 260.

9. R.I.B.A. Library.

10. HLC, Appendix III (p. 262). My account of this scene at the Academy is based on Reynolds' *Apologia*.

11. Ibid., p. 265.

12. HL, p. 193.

13. From an unidentified cutting in the Royal Academy Library.

14. R.A. General Assembly Minutes.

15. HLC, Appendix III (p. 274).

16. F, March 27, 1795.

17. HLC, p. 187.

18. HL, pp. 252-6.

19. Ibid., p. 256.

20. HLC, p. 182; W, II, pp. 134-5.

21. R.A. Notebook, September 13, 1790.

22. Leslie and Taylor, Vol. II, pp. 606-8.

23. Published in HP, Appendix II.

24. The catalogue of "Ralph's Exhibition" is printed in *A History of the Works of Sir Joshua Reynolds P.R.A.* by Algernon Graves and W. V. Cronin, Vol. IV. See also W, II, pp. 181-2.

25. *Memorials of an Eighteenth Century Painter (James Northcote)*, by Stephen Gwynn (1898, p. 226 *et seq.*).

26. Leslie and Taylor, Vol. II, pp. 610-15.

27. Malone, *Works* (1819, p. cviii).

28. R.A. Council Minutes.

29. *Diary and Letters of Madame d'Arblay*, edited by her niece (1854, Vol. V, November, 1791).

30. Somerset House.

31. HP, p. 18; F, April 3, 1807.

32. HP, pp. 18-19.

33. *The Last Illness of Sir Joshua Reynolds*, by Ernest E. Irons, M.B. (Chicago, n.d.).

34. Historical MSS. Commission (Sir Philip Wilbraham, Bt. Collection).

35. R.A. General Assembly Minutes.

36. Malone, Northcote and Leslie and Taylor all give long accounts of the funeral.

CHAPTER XIV: AFTER THE FUNERAL

1. F, January 21, 1796.

2. See Malone, *Works* (1819, pp. cclvii *et seq.*).

3. See an interesting article "The 18th Century Artist as Picture Dealer" in *The Times* of August 6, 1956.

4. I am grateful to Mrs A. T. Copland-Griffiths for details of Lady Thomond's will.

5. F, February 20, 1794.

6. National Portrait Gallery Archives: 4666.
7. F, February 14, 1794.
8. Ibid., July 10, October 14, December 31, 1795.
9. W, II, p. 151.
10. *Public Advertiser*, May 2, 1792.
11. W. P. Frith, *My Autobiography and Reminiscences*, Vol. III (1888), p. 24.
12. HL, p. 119.

INDEX

Abercorn, Duke of, 24
Abington, Mrs, 97, 122
Academy of Arts: *see* Royal Academy
Acland, Colonel, 97
Adam brothers, 215
"Age of Innocence", 125, 150, 201, 202
Albemarle, Countess of, 63
Albert Memorial, 232
Algiers, R. at, 27
Annigoni, Pietro, 235
Antwerp, R. at, 168-9
"Archers, The", 97
Ashburton, Lord (*earlier* John Dunning), 172-3, 182
Astley, John, 39, 60
Aylesford, Lord, 215

Bacon, John, 188, 193
Baker, Sir George, 174, 225, 227
Baker, Mary, 7
Baker, Theophila, 6, 7
Baker, Rev. Thomas, 6, 7
Balbi, Comtesse de, 223
Bampfylde, Lady, 155
Bampfylde, John, 153-8, 251
Bankes, John, 81
Banks, Sir Joseph, 184, 188, 189, 230
Banks, Thomas, 219, 220
Baretti, Giuseppe, 59, 93, 112-18, 132; R's parody of his travel book, 40, 112-18, 239; portrait, 117, 187
Barron, Hugh, 119
Barry, James, 34, 38, 103, 129-30, 175-6, 180, 218-19, 229
Bartoli, Professor, 112
Bartolozzi, Francesco, 92, 207
Bate, Henry, 176
Bath, Lord, 53
Bath, Order of the, R. applies for secretaryship, 196

Battoni, Pompeo, 34
Beach, Thomas, 119
Beaconsfield, 192-3, 212, 213, 231
Beattie, Dr James, 67, 124
Beattie, Margaret, 77
Beauclerk, Topham, 81
Beaufort, Duke of, 51
Beaumont, Sir George, 56, 57, 192-3, 226, 238
Beckford, Susannah, 56
Beckford, William, 55-6, 172
Beechey, Sir William, 71
Belgium: *see* Flanders
Bernini, Giovanni, 40, 224
Billington, Mrs, 208
Bingham, Sir Charles, 70
Bitumen, use by R.: *see under* Colours and materials
Blagden, Dr Charles, 153, 225
Blake, William, 100, 103-6, 231, 232, 236, 237
Blakeney, General William, 28
Blenheim, 2, 124, 160
Bonomi, Giuseppe, 192, 214-19, 229
Boringdon, Lord (*earlier* John Parker), 173
Boswell, James, proposed biography of R. by, 12, 203-4, 221; on R., 30, 58-9, 180; on meetings between Johnson and R., 57-9; Burke and, 84, 202; and wine, 134; and Crabbe's "The Village", 174; and Johnson's proposed visit to Italy, 181; on Johnson's last requests, 183; relations with R., 202-4; Royal Academy appointment, 203; portrait, 203; on R's eyesight, 211; and R's religious views, 226-7; at R's funeral, 229 (and cited *en passim*)
Bourdon, Sebastian, 56

265

Bouverie, Jacob, 63
Bowles, Jane, 124
Boydell, John, 199–201, 224
Breda, C. F. von, 139
Brentford, 112, 117, 245–6
British Institution, 232
Brodribb, C. W., quoted, 1
Brooks's ball, 208–10
Brosses, Charles de, 31–3
Browne, Solomon, 110
Bruce, Lord, 39
Brummell, "Beau", 172
Buccleuch children, 160
Bulteel, Mr (of Flete), 13–15
Bunbury, Sir Charles, 184
Bunbury, Lady Sarah, 85, 175
Burgoyne, General John, 221
Burke, Edmund, on Zachariah
    Mudge, 16; friendship with R.,
    56, 59, 82–4, 223; and Hogarth,
    66; member of "The Club", 81,
    174; and Boswell, 84, 202; in-
    feriority complex, 84; and Royal
    Academy, 92; and Baretti, 113;
    home at Beaconsfield, 124, 212;
    on R's character, 136, 228; and
    Fanny Burney's Cecilia, 144–5;
    friendship with Offy Palmer,
    150, 152; and Warren Hastings,
    162; house saved in Gordon
    Riots, 166; R's letters quoted,
    170, 171, 177; Government
    posts, 172, 173, 178; and James
    Barry, 175; and Dr Johnson, 184,
    188, 192–3; and R's Discourses,
    185–6; and Boydell, 199; pro-
    posed biography of R., 203–4;
    and French Revolution, 213; R's
    executor, 226; R's bequest to,
    226; obituary notice of R., 228;
    at R's funeral, 229; talkative and
    eloquent, 230; portrait, 249
Burke, Richard, 90, 172, 180–1
Burlington, Lady, 75, 236
Burney, Dr Charles, 167, 222
Burney, Fanny, on R. at Minorca, 28;
    and Burke, 84; R's copy of

Evelina, 142; meetings with R.,
    142–5, 225–6; Cecilia published,
    144–5; on Offy Palmer, 151; and
    George Huddesford, 154; and
    trial of Warren Hastings, 162;
    quoted, 40, 86, 167
Burwood, 48
Bute, Lord, 79
Buttery, Horace A., 55, 248

Caricaturist, R. as, 40, 41, 112
Carlisle, Countess of, 86
Carmine, use by R.: see under Colours
    and materials
Carracci, Agostino, 40
Cathcart, Lord, 51
Catherine the Great of Russia, 196–7
Cats, Jacob, 10, 12
Catton, Charles, 77, 92
Cavendish, Lord Richard, 166
Centurion, H.M.S., 26–7
Ceracchi, G., 214, 232
Chambers, Catherine, 46, 47
Chambers, Sir William, character
    sketch, 45–6, 88–9; R's meeting
    with in Paris, 45–6; Swedish
    affinity, 46; on travelling, 46;
    taste for chinoiserie, 46, 76; and
    Society of Arts, 60, 61, 78; rela-
    tions with R., 88–9, 95–6, 165,
    206–7, 233; court posts, 89; and
    Incorporated Society of Artists,
    90; and Royal Academy, 90,
    91; aspirations to presidency of
    Academy, 91, 94, 96; elected
    treasurer, 92–5; Swedish knight-
    hood, 95; established at Whitton,
    107, 112; architect of Wick
    House, Richmond, 108–12; dis-
    courses on architecture, 108–9;
    R's "Journey" possibly written
    for, 112, 116; and uniform for
    academicians, 126–7; on sex life,
    137; portrait, 139, 165, 166; and
    Hone's "The Conjuror", 140–1;
    short disappearance (1780), 165;
    hostility towards R., 178, 221;

and Johnson statue, 189–91, 224–5; and Bonomi affair (1790), 216–17, 219–20; and R's resignation from Academy, 219–20; takes chair at Academy meeting (1791), 225; objects to R's body lying-in-state at Somerset House, 228; at R's funeral, 229; death (1796), 233; in close proximity to R. on memorials, 232–3; mentioned, 77, 78, 154, 167

Chamier, Anthony, 81–2

Charlemont, Lord, 39, 108

Charlotte, Queen, 164, 166, 250

Child, Sarah Anne (*later* Countess of Westmorland), 122

Chinoiserie, 46, 76

Cholmondeley, Lord, 209

Cholmondeley, Mrs, 143, 154

Churches, decoration of, 2, 125, 169

Cipriani, G. B., 101

"Club, The": *see* Literary Club

Coach used by R., 77–8

Cockburn (Lady) and her children, 124

Cocks, Miss, 208–10

Coleorton, cenotaph at, 193, 238

Collection of pictures formed by R., 56, 76–7, 196–7, 223–4, 231

Colman, George, 107, 110–11, 184

Colours and materials used by R., imperfections, 54–5, 75–6, 121, 163, 166, 232, 234, 248–50; preference for carmine, 54, 75, 248; use of bitumen, 197, 203, 234, 248–50

Constable, John, 193

Constant, Benjamin, quoted, 236

"Continence of Scipio", 199

Copley, J. S., 71, 88, 220

Copying, R. and, 34, 35, 179

Cosway, Richard, 61, 133

Cotes, Francis, 53, 78, 90, 92, 96

Cotterell, Misses, 57

Cotton, William, 10

Courtenay, John, 137, 212

Coutts, Thomas, 19

Cowdray House, 213

Crabbe, George, 174–5

Craunch, Mr, 14, 15

Cremorne, Lord, 51

Crewe, Frances, 150, 160

Crewe, Master, as Henry VIII, 36, 150, 160, 235

Cumberland, Duke of, 71

Cust, Sir John, 86

Cutcliffe, Mr (of Bideford), 14–15, 18, 20

Cutcliffe, Thomas, 17

Dance, George, 92, 139

Dance, Nathaniel, 92, 139–40

Dantan, Jean-Pierre, 41

Dartmouth, Lord, 85

Daulby, Daniel, 160–1

Davis, Rev. John, 21

Dawson, Lady Anne, 51

"Death of Cardinal Beaufort", 186, 200, 201

Delany, Mrs, 144

Devon dialect, 9

Devonport: *see* Plymouth Rock

Devonshire, Duke of, 51

Devonshire (Georgiana, Duchess of) and her daughter, 159, 166, 172, 197, 249

Devonshire Club, 208

Dilettanti Society, 60, 88, 160, 208, 236

Discourses by Reynolds, 64, 65, 93, 102–3, 198, 199, 222–3; "Ironical Discourse", 112, 223; help of Johnson and Burke, 185–6; collected edition (1797), 186, 232; fifty editions, 186; First Discourse (1769), 97–100; Second, 33–5, 101–2; Third, 65, 66, 105, 185; Fourth, 121; Fifth, 38; Sixth, 37, 105; Tenth, 2; Twelfth, 35, 36, 185; Thirteenth, 2; Fourteenth, 65, 68, 159, 204–7; Fifteenth (1790), 103, 222–3

Dodsley, Robert, 55

Domenichino, D. Z., 40

Doughty, William, 119
D'Oyly, Sir John, 208, 209
Drawings by R., 41–2
Drinking-songs by R., 135
Drury, Alfred, 232
Du Fresnoy, C. A., 131, 172
Dunning, John: see Ashburton, Lord
Dysart, Earl of, 107–8

Edgcumbe, George, Lord: see Mount Edgcumbe, Earl of
Edgcumbe, Richard, 1st Lord, 26, 27, 34
Edgcumbe, Richard, 2nd Lord, 13, 15, 60
Edgcumbe, Sir Robert, 152
Edwards, Edward, 216–19
Elford, William, 120
Eliot family, 24, 25
English Academy, Rome, 60
Esdaile, Mrs Arundell, 2
Eumelian Club, 208
Execution, public, R. witnesses, 203
Exhibition of R's paintings (1813), 54, 232

Farington, Joseph, visits Plympton, 9–10; and Royal Academy, 91–2, 126; on Angelica Kauffmann, 139–40; on Academy students and bread, 174; cited *en passim*
Fischel, Oskar, quoted, 31
Fisher, Kitty, 70, 71, 86, 136
Fitzherbert, William, 113
Fitzwilliam, Lady Charlotte, 51
Flanders, R. visits, 167–71, 196–7, 249
Flaxman, John, 137, 232
Foley, J. H., 232
"Fortitude", 148
Foster, Lady Betty, 197, 235
Fouquières, Jacques, 56
Fox, Charles James, 85, 111, 173, 174, 176
Freemasons' Tavern, 216
French Revolution, 195, 212, 213, 223
"Fresnoy", 131–2, 136
Fresnoy, Du: see Du Fresnoy

Fry, Roger, 102
Fuseli, Henry, 139, 166, 219

Gainsborough, Thomas, contrasted with R., 2, 102, 158–9; patronized by George III, 71; tribute to R., 75; original member of Royal Academy, 92; candidate for presidency, 96; Reynolds sits to, 144, 173, 204–5; withdraws from 1784 Academy exhibition, 176, 205; rival exhibition, 176; candidate for appointment as King's Principal Portrait Painter, 176–7, 205; R's appreciation of, 204–7; R's deathbed reconciliation with, 204–5; death (1788), 205; mentioned, 85, 166, 235
Galt, John, 91, 92
Gandy, William, 25
Gardiner, Luke, 124
Gardiner, William, 111
Garrick, David, friendship with R., 59, 107; and Society of Arts, 61; portraits, 70, 83, 122–3; gift of chest to R., 77; R's critical account of, 82–3; and Baretti, 113; and Joseph Palmer's play, 148
"Garrick between Tragedy and Comedy", 64, 150
Gentleman's Magazine, 230
George I, statue of, 72
George III, King, proclamation, 4; portraits, 71, 166, 250; taught drawing by Chambers, 89; and Royal Academy, 90–3, 95; attitude to R., 92–4, 164; naval review, 123; and Gordon Riots, 166; and Dr Johnson, 181–2; vetoes Academy contribution to Johnson statue, 191; recovery from insanity, 208, 210; on Tyler, 216; and R's resignation as P.R.A., 220, 221; authorizes lying-in-state of R's body at Somerset House, 208; loses patience with Chambers, 233

Ghezzi, P. L., 40
Giardini, Felice de, 112
Gibbon, Edward, 31, 145, 166
Gibraltar, R. at, 27
Gill, Charles, 99, 100, 119
Gilpin, William, 223
Goldsmith, Oliver, friendship with R., 59, 80, 91, 107; member of "The Club", 81; R's account of, 83; portraits, 83, 96, 187; "The Deserted Village" dedicated to R., 83, 138; Royal Academy appointment, 93; mock-epitaph on R., 104–5; on Baretti, 113; Turnham Green anecdote, 115–116; death (1774), 127; memorials, 127; and Angelica Kauffmann, 138; Mrs Gwyn and, 142; Offy Palmer and, 149–50
Gordon, Duchess of, 86
Gordon, Frances Isabella, 201
Gordon Riots (1780), 4, 166
"Graces adorning a term of Hymen", 124, 167, 175
Grafton, Duke of, 94
Grant, Albert, 72
Grant, Sir Francis, 74
Great Newport Street, R's house in, 50, 57
Green, Valentine, 85
Grimaldi, William, 207
Guercino, 19, 40
Gwatkin, Robert Lovell, 152, 172, 229
Gwatkin, Theophila "Offy" (earlier Theophila Palmer) (niece), 48, 97, 115, 130, 149–53, 163, 226; portrait, 97, 150, 152, 172; marriage, 152; death (1848), 232
Gwatkin, Theophila (great-niece), 202
Gwyn, Mary (earlier Mary Horneck), 142, 226

Hamilton, Duchess of, 85
Hamilton, Captain the Hon. John, 24, 25

Hamilton, Mary, 142
Hamilton, William, 93
Harcourt, Earl, 51
Hastings, Marquis of, 211
Hastings, Warren, 161–2
Hawkins, Sir John, 82, 93, 183, 184
Haydon, B. R., 19, 130, 132, 147, 232
Hayman, Francis, 60, 61, 74, 92
Hazlitt, William, 129–32
"Heads of Angels", 150, 201, 235
Heathfield, Lord, 194, 197–8
"Hercules", 198, 199
Herschel, Sir John, 42
Hickey, Joseph, 108
Hickey, Thomas, 161
Hilles, Prof. F. W., cited or quoted, 9, 33
Hodges, William, 198
Hogarth, William, 2, 4, 15, 25, 51, 65–9, 72
Holland: see Netherlands
Holland, Lord, 115, 230
Holland House, 115, 213
"Holy Family", 201
Hone, Nathaniel, 9, 39–41, 78, 92, 140–1
Hoppner, John, 71
Horn, Count de, 140
Horneck, Mary: see Gwyn, Mary
Houghton collection, 180
Huddesford, Rev. George, 153–7, 251
Hudson, Thomas, 14–22, 45, 47, 51, 60, 248
Hull, Thomas, 101
Humphry, Ozias, 86, 211–12
Hunter, John, 227
Huntingdon, Earl of, 51

Idler, 65–8, 79, 138
Inchiquin, Earl and Countess of: see Thomond
Incorporated Society of Artists, 61, 78, 88, 90–4, 131
"Infant Academy", 201, 250
"Infant Samuel", 160
"Ironical Discourse", 112, 223
Irons, Dr Ernest, 29

Italy, R. in (1750-2), 23-5, 32-47; influence of visit, 248, 250; conduct of English visitors to, 31-2

Jackson, William, 155-7
Jervais, Thomas, 163
Johnson, Betsey (niece), 148, 163
Johnson, Elizabeth (sister), 8, 13, 22, 26, 48-9, 148-9
Johnson, Samuel (nephew), 148, 149
Johnson, Dr Samuel, on living in London, 17-18; on Minorca, 28; life of Richard Savage, 50; first meeting with R., 57, 60; friendship with R., 56, 57-9, 62; and Society of Arts, 60-2; meets Prebendary Mudge, 80; Irish "bull", 80; eccentric behaviour, 81; and Literary Club, 81-2; regard for R., 87; and Royal Academy, 92, 93; and R's knighthood, 93; and R's Discourses, 102, 185-6; state pension, 79; Devonshire holiday with R., 10, 80; and Burke, 84; on Baretti, 113; on wine, 134; and Fanny Burney, 145; on R. and marriage, 145-6; regard for Fanny Reynolds, 146, 148; Offy Palmer and, 149; on R's illness (1782), 174; ill-health, 174, 176, 180; on R's royal appointment, 178; R's relations with in 1784, 180-3; projected visit to Italy, 181-2; King's attitude to, 181-2; death (1784), 183; R's memoir of, 183; three requests of R., 183; will, 183; funeral in Westminster Abbey, 184; influence on R., 184-5; R's campaign for public monument, 188-93; Royal Academy and a statue, 189-91, 224-5; statue placed in St Paul's, 193; portraits, 57, 96, 167, 187-8, 198
Johnson, William (brother-in-law), 49, 79, 148

Johnson, William (nephew), 148, 161-2, 207
Jordan, Mrs, 208
"Journey from London to Brentford", 35, 40, 60, 112, 114-18; text, 239-47

Kauffmann, Angelica, 29, 92, 138-42, 214
Kearsley's Pocket Ledger, 195-6
Keats, John, 130, 136
Kemble, Fanny, 176
Kendall family (of Pelyn), 20
Keppel, Augustus, Viscount, 26-8, 52, 70, 156, 160, 172, 198, 235
Keppel ladies, 57
Kew Pagoda, 76, 89
Kildare, Countess of, 51
King's Principal Portrait Painter, 164, 176-9, 196, 205
Kirby, Joshua, 91
Kirkley, Ralph (servant), 76, 78, 86, 224, 226, 229
Kneller, Sir Godfrey, 52, 74
Knowles, Sir James, 72
Kraye, Lambert, 170-1

Lambe's auction rooms, 95, 96
Landscapes by R., 24, 57, 108, 159
Langton, Bennet, 59, 81, 183, 184, 202
Lansdowne, Lord, 57, 70
Lantrow, Mr, 17
Lawrence, Thomas, 179, 224
Leeson, Joseph: see Milltown, Lord
Leicester Fields, R's home in, 3, 69-77, 85, 112; district described, 72; name displaced by Leicester Square, 214
Leicester House, 71, 72
Leicester Square: see Leicester Fields
Leland, John, 5
Leslie, C. R., cited, 21, 23
Lethaby, W. R., quoted, 234
Lever, Sir Aston, 180
Ligonier, Lord, 70
Literary Club ("The Club"), 81-2, 84, 103, 174, 184, 188, 189, 204, 212, 213, 221

London, in R's day, 4; R. arrives in (1740), 15; (1744), 20–1; (1753), 50; proposed commissioning of historical pictures by Lord Mayor, 224
London Chronicle, 79, 80
Lowe, Mauritius, 167
Lowth, Bishop Robert, 9
Lowther, Sir William, 39, 41, 51, 62
Ludlow, Lord, 57

MacArdell, James, 85
"Macbeth and the Witches", 200, 201
Malin, John and Elizabeth, 95, 96
Malone, Edmond, editor of R's "Works", 103, 171, 185–6, 225, 232; on R. and women, 137; and Dr Johnson statue, 188, 189; visits Burke at Beaconsfield, 212, 225; R's executor, 226; at R's funeral, 229; cited *en passim*
Manners, Lord Robert, 173
Maquignon, P., 221
Maratti, Carlo, 36, 41
Marchi, Giuseppe, 43–5, 51–3, 62, 119, 163, 229
Marlborough, Duchess of, 54
Marlborough family group, 160
Mason, William, 74, 131, 165, 172, 200
Mayo, Lord, 39
Melbourne, Lord, 19
Metcalfe, Philip, 167–9, 188, 204, 213, 226, 229
Meyer, Jeremiah, 216, 218
Michelangelo, R. and, 35–8, 103, 138, 186, 223
Milbanke, John, 89
Millidge, Josiah, 155, 157, 251
Milltown, Lord (*earlier* Joseph Leeson), 39, 41
Minorca, R. at, 23, 27–30
Moira, Earl of: *see* Hastings, Marquis of
Mola, Pier Francesco, 41
Monckton, Miss, 145
Montagu, Mrs, 53, 144

Montgomery, Misses, 124, 175
Morland, George, 61, 73
Morland, H. R., 73
Morley, Lord, 5, 25
Morning Herald, 230
Moser, G. M., 50, 78, 90, 92, 174, 216
Moser, Mary, 92
Mount Edgcumbe, Countess of, 85
Mount Edgcumbe, Earl of (*earlier* Lord Edgcumbe), 24, 60, 123, 125
Mudge, Dr John, 50, 80, 120
Mudge, Zachariah, 16, 50, 57, 80

"Nativity, The", 163
Neate family, 25
Netherlands, R. in, 167–71
New Memorandum Book Improv'd, 55
Newton, F. M., 60, 92, 96, 216
Nollekens, Joseph, 127, 141, 219
North, Lord, 172, 173
Northcote, James, character sketch, 119–22, 127–30; first sight of R., 81; student-pupil of R., 53, 108, 120–2; on R. and Velasquez, 39; relations with R., 120–2, 127–32; leaves R's studio (1776), 128; later life, 128–30; on R's character, 129, 224, 236; Hazlitt's "Conversations", 129–32; at R's funeral, 229; death, 132; cited *en passim*
Northcote, Samuel, 108, 124, 125
Notebooks, Reynolds', 32–3, 35–6, 40–3, 51, 55–6; 1774–6 missing, 127; quoted *en passim*
Noverre, J. G., 107
Nugent, Dr Christopher, 81

O'Brien, Nelly, 70, 71
"Offy": *see* Gwatkin, Theophila
Old Slaughter's, 21, 51
Omai, 160
Opie, John, 199, 219, 229
Orkney, Countess of, 232
Ossory, Lord and Lady Upper, 212–213, 226

Ourry, Captain Paul, 25, 125

Oxford University, R. receives D.C.L., 123–5; window in New College chapel by R., 148, 162–3

Paine, James, 74, 90

Painters' Company, 182

Painting methods and technique, Reynolds'—assistants' work on pictures, painting accessories, etc., 52–4, 119–20, 122, 128, 179, 249; borrowings of detail from earlier artists, 36–7; colours and materials: see Colours; draughtmanship weak, 41–2, 44; studio practice, 74–5, 160–2; technique, 52–5, 248–50

Palettes used by R., 52, 74

Palmer, John (brother-in-law), 48

Palmer, Joseph (nephew), 148

Palmer, Mary (niece): see Thomond, Marchioness of

Palmer, Mary (sister), 9, 15, 21, 26, 29, 48, 149

Palmer, Theophila "Offy" (niece): see Gwatkin, Theophila

Palmerston, Lord, 154, 226

Paoli, General, 184

Paris, R. in, 45–6, 90

Parker, John: see Boringdon, Lord

Parliament, R. and, 125

Parr, Dr Samuel, 191

Patch, Thomas, 41

Penny, Edward, 91, 92, 96

Percy, Bishop Thomas, 134

Petersham, 108, 111

"Pindar, Peter": see Wolcot

Pitt, William, 196

Plympton, 5–10, 21; Grammar School, 6, 10, 21; R. chosen as mayor, 124–5

Plymouth Dock (Devonport), 20, 21

"Plymouth Sound from Cattedown", 24

Pope, Alexander, 1–2, 18, 81

Potter, Rev. Humphrey, 7

Potter, Rev. John, 7

"Potter, Matthew", 6–7

Potter, Philip, 7

Potter, Theophila: see Reynolds, Theophila (mother)

Poussin, Nicolas, 197, 231

Pozzo, Padre, 10, 12

Praed, W. M., quoted, 7–8

Price, Lady Caroline, 197, 235, 249

Prices for portraits charged by R., 28, 51, 70, 86, 160, 178

Public Advertiser, 174, 231

"Puck", 201

Ramsay, Allan, 25, 52, 164–5, 176–8

Raphael, R. and, 35–8, 40, 104, 131, 186

Rawdon, Lord: see Hastings, Marquis of

Religious pictures by R., 162–3, 201

Religious views of R.: see under Reynolds

Rembrandt, R. and, 19, 37, 44, 168

Reynolds, Elizabeth (sister): see Johnson, Elizabeth

Reynolds, Frances (Fanny) (sister), character, 8, 9, 49, 147–8; portrait, 22; R's housekeeper in London from 1753, 50, 56, 82; friendship with Dr Johnson, 58, 146; relations with R., 88, 120–1, 147–8; and R's coach, 78; in Paris (1768), 90; and Northcote, 120–2; poems, 146–7; leaves R's household, 147–8; R's bequest to, 226

Reynolds, Humphrey (brother), 18

Reynolds, John (uncle), 6, 17

Reynolds, Rev. Preb. John (grandfather), 6

Reynolds, Rev. Joshua (uncle), 6

Reynolds, Sir Joshua (see also under names of persons and subjects throughout the index), birth (July 16, 1723), 5, 6; parentage, 5–8; baptism, correction in church register, 6; home life and education, 9–16; influenced by

Richardson's "Theory of Painting", 10-11; attack of smallpox, 11-12, 14; early artistic attempts, 12-15; apprenticed to Thomas Hudson in London (1740), 15-21; returns to Devonshire (1743), 20; paints first portraits, 20; returns to London (1744), 20; death of father, 21; moves to Plymouth Dock, 21; meets Keppel, 26; voyage to Minorca, 26-7; at Minorca (1749-50), 27-8; riding accident, 28-9; in Italy (1750-2), 23, 25, 31-47; meeting with Chambers in Paris (1752), 45-6; returns to England (1752), 47; stays in Devonshire, 48-50; returns to London (1753), 50; first meeting with Johnson (1756), 57, 60; death of mother, 62; first essays published (1759), 65-8; exhibits at Society of Arts exhibition (1760), 61, 63; moves to Leicester Fields, 70, 71; founds Literary Club (1764), 81; elected President of Royal Academy (1768), 91-3; King's attitude towards, 92-4, 164; knighted (1769), 93-4, 164; opening address at Academy, 97-101; writes "Journey from London to Brentford" (1770-1), 114-18; Wick House, Richmond, completed (1772), 110-12; attends naval review (1773), 123; D.C.L., Oxford, 123-4; mayor of Plympton, 124-5; deeply moved by Goldsmith's death, 127; Fanny Reynolds leaves household, 147-8; achievements between 1774 and 1780, 160; visits Flanders and Holland (1781), 167-71; second stroke (1782), 144, 173; appointed Principal Portrait Painter to the King (1784), 176-9; freedom of the Painters' Company, 182; memoir of Johnson (1784), 183; attends Johnson's funeral, 184; influence of Johnson on his adult life, 184-6; unsuccessful application for secretaryship of the Order of the Bath (1785), 196; attends public execution, 203; last visit to the continent, 196; paints pictures for Catherine the Great, 198-9; loses sight of left eye (1789), 210; ceases serious painting, 210, 211, 221; resigns as P.R.A. after Bonomi affair (1790), 219; restored to presidency, 220-1; delivers last Discourse, 222; health deterioration (1791), 225; last illness, 226-7; death (February 23, 1792), 227; lying-in-state and funeral, 228-9; burial in St Paul's, 229; royal portraits sold after his death, 179

Appearance, 18, 22, 29; face scarred by smallpox, 11-12; deficiencies of upper lip, 28-9

Biography by Boswell or Burke, considered but not written, 12, 203, 204, 221

Birds, fondness for, 213-14

Characteristics, 3-4, 29-30, 214-15, 236-7

Children, fondness for, 116, 150-1, 201-2

Collection of pictures: see Collection

Deafness, 29, 38, 162, 207

Devon dialect, authority on, 9

Discourses: see Discourses

Dress, 33, 77

Eyesight, failing, 197; threat of blindness, 207; wearing of spectacles, 207-8; loses sight of left eye, 210, 211; fears for other eye, 221, 222, 225-6; possible cause of blindness, 227

Family, relations with, 148-9

Foreigners, attachment to, 214

Friendly and tolerant, 88, 89

Reynolds, Sir Joshua (*contd.*)
Handwriting, 32, 208
Health, attack of smallpox, 11–12, 14; slight stroke (1764), 86–7; second stroke (1782), 144, 145, 173–4; disease of the liver, 210, 213, 221, 226; doctors' failure to diagnose illness (1791), 225; last illness (1792), 226–7; post-mortem revelations, 227 (*see also* Eyesight, above)
Host, success as, 82, 230
Humour, turn for, 112
Marriage, attitude to, 137, 140–2, 145–6
Memorials, 192–3, 238
Money matters, attitude to, 19–20, 62, 76, 196
Notebooks: *see* Notebooks
Painting methods and technique: *see* Painting
Parody, gift for, 40–1, 114
Poem by, 151
Portraits of Reynolds by other artists, 29, 138–9
Prices for portraits: *see* Prices
"Prince of Portrait Painters", 2
Pupils, 119–20, 130
Reading, 33
Religion, attitude to, 8, 9, 121, 125, 226–7
Self-portraits, 18, 22, 24, 25, 29, 52, 125, 138–9, 207
Sitters, numbers of, 56, 123; methods with, 74–5, 160–2
Speech, indistinctness, 29, 222
Spelling, versatility in, 10, 40, 90
Statues and busts, 72, 214, 232–3
Temper, uncertainty of, 214–15, 221, 236–7
Will, 226; assessment of fortune, 231
Wine, fondness for, 134–6
Women, relations with, 49, 136–45
Writer, as, 64–5, 186; humorous sketch, 79; editions of "Works", 102–3, 171, 186, 232
Reynolds, Martin (brother), 18

Reynolds, Mary (sister): *see* Palmer, Mary
Reynolds, Robert (brother), 22, 49, 56
Reynolds, Rev. Samuel (father), 5–20, 22, 62; date of death, 21–2
Reynolds, Theophila (*earlier* Theophila Potter) (mother), 6, 7, 21, 48; death (1756), 62
Richards, John, 218
Richardson, Jonathan, 10–15, 68
Richardson, Samuel, 59
Richmond, R. and, 107–11 (*see also* Wick House)
Richmond, Duke of, 63
Rigaud, J. F., 139, 219
"Rinaldo" (pseudonym of R.), 114, 239
Roberts, Captain, 24–5
Robinson, Mrs "Perdita", 176, 208
Rockingham, Marquis of, 172–3, 249
Rome, R. in: *see* Italy
Roscoe, William, 238
Roth (painter), 179
Roubiliac, L. F., 45, 60
Royal Academy, efforts to establish, 60, 68, 78, 90–4; established (1768), 78, 92, 106; R. elected first president, 91–4; original members, 92; treasurer, 92–5; honorary appointments, 93; porter and "sweeper", 96; annual exhibitions and dinners, 96, 101, 166, 233–4; R's opening address, 97–101; Baretti's tribute to, 113–14; proposed uniform for academicians, 125–7; women founder-members, 138; moves to Somerset House (1780), 165, 166; death of first keeper, 174; ban on bread for students for rubbing-out, 174; Gainsborough withdraws from 1784 exhibition, 176, 205; contribution towards Johnson monument vetoed by the King (1791), 189–91, 225; Secretary for Foreign Correspondence, 203, 233; admission

of foreigners, 215-16, 219; attempt to elect Bonomi professor of perspective (1790), 215-21; secretaryship, 216, 218; early academicians, 216; R. resigns as president (1790), 219-20; R. restored to presidency, 220-1; R. removes picture from exhibition, 221; R's last Discourse (1790), 222-3; R. absent from meeting (1791), 225; West president after R's death, 228; R. lies in state at Somerset House, 228-9; payments for R's funeral, 229; medal in R's honour, 232; Sir William Chambers' disruptive manœuvres, 233; progress under R's presidency, 233-4

Royal Society, 88

Rubens, R. and, 167-72, 196-8, 249

Ruskin, John, 2

Rutland, Duke of, 148, 163, 173, 178, 188, 196, 198

"Saint Cecilia", 208

St John, Mrs, 168

"St John Baptist", 160

St Martin's Lane, R's apartments in, 21, 50-1

St Paul's Cathedral, proposed decorations in, 125, 140-1, 169; statue of Johnson in, 188-93; thanksgiving service for King's recovery (1789), 210; R. buried in, 228-9; statue of R. in, 232

Sandby, Paul, 61, 92

Sandby, Thomas, 92, 219, 220

Sandwich, Lord, 205

Savile House, 4, 71, 72, 166

Schomberg House, 176

Scott, Dr William: see Stowell, Lord

Self-portraits: see under Reynolds, Sir Joshua

Serpentine line, 65-7

Shakespeare, R's interest in, 79; Boydell's Shakespeare Gallery, 199-201

Sharpe, Joshua, 197-8

Sheridan, Mrs, 163

Sheridan, R. B., 143-4, 162, 208

Siddons, Mrs, 182, 208, 209, 235

"Siddons (Mrs) as the Tragic Muse", 131, 175-6

"Simplicity", 150, 202

Smart, Rev. Thomas, 13, 15, 41

Smith, Adam, 68

Smith, J. T., 141, 214

"Snake in the Grass", 186

Snuff, 133, 212

Society of Artists: see Incorporated Society of Artists

Society of Arts, 60-3, 78, 85, 88, 98, 175, 195

Society of Sons of the Clergy, 88

Somerset House, 96, 138, 160, 165, 166, 222, 228-9

Somerset Palace, 96

Southey, Robert, 155, 156

Spectacles worn by R., 207-8

Spencer, Lady, 63, 159, 172

Sterne, Laurence, 64, 70, 198, 235

Stothard, Thomas, 147

Stowell, Lord (earlier Dr William Scott), 183

Strange, Sir Robert, 104

"Strawberry Girl", 97, 150

Stuart, James, 60

Sydney, Lord, 97

Tavistock, Lord and Lady, 54

Taylor, Tom, cited or quoted, 12, 20, 90, 168, 170

"Thames from Richmond Hill", 57

Thomond, Marchioness of (earlier Mary Palmer and Countess of Inchiquin) (niece), character sketch, 152-3; R's regard for, 48, 149, 151; takes charge of R's household, 148, 152; letter on Brooks's ball, 208-9; dislike of Wick House, 108; and Boswell, 204; on imperfections of R's pictures, 54; suitors, 153, 155-7, 225, 251; R's bequest to, 226;

Thomond, Marchioness of (*contd.*) assessment of inheritance, 231; letter to R's doctor, 227; sells stock of royal portraits, 179; marriage (1792), 153, 231; portrait, 152; loyalty to R's memory, 232; and memorial exhibition of R's works (1813), 54; death (1820), 232; mentioned, 175, 196, 202, 210–13

Thomond, Marquess of (*earlier* Earl of Inchiquin), 153, 157, 231

Thurlow, Lord, 181

Thrale, Mrs, 85, 127, 236

Thrales, The, 58, 113, 142

Tintoretto, 248

Titian, 248

Tolcher, Henry, 120

Toms, Peter, 53, 92, 119

Torrington, 21, 48–9, 62

Turk's Head, Gerrard Street, 82, 134

Turner, Sir Charles, 39

Turner, Charles, 85

Turner, J. M. W., 219, 229

Turnham Green, 115–16, 244

"Two Gentlemen", 153–7

Tyler, William, 78, 92, 216–20, 229, 233

"Ugolino and his Children in Prison", 103, 123

Upper Ossory, Lord: *see* Ossory

Vanbrugh, Sir John, 2, 160, 231

Van Dyck, Sir Anthony, 24, 52, 168, 169, 197, 231, 248

Vandyke, Peter, 53

Van Eyck, 102, 168

Vatican, R. at the, 37–8

Velasquez, R. and, 37–9, 201

Venice, influence on R., 44–5, 47, 54

Vernon, Joseph, 101

Victoria and Albert Museum, 133, 233

Vinci, Leonardo da, 99

Waldegrave, Ladies, 166, 167

Wale, Samuel, 215

Wales, Prince of, 179, 199, 208

Wales, Princess Dowager of, 89

Walpole, Horace, 31, 36–7, 57, 103, 107, 165–7, 175, 185, 198, 212

Walpole, Sir Robert, 18

Wang-y-Tong, 76, 160

Warburg Institute, 36

Warmell, Mr, 14, 15

Warren, Dr Richard, 225

Warton, Joseph, 59, 153

Warton, Thomas, 162

Waterhouse, Prof. E. K., cited, 25, 160, 172

Watson, George, 119

Watteau, Antoine, 197, 231

Weekes, H., 72

West, Benjamin, 71, 90–2, 94, 189, 216, 228, 234

Westmorland, Countess of: *see* Child, Sarah Anne

Weston, Miss, 23–4, 27, 28, 39

White, George (model), 123, 140

Whitefoord, Caleb, 125, 159–60, 219

Whitton Place, 89, 107

Wick House, Richmond, 108–12, 223

Wilkes, John, 56, 117, 203

Wills, Rev. James, 131

Wilson, Richard, 39, 61, 92, 166

Wilton, Joseph, 43, 91, 92, 139, 174, 229

Windham, William, 184, 212, 230

Wolcot, John ("Peter Pindar"), 128, 191

Wordsworth, William, lines on R., 238

Worsley, Lady, 166

Wouwerman, 169

Wright, Richard, 53

Wyatt, James, 233

York, Duke of, 71

Zoffany, Johann, 30, 71, 86, 92, 166, 219

Zuccarelli, Francesco, 34–5, 92

142. ?Edna

Brentford

Brentford
Butts

Chiswick Park

London Stile

Kew Green

Turnham
Green

to Richmond

Strand·on·the
·Green

Reynolds house
at
Richmond

Chiswick
House

Chiswick
Green

1 7 7 0

A Journey from
LONDON to BRENTFORD
through KNIGHTSBRIDGE
KENSINGTON, HAMMERSMITH
& TURNHAM GREEN
by RINALDO

One English Mile